# SHADOW OF
# COLOSSUS

A SEVEN WONDERS NOVEL

# SHADOW OF
# COLOSSUS

A SEVEN WONDERS NOVEL

# T.L. HIGLEY

PUBLISHING GROUP
Nashville, Tennessee

ISBN-13: 978-1-60751-185-4

Published by B&H Publishing Group,
Nashville, Tennessee

Dewey Decimal Classification: F
Subject Heading: HISTORICAL FICTION \
COURTESANS—FICTION \ GREECE—
HISTORY—281–146 B.C.—FICTION

Scripture quotation was taken from the Holy Bible,
New International Version, copyright © 1973, 1978,
1984 by International Bible Society.

To my mother, Iris Strauss
Who shares my love of Greece

And to my father, Joe Strauss
Who shares my love of writing

Thank you both, for always encouraging,
always loving, and always believing in me.
I love you.

# Acknowledgments

I've had a desire to write books about the Seven Wonders for years. Thank you to all the folks at B&H Publishing Group for partnering with me to bring this series to life. Thank you, Karen Ball and David Webb, for championing the project. David, your outstanding editing made the book much stronger. Julie Gwinn, your enthusiasm for fiction and for marketing has been awesome, and so much fun to work alongside!

Thank you to my agent, Steve Laube, for also believing in the concept, and for giving sound guidance. You're terrific!

Joan Savoy, my personal patron of the arts, what can I say about all you have contributed to this book? Quiet places to write, cheerleading, hand-holding, prayer, phone calls encouraging me to "press on, sister," food and chocolate, reading the manuscript (twice!) before anyone else had read it, and finally, being my travel companion for our adventure in Rhodes. You are so dear to me, and your touch is woven through the pages of this book. Thank you.

Matt Savoy and Sarah Higley, thanks for the brainstorming! Rachel Higley, thank you for helping me create Web pages that reach people.

And to my husband Ron, and our kids, Rachel, Sarah, Jake and Noah—you all give so unselfishly of yourselves to allow me to write books. I continue to be amazed at the blessing you are in my life. Thank you for loving me, even when things get crazy. I love you!

# GLOSSARY OF ANCIENT GREEK

**agora**—an open marketplace where merchants keep stalls or shops for the selling of goods

**amphorae**—a ceramic vase with two handles and a long neck that is narrower than the body of the vase

**andrôn**—a room in the house that is reserved for the men, largely for the purpose of entertaining guests

**bouleuterion**—an amphitheater-style structure used primarily for meetings of the *boule*, a council of citizens who assemble to confer and decide matters of public interest

**cella**—a room at the centre of a Greek temple, usually containing a statue representing the deity venerated in the temple

**chitôn**—a loose-fitting outfit made of two sheets of light drapery worn directly over the body, usually girded with a belt under the breast or around the waist; often depicted as the clothing of the goddess Aphrodite

**emmeleia**—a solemn and stately dance depicting a tragedy

**epistates** (ĕpistătēs)—local official charged with maintaining order; a police chief

**hetaera** (hĕtairah)—a courtesan, or professional female companion; often well educated, sometimes influential, and the only woman allowed to actively participate in the men's symposia

**himation**—outerwear, similar to but made of a heavier drape than the chitôn; a cloak

**parados**—a corridor at the front of the stage of a theater from which the Greek chorus enters

**proaulia**—the day before the wedding; a ritual in which the bride-to-be makes sacrifices in preparation for marriage

**skene**—in a theater, the building in which costumes are stored and to which the painted backgrounds are connected

**stoa**—a covered walkway or portico, commonly for public usage

**strategos** (strătēgōs)—literally, "army leader"; one of ten men elected to direct political affairs of the island; plural, *strategoi*

**strigil**—a small, curved metal tool used to scrape dirt and sweat from the body (perfumed oil is applied to the skin, often by a slave, then is scraped off along with the dirt)

**taverna**—an establishment serving wine, vinegar, and snacks

# Part I

*"The finest of all the votive gifts and statues in the city of Rhodes is the Colossus of Helios. Now it lies on the ground, overthrown by an earthquake, severed at the knees."*

Strabo, *The Geography*, c. AD 23

*"Even lying on the ground it is a marvel. Few people can make their arms meet round its thumbs, and its fingers are larger than most statues."*

Pliny the Elder, *Natural History*, AD 77

*The wealthy island of Rhodes,*
*Desired by the Ptolemies of Egypt,*
*Coveted by the Seleucids of Syria,*
*Admired by the Romans, now birthing an empire.*

*Rhodes, last stronghold of democracy,*
*Patron of arts, center of learning, pride of Hellenism,*
*An island of people awaiting their destiny*
*Shifting even now beneath their feet.*

# ONE

# Rhodes, 227 bc

✦ *Seven Days before the Great Quake* ✦

In the deceitful calm of the days preceding disaster, while Rhodes still glittered like a white jewel in the Aegean, Tessa of Delos planned to open her wrists.

The death of her body was long overdue. Her soul had died ten years ago.

*Ten years this day.*

Tessa took in a breath of salty air and shivered. From her lofty position outside Glaucus's hillside home, she watched the populace's torches flicker to life in the dusk. Across the city the day's tumult at the docks slowed. The massive statue of Helios at the harbor's frothy mouth caught the sun's last rays as it slipped into a cobalt sea. The torch he thrust skyward seemed to burst aflame, as though lit by the sun god himself.

He had been her only constant these ten years, this giant in the likeness of Helios. A silent sentinel who kept vigil as life ripped freedom and hope from her. Painful as it was, tonight she wanted only to remember. To be alone, to remember, and to mourn.

"Tessa!" A wine-sodden voice erupted from the open door behind her.

The symposium had begun only minutes ago, but Glaucus was already deep into his cups. Bad form in any company, thought Tessa, but Glaucus rarely cared. Tessa inhaled the tang of sea air again and placed a steadying hand against the smooth alabaster column supporting the roof. She did not answer, nor turn, when she heard her fat master shuffle onto the portico.

"Get yourself back into the house!" Glaucus punctuated his command with a substantial belch.

"Soon," she said. "I wish to watch the sun god take his leave."

A household servant crept out and set two torches blazing. An oily smell surged, then dissipated. From the house floated harsh laughter mingled with the tinny sound of a flute.

Glaucus pushed his belly against her back and grabbed her arm. The linen *chitôn* she'd taken care to arrange perfectly fell away, exposing her shoulder. She reached to replace it, but Glaucus caught her hand. He brought his mouth close to her ear, and she could smell his breath, foul as days-old fish.

"The others are asking for you. 'Where is your *hetaera*?' they say. 'The one with more opinions than Carthage has ships.'"

Tessa closed her eyes. She had long entertained Glaucus's political friends with her outspoken thoughts on government and power. While his wife remained hidden away in the women's quarters, Glaucus's hetaera was displayed like an expensive pet with sharp teeth. Tessa had once believed she led an enviable life, but the years had stripped her of her illusions.

She stroked the polished filigree of the gold necklace encircling her throat and remembered when Glaucus fastened it there, a gilding for his personal figure of bronze.

"Now, Tessa." Glaucus pulled her toward the door.

Her heart reached for the statue, clinging to her first memory of it, when Delos had been home and innocence had still been hers. *When I open my wrists, I will do it there.*

Ω

The *andrôn*, central room of the men's quarters, smelled of roasted meat and burning olive oil. Glaucus paused in the doorway, awaiting the attention of those who had curried enough of his favor to be invited tonight. When the small crowd lounging on low couches at the room's perimeter turned his way, he pushed her into the lamp-lit center. "Tessa, everyone," he shouted. "Making a grand entrance!"

The room laughed and clapped, then returned their attention to the food and wine on the low tables beside them. In the corner, a young girl dressed in gauzy fabric blew thin streams of air into a small flute. Tessa's eyes locked onto the girl's for a moment. A private understanding passed between them that they were both objects of entertainment, and the girl looked away, as though ashamed to be seen so clearly. A desire to protect the girl surfaced in Tessa, a maternal feeling that of late seemed only a breath away.

Glaucus pulled her to a couch and forced her down onto the gold-trimmed red cushions. He lowered himself at her right and leaned against her possessively. A black bowl with gold designs waited in the center of their table, and Glaucus ladled wine from it into a goblet for her. To the room he said, "To Tessa—always the center of attention!" He raised his own cup, and his guests did the same.

Tessa's gaze swept the room, taking in the majority of men and the few women reclining against them. The moment was suspended, with cups raised toward her, drunken and insincere smiles affixed to faces, lamplight flickering across tables piled with grapes and almonds and figs, and the flute's lament behind it all.

*Will I remember this night, even in the afterlife?*

"To Tessa!" Shouts went round the room, cups were drained and thumped back to tables, and the party quickened around her. Glaucus reached for her, but she pushed him away.

He laughed. "It would appear my Tessa is a bit high-spirited tonight," he said to the others. "And what shall be done with a mischievous hetaera?" His thick-lipped smile and raised eyebrow took in the room and elicited another round of laughter. He nodded, then turned his attention to the man on his right, resuming a conversation whose beginning she must have missed.

"Your objections earlier to the naturalization of the Jews are noted, Spiro. But to extend citizenship to the foreigners among us can often be expedient."

Tessa could not see Spiro, his frame completely blocked by the bulk of Glaucus beside her, but his voice poured like warm oil. Yet underneath his smooth tones, Tessa heard the cold iron of anger. He was one of few among the *strategoi* to contradict Glaucus publicly.

"Like-minded foreigners, perhaps," Spiro said. "But the Jews make it no secret that they despise our Greek ways. They disdain even our proudest achievement, our Helios of the harbor. They must be expunged, not embraced by weak-willed politicians who—"

Glaucus raised a pudgy hand. "You presume an authority not yours, Spiro."

"Only a matter of time, Glaucus."

Glaucus snorted. "Again you presume. The people of this island are too clever to choose seductive charm over solid leadership."

Spiro laughed quietly. "Why, Glaucus, seductive charm? I didn't realize you had noticed."

Glaucus shook his head. "Perhaps the women are affected, but it is the *men* who vote."

Tessa sensed Spiro lean forward, his eyes now on her. "And we both know where men find their opinions."

Glaucus snorted again and swung his legs to the floor. It took several tries to raise his ponderous body from the cushions. "Get drunk, Spiro. Enjoy your delusions for one more night. But next week I sail to Crete, and I expect them to fully support my efforts." He nudged Tessa with a sandaled toe. "Don't go anywhere. I will be back."

Tessa watched him leave the room, relief at his temporary absence flooding her. She was to travel to Crete with him next week, though she had no intention of ever stepping onto the ship.

The previously unseen Spiro slid to her couch now, an elbow on the cushion Glaucus had just vacated. He was older than she, perhaps thirty, clean-shaven like most of the others but wore his jet-black hair longer, braided away from his face and falling just above his shoulders. His eyes, deep set and darker than the night sea, studied hers. A smile played at his lips. "What are you still doing with that bore, Tessa? You could do better."

"One slave master is as another. To have something better is only to be free." She was not truly Glaucus's slave in the usual sense, and Spiro knew it, but it made little difference.

Spiro smiled fully now, and his gaze traveled from her eyes, slowly down to her waist. He took liberties, but Tessa had long ago become heedless of offense.

"That is what I like about you, Tessa. One never meets a hetaera who speaks of freedom; they are resolved to their place. But you are a woman like no other in Rhodes."

"Why should I not be free?"

Spiro chuckled softly and inched closer. "Why, indeed? Ask the gods, who make some women wives and give others as slaves." Spiro's hand skimmed the cushions and came to rest on her thigh. "If you were mine, Tessa, I would treat you as the equal you deserve to be. Glaucus acts as though he owns you, but we all know he pays dearly for your favors. Perhaps it is *you* who owns *him*."

Spiro's fingers dug into her leg, and his eyes roamed her face and body again. Tessa felt neither pleasure nor disgust, a reminder that her heart had been cast from bronze. But a flicker of fear challenged her composure. Spiro, she knew, was like one of the mighty Median horses: raw power held in check, capable of trampling the innocent if unleashed.

A shadow loomed above them, but Spiro did not remove his hand. Instead, he arched a perfect eyebrow at Glaucus and smiled. Tessa expected a flash of anger, but Glaucus laughed.

"First, you think to rule the island, Spiro, and now you think to steal Tessa from me, as though she has the free will to choose whom she wants?" Spiro shrugged and moved to the next couch. Glaucus plopped down between them again. "She will never be yours, Spiro. Even when I am dead, her owner will only hand her to the next man in line to have paid for her." He waggled a finger at Tessa. "She is worth waiting for, though, I can tell you." Another coarse laugh.

Something broke loose in Tessa then. Caused perhaps by the vow taken while drinking in the sight of the harbor's bronze statue, and the assurance that soon nothing she did now would hold consequence for her. Or perhaps it was ten years of bondage, commemorated this night with nothing more than continued abuse. Whatever the reason, she rose to her feet. The room silenced, as though a goddess had ascended a pedestal. She lifted her voice.

"May the gods deal with you as you have mistreated me, Glaucus of Rhodes. I will have no part of you."

Glaucus grabbed her arm. "Your heart is not in the festivities tonight, my dear. I understand. I will meet you in the inner courtyard later."

He did this to save face, they both knew. Tessa wrenched her arm free of his clutches, glanced at Spiro, and felt a chill at the look in his eyes. She raised her chin and glided from the room.

In the hall outside the andrôn, she looked both directions. She had no desire to stay, yet the world outside the house was no more pleasant or safe for her. She turned from the front door and moved deeper into the house.

The hallway opened to a courtyard, with rooms branching in many directions. Along the back wall, a colonnaded walkway, its roof covered with terra-cotta tiles, stretched the length of the courtyard. A large cistern gaped in the center. Beside it stood a large birdcage; its lone inhabitant, a black mynah with an orange beak, chirped in greeting.

Glaucus had said he would meet her here later, but from the sounds of the laughter behind her, the party raged without her. She should be safe for a few minutes at least. She crossed to the bird she had adopted as her own and simply named Mynah. Tessa put a finger through the iron bars and let Mynah peck a hello.

Her head throbbed, as it always did when she wore her hair pulled back. She reached above her, found the pin that cinched her dark ringlets together, and yanked it. Hair loosed and fell around her, and she ran her fingers through it in relief.

A sharp intake of breath from across the room startled her. She whirled at the sound. "Who's there?"

A soft voice in the darkness said, "I am sorry, mistress. I did not mean to startle you."

Tessa's heart grasped at the kindness and respect in the voice, the first she had encountered this evening. She put a hand to her unfastened hair. Somehow she still found it within herself to be embarrassed by this small impropriety.

The man took hesitant steps toward her. "Are you ill, mistress? Can I help you in some way?" He was clean-shaven and quite tall, with a lanky build and craggy face, Glaucus's Jewish head servant, Simeon.

"No, Simeon. No, I am not ill. Thank you." She sank to a bench.

The older man dipped his head and backed away.

Tessa reached out a hand. "Perhaps—perhaps some water?"

He smiled. "I'll only be a moment."

She had disgraced Glaucus tonight, in spite of his effort to laugh off her comments. How would he repay the damage she had done him? His position as a strategos of the polis of Rhodes outranked all other concerns in his life, and he would consider her disrespect in the presence of other city leaders as treasonous.

In the three years since Glaucus had paid her owner the hetaera price and she had become his full-time companion, they had developed an unusual relationship. While he would not allow her to forget that she was not free, he had also discovered her aptitude for grasping the intricacies of politics, the maneuvering necessary to keep Rhodes the strong trading nation that it was, and to maintain Glaucus's hold on leadership within this democratic society. Power was a game played shrewdly in Rhodes, as in all the Greek world, and Glaucus had gained a competitive edge when he gained Tessa.

Rhodian society had declared her to be a rarity: beautiful, brilliant, and enslaved. But the extent to which the decisions of the city-state passed through her slave-bound fingers was unknown to most. And in this she held a measure of power over Glaucus. She recalled Spiro's astute comment earlier: *Perhaps it is you who owns him.*

Simeon returned with a stone mug in his hands. He held it out to her and covered her fingers with his own gnarled hand as she reached for it. His eyes returned to her hair. "I—I have never seen you with your hair down," he said. He lowered his gray head again but did not back away, and his voice was soft. "It is beautiful."

Tessa tried to smile, but her heart retreated from the small kindness. "Thank you."

He didn't look up. "If you are not ill, Tessa, perhaps you should return to the symposium. I should not like to see Glaucus angry with you."

Tessa exhaled. "Glaucus can wait."

Another noise at the courtyard's edge. They both turned at the rustle of fabric. A girl glided into the room, dressed in an elegant yellow chitôn, her dark hair flowing around her shoulders. She stopped suddenly when she saw them.

"Simeon? Tessa? What are you doing here?"

Simeon bent at the waist, his eyes on the floor. "The lady was feeling ill. She requested water." His eyes flicked up at Tessa, their expression unreadable, and he left the room.

Tessa turned her attention to the girl, inhaling the resolve to survive this encounter. At fourteen, Persephone hovered on the delicate balance between girl and woman. Glowing pale skin framed by dark hair gave her the look of an ivory doll, but it was her startlingly blue eyes that drew one's attention. In recent months, as she had gained understanding of Tessa's position in her father's life, Persephone had grown more hostile toward her.

She raised her chin and studied Tessa. "Does my father know you're out here?" Her tone contradicted the delicacy of her features.

Tessa nodded.

"So he let his plaything out of her cage?"

Tessa's eyes closed in pity for the girl, whose mother had abandoned her for the comfort of madness.

The girl flitted to where Mynah cheeped inside its bars. She picked a leaf from a potted tree and held it out to the bird. "But who am I to speak of cages?" she said. She raised her eyes to Tessa. "We are all trapped here in some way. You. Me. Mother."

"Cages can be escaped," Tessa said, surprising herself. She had never dared to offer Persephone wisdom, though her heart ached for the girl.

Persephone turned toward her, studying her. "When you find the key, let me know."

"Tessa!" Glaucus's voice was thick with wine and demanding.

Tessa turned toward the doorway. The girl beside her took a step backward.

"There you are," he said. "I've sent them all away." He waddled toward them. "I am sick of their company." He seemed to notice the girl for the first time. "Persephone, why are you not in bed? Get yourself to the women's quarters."

Tessa could feel the hate course through the girl as if it were her own body.

"I am not tired. I wished to see the stars." She pointed upward.

Glaucus stood before them now, and he sneered. "Well, the stars have no wish to see *you*. Remove yourself."

"And will you say goodnight to Mother?" Persephone asked. The words were spoken with sarcasm, tossed to Glaucus like raw bait. Tessa silently cheered the girl's audacity.

Glaucus was not so kind. "Get out!"

"And leave you to your harlot?" Persephone said.

In a quick motion belying his obesity, Glaucus raised the back of his hand to the girl and struck her against the face. She reeled backward a step or two, her hand against her cheek.

Tessa moved between them. "Leave her alone!"

Glaucus turned on Tessa and laughed. "And when did you two become friends?"

Persephone glared into her father's corpulent face. "I despise you both," she said.

Glaucus raised his arm again, his hand a fist this time, but Tessa was faster. She caught the lowering arm by the wrist and pushed it backward. Glaucus rocked back on his heels and turned his hatred on her.

Tessa kept her eyes trained on Glaucus but spoke to the girl, her voice low and commanding. "Go to bed, Persephone." She sensed the girl back away, heard her stomp from the room.

The anger on Glaucus's face melted into something else. A chuckle, sickening in its condescension, rumbled from him.

"High-spirited is one thing, Tessa. But be careful you do not go too far. Remember who keeps you in those fine clothes and wraps your ankles and wrists in jewels. You are not your own."

*But I soon will be.*

Glaucus reached for her, and she used her forearm to swat him away like a noisome insect. "Don't touch me. Don't touch her. Take your fat, drunken self out of here."

The amusement on Glaucus's face played itself out. The anger returned, but Tessa was ready.

Glaucus's words hissed between clenched teeth. "I don't know what has come over you tonight, Tessa, but I will teach you your place. You belong to me, body and spirit, and I will have you!" His heavy hands clutched her shoulders, and his alcohol-soaked breath blew hot in her face. Every part of Tessa's inner being rose up to defend herself.

It would all end tonight.

# TWO

S piro lifted his fourth cup of the night, spilled three drops onto the andrôn's floor in a libation to Helios, and drained the cup. He would wait for his moment.

Glaucus had called an end to his symposium and tossed Spiro and the other city leaders into the street before Spiro had drunk his fill of wine. And so the party simply moved to another's home, Xenophon's men's quarters, a double of the andrôn where Glaucus served them.

Across the room, their new host bowed low. "Welcome, men. Glaucus's headache is my gain. I am honored to host you this evening." Xenophon smiled as one who had bested an opponent in the gymnasium. He and Glaucus served as two of the ten strategoi, leaders who had proven themselves militarily. These men formed alliances when it suited them, but always there was rivalry.

Spiro knew that if he were to lead Rhodes to the place he dreamed of, both Glaucus and Xenophon must be dealt with, along with the other three who opposed him. Many of these were present tonight.

Spiro surveyed the room through narrowed eyes. Dim-witted, most of them, believing they understood the game of power. Did any of them believe the headache Glaucus claimed? Or did they know the truth, that Tessa's disrespect had prompted him to end the party and deal with her properly?

*Tessa.* The image of her shimmered in his mind, like a treasure longing to be possessed. Spiro smiled, amusing himself with thoughts of Glaucus dealing with her even now. Would he strike her? Hold her down until fear sparked from her eyes, overcoming her insolence? Would he wait for her to weep, to beg for mercy? Spiro indulged the delicious images a few moments longer, until the conversation around him drew his attention away from the pleasure.

"Glaucus will lead Rhodes to future prosperity we have only dreamed of," an aging politician was saying beside him.

Spiro leaned back and sipped his wine. This conversation was his reason for coming. "Glaucus is a fool," he said, tossing the comment into the center of the room and waiting for it to burst into flame.

As he hoped, all eyes turned toward him and bodies tensed. Spiro relaxed into the cushions and raised his cup to the others. "We in this room understand the value of powerful leadership. Glaucus continues to undermine that leadership, forcing us to be led by the populace, by the majority's will—the majority of whom are also fools."

"You go too far, Spiro," another magistrate said. "Democracy in Rhodes remains intact in spite of the Macedonian, who conquered nearly every other city-state of Greece. Would you have us bow to Alexander as well, even though he is dead these hundred years?"

Spiro swung his legs to the floor and set his cup on the table beside him. "The Macedonians have much to offer. We could all learn from the Great Alexander." He dropped the pitch of his voice, cool water to quench hot tempers. "Membership in the Achaean

League would grant us a military strength we must have if we are to remain free. And one of our own would still lead here, one who could do far more than Glaucus ever could."

Xenophon chuckled from the other side of the room. "One such as yourself, Spiro?"

He returned the question with a small smile.

"Come now, Spiro, it is no secret that you seek to rule Rhodes as your father rules Kalymnos."

Muted conversations buzzed around the room at Xenophon's daring challenge.

"I seek only the wealth and peace of Rhodes," Spiro said. He skewered Xenophon with a lethal stare. "And you know nothing of my father."

Hermes lifted a cup. "He is a great leader, your father. A pity the son cares more for wine and women and does not offer the same potential."

Private whisperings ceased, creating a heavy silence that waited for Spiro's reaction. But he only surveyed the room calmly, then reclined and crossed his arms.

Demetrius was the first to speak, as Spiro knew he would. "You shame yourself with rash words, Hermes. The name of Spiro commands respect in Rhodes and beyond."

Hermes shrugged but did not argue.

Spiro watched him through narrowed eyes. "We are all aware that we strategoi are evenly divided on the issue of the League. But we are also men of honor, and as such we confine our debate to politics." He dipped his head. "Your envy has no place here."

Hermes sputtered, then wiped his mouth with the back of his hand. "Envy!"

Spiro smiled. "As you mentioned, I have a discerning palate for quality."

Xenophon weighed in. "Quality? Like Tessa?"

Laughter around the room lit a slow-burning flame in Spiro's gut. It was true, he wanted Tessa nearly as much as he wanted to rule Rhodes. The thought of her quickened his pulse.

"Our history is full of great leaders with great women at their side," he said.

Hermes laughed. "Ah, but I have heard it is your father's *mistress* who has commanded his attention and given him a son he favors over you."

Spiro inhaled to relieve the pressure on his chest. "And I am flattered that you have spent so much time studying my private life, Hermes. What is it our philosophers say? 'That which consumes us becomes our center.'"

A bare-chested slave entered, toting a small plate of nuts and figs, and placed it on a table before Xenophon. He exited with a bow.

"Come," Xenophon said, holding a fig aloft. "Let us leave off talk of government and turn our minds to other things."

At that moment a girl somersaulted into the room and jumped to her feet, hands high. The music from the corner picked up tempo, and the girl was followed by two more of her kind, wheeling into the room, hands-over-feet. The three linked arms and began an intricate series of steps in the center of the room.

The eyes and the smiles of every man in the room focused on the barely clothed young girls. Every man except Spiro. He had no interest in gymnasts. He studied Xenophon's indulgent smile, the slow way he chewed a fig as he watched the girls. He hated the man for hosting an impromptu symposium with more extravagance than most men could plan in weeks.

And then Xenophon's expression changed. Spiro thought at first that one of the girls had misstepped. He glanced around the room for the cause of the man's dismay, but no one else seemed to have taken note of anything. He looked across to Xenophon, whose face had taken on a fiery hue as he swallowed furiously. Around them the festivity continued.

Spiro raised himself from the cushions where he reclined and leaned toward Xenophon. There was no question now—the man was ill. Spiro thought to summon a slave, but before he had a chance, Xenophon jerked to his feet. The flutist ceased abruptly, the last, discordant note hanging in the air. The young gymnasts lowered themselves to the floor. All eyes turned toward their host.

Was it the fig? Was he choking? The guests were standing now, too, though no one moved to action. Xenophon sucked in air, but his breathing rasped and his eyeballs bulged.

Someone shouted, "By the gods, someone call a physician!"

Behind Spiro, a man slipped out the door in response. The two men on either side of Xenophon eased him down to the couch again. His face whitened, and flecks of foamy spittle clung to the corners of his mouth. His eyelids fluttered. And then the spasms began. A faint twitch of the head at first. Then an arm, a leg, and suddenly his entire body convulsed. The couch rocked beneath him. Those on either side held his arms.

"Where is the physician?"

"What can be done?"

Everyone spoke at once. They diagnosed, they dispensed advice, they backed away and drew close.

"Poison!"

Spiro never knew who first spoke the word, but once it had been said aloud the crowd knew it to be true. Someone knocked the plate of figs to the floor. Another attempted to pour wine down Xenophon's throat, as if it would ward off the poison's evil effects.

Behind him, someone moved to leave, but Hermes prevented his exit. "No one leaves this room until it is known what has happened here."

The attention returned to Xenophon. Another convulsion gripped him. A moment later his body stiffened as though he were a sculpted figure instead of living man. His head jerked toward Spiro. Xenophon's eyes fixed upon him. Spiro held the stony, unblinking stare for several moments, and then Xenophon's body sagged. His head dropped to his shoulder, and his tongue lolled from his mouth like a sleeping dog's.

The man was quite dead.

## Ω

They were held there, every guest, and questioned by city officials. Had anyone been seen tampering with Xenophon's figs? Who was the slave who had brought them in? Did anyone have reason to see harm come to Xenophon? Spiro had nearly laughed at that question. At least five men in the room vehemently disagreed with Xenophon's politics. Who among them did *not* have a reason to see harm come to him? The question should have been, who had the stomach to do it?

When they had all been sufficiently interrogated and allowed to leave, Spiro headed down toward the docks. The memory of Xenophon's final, glassy stare held Spiro transfixed. It was as though Spiro's hatred had distilled into a poison and found its way in Xenophon's body. The surge of power intoxicated him, even as he admitted he had not truly caused the man's death.

But what did it matter who had murdered him? Xenophon's death would mean change for Rhodes. Along with Glaucus and Xenophon, three other strategoi had stood in opposition to the Achaean League. With Xenophon gone, a power void had been created, awaiting the first man to step into it.

Spiro slowed at the quay near the statue of Helios and watched the men hauling grain onto a ship. Such a simple task. And yet the island's blessed position made it central to nearly all Greek trade and brought riches to its people, washed in on every high tide.

Rhodes was greater even than Kalymnos, his father's island.

*And I could be greater than he.*

His mind played with the thought. Xenophon was dead, and somehow Glaucus would have to be managed.

*I have spent too many years debating, flattering, cajoling.*

Did he have what it would take to seize the city for himself?

$$\Omega$$

Tessa raised both fists to her face, jerked them outward, and broke Glaucus's grip on her shoulders. She took a step backward. "Get away from me, you filthy beast."

Glaucus seemed to accept the insult as a challenge. A fire sparked in his eyes, one she had not seen before—cause for fear. She backed away farther, placing distance between them in the courtyard. A rare breeze blew into the enclosure as though to cool her anger, to save Tessa from herself.

But she had no desire to be saved. Not tonight.

"What did you think, Tessa?" Glaucus said, his speech slurred. "Did you think you are my equal, simply because I humor you with news of the city?"

"Humor me?" Tessa straightened. "You humor *me*? You could not lead a carrion bird to a carcass without me, let alone lead a city."

His hand shot forward, and the slap rang out in the silent courtyard, its echo bouncing back from the colonnade's tiled roof.

Tessa placed a cool hand against her stinging cheek.

"Strike me, beat me, kill me if you like, Glaucus. But the truth remains unchanged: You need me. You need my insight, my opinions, the information I glean in places you wouldn't dare enter. If that doesn't make me your equal . . ."

Glaucus laughed and folded his arms across his girth. "Finally you speak reason! Nothing can make you my equal. You are and always will be a pleasant, if challenging, distraction. Nothing more."

Movement at the side of the courtyard caught her eye.

"Is there anything you need, Master?" Simeon's question was for Glaucus, but his eyes were on Tessa.

Glaucus half-turned and waved the man off. "Leave us, Simeon. This is no concern of yours."

Simeon bowed his way out, and Glaucus scowled. "That old goat has outlived his usefulness. I have arranged for his replacement already."

"Do you have affection for *anyone* other than yourself?" Tessa said. She counted on shaky fingers as his expression grew rancid. "Your wife, your daughter, Simeon—faithful to you always." She paused. "And me. None of us are more to you than useful tools, amusing toys to be discarded or abused as you wish."

Glaucus reached to Tessa and touched the gold circlet at her neck. There was a cunning behind his drunken half-smile, a slyness that Tessa had never seen before. "I think at last my hetaera understands me," he said. "You exist to be used, Tessa. That is your purpose. Did you think you were entitled to more? Do you dream of happiness, of a *family* perhaps?"

His mockery of her unspoken desire jolted her. "I hate you," she hissed.

Glaucus stared deeply into her eyes. He shook his head and shrugged one shoulder. "Why should that concern me?"

It was a simple question, quietly asked, but it caused Tessa to stagger backward a step. She had nothing left then, nothing at all. The power she believed she wielded over Glaucus was an illusion. The role she played, of politically astute companion to one of the country's most powerful men, was nothing more than a bit of theater, a mask she assumed. And she would never have her secret wish.

The decision she'd made before the symposium hardened. She swore to Helios that before his first rays lit the Rhodian sky in the morning, she would offer herself at his feet and be free.

While her thoughts ran unbidden, Glaucus sidled closer until he stood only inches from her. As if from outside herself, she watched his hands caress her arms, felt him pull her into a harsh embrace.

*Yes, a family. A child, yes. A way to redeem the past.* Release came with the acknowledgment.

She whispered into his ear the first thing that came into her mind, a familiar thought she had never before given voice. "I will kill you while you sleep."

There was no reaction, save for his hands traveling up her arms, to her throat. His fingers dug into her flesh, restricting her air slightly.

She lifted her arms to fight him off, but then relaxed.

*Go ahead. Do it. Perhaps I haven't the courage to do it myself.*

More pressure. Less air. Tessa sucked in breath in tiny gasps, but she did not resist.

*Ten years. Ten years tonight.*

She remembered that girl who stood at the rail of the ship from Delos, not much older than Glaucus's daughter, naïve and carefree. She remembered her and mourned for her. Rhodes was her prison, her cage, as Persephone had said. It was time to escape.

*And yet . . .*

Would she die as she had lived, at the whim of another?

A deep passion to control her own fate, in this, her last act before she entered the underworld, surged up from an unknown place.

She scrabbled at Glaucus's meaty fingers on her neck, but she could not tear them away. Cold spots of black trembled in her vision.

*Not you. Not you. I will do it myself.*

She called on the hatred of ten years, let it boil inside of her until it flowed into her arms, her hands, her fingers. She reached out and dug her fingers into Glaucus's eyes.

He yelped like a dog who'd been kicked and released her immediately. Tessa filled her lungs with sweet air and pushed him backward. She tried to step around him, but he wrapped an arm around her waist.

"You're not going anywhere," he gurgled. He turned her to him and pulled her close, and Tessa realized with horror that her attack had excited him more. She beat at his face with her fists. His breath was labored, and he was still unsteady from too much wine, but he was twice her size. "I've had enough of the high-spirited hetaera," he said. "I think I shall put an end to her tonight."

In desperation, Tessa brought her knee up, hard. Glaucus howled and bent forward. Tessa grabbed his shoulders and shoved him away from her. He stumbled backward one step, then two. His balance shifted. She watched as his weight fell against one of the columns supporting the roof that covered the walkway.

It happened slowly yet all at once. The column shook under Glaucus's weight. His feet shuffled but lost purchase. The wine did its work, and he fell. One shoulder bore the impact, and Tessa heard a crack. He lay at her feet at the edge of the walkway, face up, eyes closed but breathing hard.

And then there was a sliding sound above her, like a cooking pot being dragged across a stone floor. Tessa looked up. One single terra-cotta tile slid down the roof, one large square of baked earth shaken loose by the jolt to the column. Down it slid, until it tipped over the lip of the roof, spun twice as it fell, and buried itself in the center of her master's forehead, cleaving flesh and then bone.

Tessa did not move, did not breathe.

She watched his chest for his next breath, but it did not come.

She braved another look at his face. Blood pooled on the floor beneath him. The tile remained upright, embedded in his skull. Tessa was reminded of the way the men at the docks sometimes left their knives buried in the cutting blocks after chopping the head from a fish.

Glaucus had crossed to the afterlife.

Tessa looked away and clutched her stomach, waiting for the remorse that did not come.

Two beats of silence, then Simeon returned to the courtyard.

# THREE

A half-mile away, thirty-two dockworkers labored beside the dark sea, hauling sacks of grain from dock to barge.

Thirty-two workers, all but one a slave.

Nikos paused in his trek from the mountain of grain on the quay, a large sack resting in well-muscled arms. Arms once accustomed to this very labor, arms that remembered the former days as easily as Nikos did.

A grizzled old man bumped against him, then shoved an elbow into his gut. "Stand about while we work, will you?"

He turned to the man, searched the scratchy beard and greasy hair for what might remain of the old slave's humanity. Is this what Nikos would have looked like in a few score years had his father not acknowledged and rescued him?

Behind him, a jab in the back. "Get to work, man!"

Nikos continued to the barge that dipped and bucked at the water's edge, flung his sack in line with others, and returned to the pile. The dock master's stick found the legs of another slave.

*I could find a better use for that stick.* He laughed to himself. *Another hour, at most.*

His masquerade as a work-for-hire free man at the *agora* had served him well. He had caught the attention of the man he had targeted and been offered a position within his home. He was to report tonight, after his shift at the docks.

"What's your name?" a voice behind him demanded.

He turned from the grain, taking in a man dressed in a short tunic, the dark harbor behind him, the water lapping at the stone wall's edge. His eyes were drawn toward flames a few hundred yards distant to his right, circling the base of the mighty Helios. Torches illuminated the statue's circular base and the bare feet and legs that rose from it. The body and head disappeared into the darkness, as though Helios communed with the gods of the night sky.

Another poke in his stomach, this time with the end of that stick. "I said, what's your name, water rat?"

Caution told him to remain unknown. He shrugged.

The man before him, younger than him by ten years, sneered. "Well, No-Name, either start carrying grain or find yourself in the sea. We've no use for pretty men standing about."

To avoid another jab from the stick, Nikos lurched forward with the others to pick up sacks and tote them to the barge. Out in the harbor a ship rested at anchor, waiting for the load of grain.

Nikos watched the dock master stroll along the harbor's edge, swinging his stick, then engage in conversation with an older, well-dressed man. An angry scar like a crescent moon was etched across the older man's cheek. Nikos frowned and studied the scar. Where had he seen this man before?

Head down, Nikos continued carrying the sacks of grain. Everything depended on his not being identified. If he were recognized and hailed, his careful plan to enter the inner circle of Rhodian politics and gain valued information would come to nothing.

From the corner of his eye, Nikos watched the younger man shake his head, then extend a hand around the dock, as if inviting the older man into his domain. The two parted before Nikos had a chance to contemplate disappearing. The well-dressed man faded into the darkness, moving toward the other end of the dock, and the dock master wandered in Nikos's direction.

"You! What did you say your name was?"

Nikos hesitated, then kept moving, head down. "Dimitri."

The man tilted his head and chewed his lip. "Have you gotten yourself in some trouble?"

Nikos shook his head.

"Because the law is looking for a fine-looking free man like you. He seems very eager to find him. A murderer, perhaps? A thief?"

Nikos hefted a crate to rest on his shoulder and kept walking. The dock master stepped in front of him. "I should think there would be a reward for finding a man so hotly pursued."

Nikos weighed his options. If he continued this charade, he might be identified and he would fail in the task his father had set before him. If he ran, he would surely be pursued. A shout and a crash arose from the end of the slave-line behind him. Nikos turned.

In its frantic rush to accept and disgorge as much trade as possible, Rhodes had begun to employ pulley systems to lift the heaviest items, treasures such as Athenian marble and ship-building timber from the wooded hills of Thrace. One of these pulleys had failed, releasing a cache of logs to the dock below.

A scream sliced the night air. Nikos ran toward the source.

Only one slave had not escaped the falling timber. This one lay on the quay, his lower leg bent at a perverse angle. Nikos pushed through the workers around the injured man, his instinct erasing all thoughts of exposure.

In the days before he had been lifted from the life of these men and placed within the wealth of his father's favor, Nikos had been more than a dockworker. He had been a champion of the working conditions of slaves. And in his years of exposure to injuries suffered, he had developed a working knowledge of and a fiery passion for the healing arts.

"Let me see the leg," he said. The authority in his voice created a breach in the crowd.

The man moaned from the ground, his face a grimace of pain. Nikos recognized him as the old man who had elbowed him earlier. A boy knelt beside him, holding the injured man's head in his hand.

Nikos ran a gentle hand down the leg, whispering comfort. The man had suffered a nasty break, there was no doubt. He would not work the docks again. But with proper treatment, he might live out his days as a household slave.

"The leg must be set," Nikos said to no one in particular. "Fetch a narrow plank and tear some clean rags."

Nikos looked over his shoulder. Through a gap in the crowd, he spotted the well-dressed man with the scar emerging from the darkness, his eyes darting about like a hound on a scent.

Recognition flashed. The man was an enemy. More precisely, the right-hand man of his father's chief adversary.

Nikos reached a hand beneath his tunic, to a pouch belted at his waist. He drew out two drachmas and pressed them into the hand of the young slave holding the old man's head. The boy raised incredulous eyes to Nikos who whispered, "Use this to pay the physician. Be certain the leg is set and allowed to heal. He will walk again." He patted the old man's arm. "Courage," he said.

Wishing he could do more, Nikos fled into the night, away from the harbor and its guardian statue, away from his father's enemy.

He would be hunted. But by the time he was found, he must be well-entrenched in the home and life of the man who was the key to his success: Glaucus of Rhodes.

## Ω

Tessa watched Simeon enter the courtyard, saw the concern on his face. She observed him looking toward Glaucus at her feet, perceived that he crossed the courtyard in haste and kneeled beside his master. All this she saw from a vague and hazy place within her mind, oddly detached. A place that had no words to speak as Simeon questioned her.

"Oh, Tessa, what has happened?"

The kneeling servant reached a tentative hand in the direction of the tile protruding from Glaucus's forehead, then withdrew it. He lifted his head to study her.

"I heard shouting," he said. "I came to be certain you—that all was well."

"He is dead." Tessa inhaled and looked away.

"Yes."

She heard the sadness in Simeon's voice and was able to marvel that the servant held any amount of affection for his master. But then Simeon turned to her and stood.

"He pushed you too far, Tessa. This was foreseeable. A woman such as yourself, forced to submit to him . . ."

Tessa did not at first grasp his meaning. Then realization came. She lifted a weak hand toward Glaucus. "Do you think that I did this?"

Simeon gripped her arm. "I do not blame you, Tessa. But we must think now. We must think about how to protect you!"

She shook her head. "The tile. The column," she pointed upward, "it came from the roof."

"Tessa! It makes little difference now. You must listen!" Simeon led her a few paces from the body. "All who attended the symposium tonight heard your imprudent words. All have seen the way he demeans you, in spite of the respect you command in this city. No one will doubt that you have killed him."

Tessa could focus only on fragments of Simeon's words. Such a strange feeling. "What will happen to me?"

Simeon glanced at Glaucus. "If you are found guilty of murder, you will be executed."

"But I am not guilty."

"And if you are found innocent, you will be passed to the next patron who has paid your hetaera price."

"I will run," she said. "Disappear."

Simeon smiled sadly. "You are the most well-known hetaera on the island, Tessa. Where could you go that you would not be recognized? Who would not return you to Servia for the price of the reward?" He sighed. "Stay here a moment."

He left, and sparks of panic surged to Tessa's fingertips. Even if she could make people believe, could escape execution, who knew what her next patron might be like?

Simeon returned a moment later, a dark swath of fabric in his hands. He flicked his wrists to snap the fabric taut in the air, then let it float to the ground where it covered Glaucus's bulk. Tessa breathed again, began to think.

"I must know who is next, Simeon."

The Jewish man nodded. "I will pray that it is a better man, for your sake."

Tessa wrapped her arms around herself. "Tell no one, Simeon. Promise me that you'll tell no one until I return!"

Simeon smiled, sadness in his eyes. "We cannot hide him for long, Tessa. He will be missed as soon as the day is new."

Tessa looked at the fabric-draped body and thought of her vow to Helios, to offer herself before sunrise. But perhaps the god had heard her cry and answered with a different sort of freedom, one she had not dared to dream. She was tasting it now, she knew. And once tasted, it could not be relinquished.

"Help me drag him out of sight for now, Simeon." The older man frowned. She took in the dark courtyard, with all its shadow. "There," she pointed. "Behind the gardener's tools and pots. He will not be seen so easily."

They accomplished the heavy task in a few minutes, leaving the covered body half-hidden in the corner, under the colonnade.

Tessa inhaled deeply, ran her hands through her hair, and nodded to Simeon. Mynah sang out a single clear note, like the starting note of a stadium race. One backward glance, then Tessa fled through the inner hall, onto the portico, and into the Rhodian night, her steps and her heart pounding a rhythm that whispered of hope.

She must learn who was to own her next. Only then could she decide. Only then could she know where her freedom would be found—in pursuing life or in embracing death.

# FOUR

The night hung heavy with the saltiness of the sea. Tessa fled through the humid air, down the hill from Glaucus's house, into the street below. Her feet followed the well-worn path home, though her mind remained in the courtyard, watching that terra-cotta tile twirl through empty air and cleave flesh.

*I have only until morning before he is discovered.*

Though Glaucus demanded her presence often, Tessa still maintained her own room in the harbor district, as it would have been scandalous not to. It was to the tiny space she called her home that she now ran, only half-conscious of where her feet landed.

*I must find Servia.*

The thought pounded in her mind. It followed the rhythm of her feet.

*Servia. Servia.*

The name brought no pleasant associations.

Tessa's steps slowed with exhaustion. Though the night air was warm, a coldness crept through her body, working its way from her heart to her fingertips. She began to shake.

*Glaucus is dead.* She panted the words aloud, then jerked her head to both sides, waiting for an accuser to leap from the darkness.

Her breathing came heavy, the only sound in the still night, and she willed it to slow.

*Who will own me now?*

Even with her head down, the city's rectangular grid and the torch-lit statue led her easily to the sea, to the harbor district where she had spent her first several years in Rhodes. Years of poverty, of begging fishermen for a day's meal, of watching her mother trade favors for fish.

And then Servia. Servia, to whom her mother gratefully handed Tessa, assuring her daughter that a better life awaited. She would be trained to be a lady, her mother said. A fine lady, with jewels and lovely chitôns, the stench of fish a thing of the past.

*Ah, mother. Did you not know you only traded one bondage for another?*

The harbor sounds grew. Shouts of dockworkers, loading barges with the Aegean's precious trade. Tessa slowed and lifted her eyes to the harbor statue, leading her forward to where she truly belonged. She soon rounded the final corner. The harbor lay before her. It crawled with slaves and hired men and was lit by a hundred flickering torches.

The neglected buildings that traced the line of the sea away from the harbor were home to tavern owners, brothels, and those unfortunate enough to find no other home. At the center of this squalor, one small building sheltered Servia's "ladies," as she called them. Those who lived there full-time, not yet ready for the market, were hardly more than girls. They spent their days under Servia's tutelage, learning the dress and the look and the allure of the hetaera. The older, more experienced ones like Tessa came and went at the whim of their current patron.

Tessa was reluctant to leave the torch-lit harbor for the darkened street that would lead her to her sometimes-home. The air felt colder here, as though the darkness sucked away the warmth of human kindness. Her sandals scraped the street, and the sound echoed back from the shacks that lined the way. Ahead, she saw a half-starved yellow cat nosing something in the street. The cat lifted its head and fixed green eyes on her. Tessa wished for a fish to ease the animal's hunger.

*But at least she is free.* Tessa stopped a few steps from the cat, and the two studied one another. *She lives her life as she pleases,* Tessa thought, *and that is more than I have.*

*But perhaps . . .*

She must find Servia and ask her the only question that mattered. Somewhere inside of her, deep within the cold, a tiny flame of hope struggled to burn. She dared to give the thought her attention. Perhaps the next patron would be a rich old man who wanted only to put her on display and nothing more. Someone who would allow her relative freedom and who would demand nothing.

Perhaps Helios *had* heard her vow this night and had intervened.

She inhaled the night air and continued walking, urged by the flicker of hope.

Not far from Servia's rooms, a voice called from a doorway, scratchy with years and soaked with wine. His words startled her. "Did you think you could get away with it?"

Tessa's sandal caught a rut in the street, and she tripped. She caught herself and kept walking. *They have come for me already.* But she did not stop.

The voice in the doorway materialized into a figure and stepped into the street. "Come on, pretty one, you can't just walk past a man and not say hello."

He darted in front of her and cut her off. Tessa took in his bare feet, the stained tunic draped over his shoulder, and his half-bare chest, scraggly with a few gray hairs. She did not look into his eyes.

His labor-roughened hands scraped up her arms. "One look. Can't you give a man one look?"

Tessa pulled her arms away. Obviously the man had no idea who she was. They moved in different worlds. She raised her eyes to his. "Get out of my way."

"Oooh, she has claws!" His lips split into a grin, revealing missing and rotted teeth. He circled her waist with one arm.

Tessa thought of the cat, free to run the streets as it wished. *Claws indeed.* She slapped his face with fingers curled inward and dragged her nails across his cheek.

He only laughed and tightened his grip on her waist. The sound sickened her, reminded her of Glaucus. She'd been treated roughly enough for one night.

"You had best release me," she said, drawing herself up to her full height and finding she stood taller than he. "Glaucus does not appreciate his hetaera being pawed by stinking dockworkers." Even as she said the words, she hated herself for seeking protection in the name of her dead patron.

Something flickered in the man's eyes. Amusement, perhaps.

"Did you think I did not recognize you, Tessa of Delos?" His fingers dug into her side, and he pulled her toward the doorway from which he'd slithered. "Servia's best, everyone says. Her finest accomplishment."

Tessa's feet dragged across the street, through the gutter's waste water, up onto the level of the buildings. The man's beard pricked at her cheek.

"Prepares them all down here, Servia does. Down here, where we can watch. Then sends the delicacies up the hill as a feast for fine men and leaves us with the scraps."

He pushed her against a door and it gave way, sucking both of them into the darkened building.

"It's time for some of us to get more than scraps, I say." He laughed in her face, and his rotten breath clouded her eyes. "Well, one of us, at least."

The small flicker of hope that began when Tessa ran from Glaucus's house now flamed into anger. She had taken down a bigger man than this only tonight. The empty street beckoned her through the open doorway.

$$\Omega$$

Nikos left the docks behind, hoping the boy into whose hands he pressed the drachmas would have sense enough to spend the money on care for the injured old man. For now, Nikos needed to remain unseen until morning. He headed for the street that lay along the docks, knowing that there would likely be a *taverna* open and serving wine even at this late hour. If he could find a dark corner, he would wait out the night and then be on Glaucus's doorstep at first light.

The street was darker than the harbor, and Nikos welcomed the shadows. He plodded down the center, seeing no one, searching for an open doorway and sounds of life.

Ahead, he heard talking, saw a flash of clothing through a door. He drew closer, looking for a place where he could sit alone in the darkness and nurse a cup of wine for a few hours. But it was only a man and woman, locked together in the doorway of an empty shack. Nikos turned his head in disgust, a comparison to animals lingering in his mind.

A sharp cry from the doorway slowed his steps. He looked again, more closely, and sauntered toward the two. An unkempt dockworker had his arms twisted around a beautiful woman. Though her hair was loosed, Nikos recognized her as a respectable woman. Her soft skin and fine fabric placed her far from these parts.

Her eyes turned on him, and the desperation there held him captive for a moment, flooding his heart with pity.

"Remove your hands from her!" Nikos leaped toward the door and surprised the preoccupied man.

"She is mine this night," the man laughed. "You can have her tomorrow!" He buried his dirty face into the woman's neck. She turned her head and closed her eyes.

Nikos's compassion hardened into anger. "I said step away." He grabbed the man's wrist and twisted him away from the woman.

"Move on!" The dockworker spat on Nikos's sandals. "This is none of your concern."

Nikos shoved the man into the abandoned building and stepped between him and the woman. "Find something else to do with your free time."

The man was small but quick. Nikos didn't expect the fist that jammed into his stomach, nor the rotted smile. Air whooshed from his lungs, and he doubled over. Beneath him, the moldy remnants of scavenged food littered the floor. But Nikos's years of experience served him well. The next punch didn't land.

He ducked to the right and threw the dockworker off balance. A stiff hand to the neck sent the man to his knees at the woman's feet. The anger on her face confused Nikos. He followed the hand with a fist to the jaw. Spittle flew. The dockworker fell, and rats scurried to their corners. The woman didn't flinch.

Nikos stepped over the man, shoulders thrown back. The woman stood in the doorway. Her chitôn had been ripped away. Nikos reached to cover her. She slapped his hand.

"Do not touch me!"

He spoke softly. "You are safe now. I want to help."

"I don't need your help!"

The man on the ground moaned and stirred. Nikos turned back to him, but the man raised a black-fingernailed hand in surrender.

Nikos kicked him in the stomach, disciplining himself to restrain the fury he felt. "Get out of here!" The man scrabbled to his knees, hauled himself to his feet, and fled into the street.

Nikos turned back to the woman. Even in the darkness he could see that she trembled. "Let me take you home."

She shook her head, and her whole body shuddered like a yellow orchid in a storm.

"You can trust me. I only want to help."

She spoke through clenched teeth. "I told you I do not need your help. Did you expect a reward? Is that why you intervened?"

"A reward?" Nikos frowned.

"Because you will get nothing. You should mind your own concerns."

Pity was quickly turning to annoyance. "Listen, woman," he said, "I saw that you were in trouble, and I helped. That's all. You could be grateful."

She backed away. "A lady has no need to express gratitude toward men who stink of sweat and fish."

Nikos narrowed his eyes. "And a *lady* would not be found on this street at this time of night."

Her jaw dropped slightly, and Nikos regretted his words. The desperation he'd seen in her eyes earlier returned. He reached out to her. "I am sorry. I should not—"

She cringed at his hand, as though it were the hand she just had fought off.

"Please, allow me to help you safely home."

She wrapped her torn chitôn around her shoulders. "You have no better chance than he of consorting with me." She whirled and disappeared into the night.

Nikos considered following her but thought better of it. She seemed capable of protecting herself with her wit alone. And his tendency toward goodwill had already drawn far too much attention this night. He cursed his inconvenient sentimentality.

This was a time to remain unseen.

# FIVE

Once more Tessa ran through the night, refusing to give thought to the demands of men—or to men who sought to rescue her. She had never met a man who wanted nothing from her, including those who disguised their demands as service.

How long until Glaucus's body was found?

One quick turn to the right at the street's end, and Tessa came to a stop in front of the building where Servia had trained her to be Glaucus's showpiece. Inside she would find her owner working with others like her. The thought made her stomach churn.

The door showed signs of age since she had been here last, and its salt-encrusted handle stuck a bit as she turned and pushed. While the outside bore the same weathered and beaten visage as the surrounding buildings, Servia had transformed the interior of her hetaera school into an upper-class home. Tessa stepped inside where the light from an oil lamp played on the fine fabrics that draped an inner arch. An expensive statue of Aphrodite graced the entry. Soft music played from somewhere deep in the house, and Tessa heard a young and feminine giggle.

One might have been in the inner halls of Glaucus's home, or that of any of the other wealthy merchants on the hill. A little bit of theater, down here in the harbor district. The comparison was apt, for it was here that young girls first donned the masks they would wear until the years, or the abuse, made them no longer interesting to their rich patrons. And then what?

Tessa had never met a hetaera who had retired from her position in comfort and wealth, though the prospect was ever held out to them, like a bit of bait on the end of a vicious hook.

Tessa walked into the house and found the andrôn. Ironic, that Servia had replicated the men's quarters in a house full of girls. Ironic, but necessary.

Three girls reclined on couches, whispering and pulling grapes from gold-painted bowls set before them. Their conversation stopped when Tessa entered.

"Servia," she said, still breathless from her run through the streets and the encounter with the dockworker.

Three wide-eyed girls stared back at her.

"Servia," she repeated. "Where is she?"

A new girl struggled to her feet and smiled shyly. She was young and pretty, with dark skin and a splash of freckles across her nose.

"You are Tessa!"

"Yes, yes," Tessa shook her head, "I need to speak to Servia!"

The other girls were on their feet now, and the newest drew close and touched Tessa's chitôn.

"So beautiful," she whispered.

"But it is torn," another said, pulling the fabric toward herself.

"What is it like?" the third asked. "What is it like to be the most admired hetaera on the island?"

*It feels like slavery.*

"Girls!" Tessa said, pulling her clothing from their curious fingers. "Tell Servia I must speak with her."

"She is not here. At night she sometimes goes to the taverna to . . ."

The girl's voice dropped away, and another filled in for her.

"To find men who need—others—of us."

Tessa nodded. She was not unfamiliar with Servia's business tactics. She took in the most promising of girls, but not all of them would prove to be fit for patrons like Glaucus. Some of them would instead produce income from the pockets of fisherman, sailors, and dockworkers. Servia split her time between training some for greatness and drumming up business for the rest.

Tessa turned to go.

One of the girls clutched her chitôn again. She was plainer than the others, much shorter than Tessa.

"Tell us something, Tessa. Tell us the most important thing you have learned as a hetaera."

She turned back and looked into the young girl's eyes, studied her unlined cheeks for a moment. "I will tell you," she said. "Soon, very soon, you will start to feel that there is something cold like a stone in your heart. Let that cold part of you grow, let it spread to all of you, until you are nothing more than a breathing piece of bronze." She let her gaze take in all three of them. "It is the only way to survive."

She fled from their youthful, perplexed faces, into the night and toward the nearest taverna.

The building was as different from the inside of Servia's home as silk from wool. Like a distorted and corrupt mirror image of Servia's andrôn, the darkness of the taverna smelled of wine and vomit, and on one of the couches lay a snoring sailor, passed out with a cup of wine still clutched in his rope-scarred hand. The air held the taste of the cheap oil used to light the lamps, and even the door felt greasy to her touch. Tessa's stomach rebelled, and she covered her nose with her hand. In a corner, two men tossed dice and placed bets under a painted fresco of a woman and child.

She spotted Servia immediately. She stood with her wide back to Tessa, gesturing and demanding attention from an unseen man on a far couch along the wall. Tessa exhaled, watched the fat under the woman's arms wobble with each punctuated sentence, and steeled herself for the encounter.

"How can you refuse?" Servia was saying. "Even those new to the island have heard that Servia's girls are the best."

Tessa could not hear the man's reply, but it did not please Servia.

"Aaachh! Two drachma, then. Two drachma, and your promise that you tell no one what a bargain you have forced Servia into."

Servia's hands went to her hips, a sure sign that she was negotiating hard.

She listened, then shook her head. "One drachma! You will not be sorry."

"I said no!"

Tessa raised her eyebrows. Few dared shout at Servia.

Tessa sensed from Servia's posture that the man had risen from the couch. "Leave me, woman," he said. "You devalue your entire sex with your haggling!"

Servia's head snapped back, and Tessa could feel her anger from across the room. Servia whirled from the insolent man and stormed across the room. She took in Tessa with some surprise and waddled over to her. Her famous gold tooth glinted in the murky light.

"Ah, here is one he would not be so quick to refuse, eh?" Servia patted her cheek and Tessa turned her head. "But she is not for sale, is she?" Servia laughed. "No, she is paid for several times over."

"Servia, I must speak to you."

The woman looked back over her shoulder. "You see the quality that Servia is known for?"

Tessa followed her gaze and found herself being watched by the man who had come to her rescue earlier. She felt her face flush and lowered her head, surprised by the unfamiliar surge of shame.

Her owner grinned at her. "What can Servia do for you, my dear?"

"Not here." Tessa glanced at the man in the corner. "Come outside."

"We can speak here." Servia extended her arm to the room. "We are all friends here."

"Outside, Servia!"

The woman shrugged. "As you wish." She shoved the door open and let it swing shut behind her, forcing Tessa to thrust out an arm to stop it.

In the street, Servia leaned against the cracked plaster wall and shook her head. "Fool," she said, tossing her head back toward the building. "He'll be thrashing himself tomorrow for the bargain he passed up tonight."

"Servia, you must tell me—"

The woman scanned the empty street. "Where is everyone tonight?" she said. "Business is not good."

"After Glaucus, Servia, who has paid next for—for my favor?"

Servia chuckled. "Ah, so delicate, Tessa. I trained you well. Glaucus must be delighted with his pet. You have made quite a name for yourself, you know."

Tessa clutched at the woman's arm, her usual aversion to touch overcome by her desperation. "Who is next, Servia?"

The woman's eyes narrowed. "Why? Are you so soon tired of Glaucus? Do you hope to do better?"

Tessa slid away and ran her hands through her hair. "I am just . . . curious. That is all. I want to know what the years ahead will hold."

"I suspect that you have not come close to expending your usefulness to Glaucus, my dear." Servia smiled and raised an eyebrow. "He strikes me as a man who does not tire easily."

Tessa curled her lip and leaned against the building. "You are right, of course. I only want to know who is next, should Glaucus . . . should he decide to find someone younger."

Servia threw back her head and laughed. "Ah, the curse of all women. We fear the passing years as men fear the loss of power. Always there is someone behind us, ready to step into our place, as my new girl, Berenice, would step into yours. But not to worry, Tessa. You have many years of beauty left."

Tessa balled her fists at her sides and ground them into the wall behind her. "Servia, tell me who is next!"

It was a mistake, always a mistake, to challenge Servia. Tessa knew it the moment she spoke the words.

The older woman folded fleshy arms over her ample chest and scowled.

"Leave the business to me, Tessa. Do not forget your place." She leaned into Tessa's face and whispered. "But I will tell you—hold onto Glaucus, my dear. The next one won't be so kind."

Ω

*The next one won't be so kind.*

Tessa retraced her steps through the harbor district street, heedless of the earlier danger, perhaps even welcoming it.

At the top of the hill lay the body of Glaucus, shrouded by dark fabric and the dark night, but soon there would be no hiding him.

Tessa considered her options. Should she return to Glaucus's home, she would face possible execution for his murder. If, by the gods' whim, she were not accused, she faced enslavement again at the hand of someone even worse than Glaucus.

Only two other choices remained. She could fulfill her vow to Helios before sunrise. Or . . .

Her steps took her toward the statue, but her thoughts were on the water beyond. Why could she not simply escape? Leave the island, start over somewhere. Simeon had said it was impossible, but was it?

One thing was certain: She would never belong to another man. She would never allow herself to be enslaved again. Escape or death—nothing more.

An early dawn gnawed at the horizon. If she were to accomplish an escape, it had to be soon. She quickened her pace, kept her focus on the statue, and breathed a fearful prayer to Helios for safe passage.

The harbor never ceased its hum of activity, earning its reputation as the busiest port on the Aegean. As Tessa crossed the street and ventured onto the stone harbor itself, her passing drew glances from slaves, masters, and freemen alike.

*I must get out of sight.*

Several crates stacked near the dark water's edge seemed a good place to survey the situation.

Tessa ran, head down, toward the sea, still dark and choppy with the night breezes. She dropped to her knees between the crates and the quay's edge and watched men load sacks onto a barge that bobbed in the harbor. Her gaze traveled outward, out to the wider sea where the ship waited for the next load of goods from the barge.

*Where is it going?* She shrugged. *Do I care? It is not staying here.*

Somehow she had to make it onto that barge—and then the ship.

For the first time since Glaucus was felled, Tessa felt the blood flow through her veins and quicken her heart.

*I am not dead yet.*

She crouched lower, wishing she could slide through the cracks in the crate, join whatever it held, and be whisked away to some foreign soil. Above her, a single gull cawed and swooped toward the sea, then lifted and sailed on moonlit wings into the night.

Resin. The crate was filled with pine resin, Tessa realized. The aroma seeped out, wrapping her in nostalgia for early days on wooded hills, before she and her mother had come to this place.

Her knees grew sore with kneeling, and dawn advanced.

She had intended to make a plan but found that her mind was unable. In the end, she waited until the barge was fully loaded, until the dockworkers had transferred their efforts to another, then sprinted along the edge of the water, bent at the waist.

No one hailed her. No one stopped her.

Tessa's breath came fast now. Her head felt light. She felt a kinship with the gull. She, too, would soar over the sea.

Two steps down into the barge. Sacks of grain, crates of treasures. There, a narrow gap between the cargo. She slipped in, then behind.

Pressed from all sides, Tessa had never felt more free.

She heard a sailor's shout, felt the barge dip, and then they were away.

*Away!*

She must still find a way onto the ship itself, but she was halfway there. Hope surged, in spite of her desire to remain cautious. She could do this.

Her mind raced. Should she alight as soon as they pulled alongside the ship? No doubt sailors would be at the rail, waiting to pull the cargo aboard. But if she waited, they would slowly but surely peel away layers of her protection until she was exposed.

She slid from behind the stack of crates, gripped the waist-high edge of the barge, and leaned over until she could see the ship. The sea below lapped at the barge's hull. She stared into the inky blackness, wondered what creatures swam beneath the surface, and hardened her resolve.

One last glance back at the harbor. A nod to Helios, who looked down on her from lofty heights with favor. The barge drew near the ship.

*It must be now.*

She gripped the edge, swung a leg over, and ignored the sharp splinters that dug at her thigh. Another leg over, a moment of indecision, and then the cold plunge into the water.

The shock of the water over her head threatened to force her mouth open. She broke the surface and pushed her hair from her eyes. Ever mindful of the barge, she tread water alongside it with silent strokes.

Within moments, they had gained the ship.

Shouts accompanied a rope thrown, the coil splashing only a few feet from her. She backpedaled to avoid detection.

All attention was trained on drawing the barge alongside the ship for the transfer of cargo. Tessa swam around to the ship's other side. Twice the choppy sea pushed her too close and banged her shoulder, then her head, into the wood. She bit her lip and kept swimming.

There, on the port side of the ship, was a rope and some toeholds, used by sailors who occasionally took to the sea for hygienic reasons.

Tessa never hesitated. Freedom was within her grasp. She clutched the rope as though it were a lifeline pulling her from a quagmire, and hauled herself up the side of the ship until her eyes were just above the railing.

The rope scorched her palms, but she held fast. All eyes were focused on the starboard side, where the crew hurriedly took on their cargo.

Up and over, she dropped with a wet thud onto the deck, then scurried for the nearest shelter. A set of steps ran down into the ship's murky hold. Darkness was her ally now, and Tessa slid down the steps without pause.

Below, a small lamp lit the center of a square room. She found another door and, behind it, a tiny compartment half-filled with supplies—and space enough for her. She pulled the door closed behind her, sank backward into she knew not what, and breathed again.

Safe. Almost free.

Again the question of this ship's destination crossed her mind. Where would her new life begin? Far from the islands, she hoped, perhaps Alexandria or Persia. Though how long a voyage could she survive under the circumstances? And if the sailors discovered her during their voyage . . .

Would they toss her overboard? Or would they—

No. No thoughts of that now. What was done was done, and she would have no regrets. Because she had no choice.

Something below her shifted, and she dropped closer to the floor. Her foot nudged the door open, and she shot a hand out to pull it shut again.

How long would it take for the ship to get underway?

She did not know how much time passed. She thought that perhaps she dozed and many hours had passed. Or it could have been only minutes. The darkness oppressed her, even as she sensed the growing light outside her small shelter.

And then voices, louder than those she'd heard above. Sailors had come below, which must mean that they were soon to push off. Her heart beat faster with a rhythm that seemed almost musical.

She struggled to make out the voices, to distinguish the words, to gain information about their destination.

With some surprise she heard a woman's voice. Did women accompany the sailors? She had never pictured it so, but perhaps they took some along to care for the needs of men on the voyage.

But this woman's voice held a particular familiarity.

The blinding recognition came only a fraction of a moment before her door jerked open.

Even in the smoky half-light of the dawn, Tessa could see the derisive smile on Servia's face.

And then Servia began to laugh. Tessa didn't move, couldn't move. The laugh had turned her limbs to iron.

A sailor drew alongside Servia. The ship's captain perhaps.

"Yes, indeed," Servia said to him, "you have precious cargo."

She reached into the folds of her *himation* and pulled out a small pouch. Tessa heard the jingle of coins as Servia pressed the pouch into the man's hand.

"I hope you will find this ample reward," she said. And then she held out a hand to Tessa, as though she were a little girl who had fallen while she played. "Come, Tessa. It is time to go home."

Tessa struggled to her feet, ignoring Servia's hand. She fought for any dignity she could muster, there in the dark with her wet clothes and hair clinging to her and the coins of her betrayal weighing down the sailor's palm.

As Servia pushed her up the steps from behind, the laughter began again. "Why did you not tell me you planned to take a holiday, Tessa? Surely you did not think you could slip away unnoticed?"

Tessa drew herself up on the deck and faced the amused stares of the sailors.

Servia nudged her forward. "You were seen the moment you stepped on to the docks." She laughed. "It is your own fault, really.

You have made yourself impossible to hide with your outspoken prominence. As soon as it became clear you intended to leave Rhodes, I had several helpful men on my doorstep, offering to lead me to you in exchange for—oh, a pittance, really."

Tessa climbed over the edge of the ship, dropped into the barge, and sat on the floor. Servia stood beside her, silent as they returned to the dock.

When they alighted, Servia wrapped an arm around Tessa's waist and whispered into her ear, "You have asked many questions tonight, Tessa. And you've done foolish things. I do not know why. You have amused me. But do not think that you can walk away from all I have done for you. If you do not return to Glaucus immediately, you will begin to feel my wrath."

Servia gave her a little shove, and Tessa stumbled forward, her mind blank. She trudged away from the water and staggered toward Helios, who had not delivered her. She found herself alone at the foot of the mighty statue and looked up at the pedestal on which he stood. Almost without thought, she climbed the pedestal, then crawled on hands and knees across the stone base until she sat between his massive sandaled feet, each one the size of a full-grown ox. She slid to one side, leaned against a bronze heel, and gazed at the city.

Morning had fully arrived now, and she absently watched three boys playing in the street below her. They had some sort of cage between them, with something trapped inside. Two of them poked sticks through the bars of the cage, and the third laughed and clapped. The animal inside the cage screeched, a sound that turned her blood even colder.

The boys shifted and Tessa leaned forward to see into the cage.

Between the bars, staring angrily out at the world, was the yellow cat with green eyes whom she had felt such jealousy toward only hours before.

The single tear that slid down her cheek surprised her. The bronze woman she had become had not shed tears in a long while. *Ah, well, it is fitting. One comes into the world squalling. And one should probably leave it with at least some sign of remorse.*

She rested her head against Helios's heel once more, wished she had thought to procure a knife before climbing up here, and watched the sun begin to rise above her prison.

# SIX

### ✦ *Six Days before the Great Quake* ✦

Spiro rose from his bed with thoughts of the night still echoing. It was time to leave aside rhetoric, to seize power through action, not words.

All around them, foreign nations challenged the Greek ideal. If Rhodes were to remain the Aegean's center of wealth, more than endless council debates were needed. Yes, action. Violence, even.

Before the sun lifted a hand's breadth from the sea, Spiro summoned a servant and cart and took to the streets to reach the agora while it was still early. If he were to embrace this path, he would need assistance.

The agora teemed with shoppers and merchants already, and Spiro dismounted his cart, choosing to command less attention by slipping through the crowds on foot. Even so, he was recognized and hailed by many. Some even dared to grasp his clothing as he passed.

"Yes, yes," he nodded and pushed aside the peasants, ignoring their tedious comments and complaints.

On the steps of the *bouleuterion*, the council building, the aged philosopher Apollonius held court, his students sitting at his feet in the tradition of Socrates and Plato, who had turned philosophy from the ramblings of old men into the pride of Hellenism. Apollonius hailed Spiro as he passed.

"What say you, Spiro? Do you not agree that although it is worthwhile to attain the good for one man alone, it is nobler and more divine to do so for nations and cities?"

Spiro smiled and waved him off. "Squander your time with philosophy, if you wish, Apollonius. War, alliances, money—these are worldly matters that must occupy those who rule."

Apollonius said to his students loud enough for Spiro to hear, "Plato said that those too smart to engage in politics are punished by being governed by fools."

Spiro stopped, smiled to himself, and considered having the man flogged. But no, he was popular among the people. Spiro chuckled good-naturedly instead. "Perhaps it is better to be a rich fool than a poor philosopher," he replied and continued on his way.

He felt a twinge of worry at the exaggerated boast. Rich? Once, perhaps. But he had been living beyond his means for some time, stretching his purse to maintain his reputation.

He swept into the slave market at last and left off his dark thoughts. The collection of men and women available pleased him, and he stopped at the fenced area to survey the latest crop. Long-haired beauties from distant lands eyed him with interest, and men milled about, hardened into surliness or broken down from abuse. A particular brute caught his eye and returned his gaze with confidence. Spiro inclined his head, a subtle request for the slave to approach. The man crossed over to him and stopped on the other side of the waist-high fence, close enough to touch. The slave was at least a head taller than Spiro and completely hairless. Spiro looked him up and down and was surprised when the giant grinned at him. He had good teeth.

"Do you like what you see?" the slave asked.

Spiro reached for the slave's upper arm and gripped it. "You're built like an ox. Let's hope you're smarter."

"Smart enough to recognize power in another when I see it."

Spiro half-smiled. "What is your name?"

"Ajax."

Named for the Trojan War hero. Perhaps fitting.

"I require discretion," Spiro said, "someone who can carry out an unpleasant task without wagging his tongue in the local taverna—or drawing unwanted attention to me."

Ajax wove his fingers together and flexed his hands. "I am at your service," he said.

Spiro studied him a moment longer, then nodded. He left Ajax and searched out the slave auctioneer.

"How much for the bald giant?"

A small man with thick lips, the auctioneer laughed. "Ah, Spiro, not surprising that you have your eye on the best of the lot. He will bring much in the auction."

"I do not wish to bid for him. I will purchase him outright, before the auction begins."

The auctioneer frowned and shook his head. "Bad business to sell off a prize steer before we see what he can bring."

Spiro leaned in. "Listen, you filthy swine, I care nothing for your profit. I do not wish to be seen acquiring this slave."

"But—"

Spiro rolled his eyes. "Are you deaf? How much?"

The little man cowered before him. "Ten minae."

Spiro snarled. A thousand drachma. Six thousand obols. He had stuffed his purse with more than he could afford, and the vermin before him was asking for nearly all of it.

He looked back at the slave pen, at Ajax who towered above the crowd and watched him with arms crossed over his massive chest. Again, the question whispered on the air last night found its mark: *Do you have what it takes to prove to your father that you are as great a leader as he?*

He pulled a sack of coins from under his himation and thrust it into the auctioneer's hands.

"Tell no one that it was I who purchased him," he instructed, ignoring the greed in the slave trader's eyes. "Direct him to come to my home after dark."

The little man nodded, and Spiro turned away from the unpleasant transaction. With a last meaningful look at Ajax, he strode back into the heart of the agora.

There was no going back now. The money was spent. Ajax would be Spiro's hands in the violence to come.

He moved through the crowd like a ship destined for a new port, heedless of the wake of people behind him.

Yes, he would seize the city for himself.

And when Rhodes was his, somehow he would have Tessa, too.

## Ω

Helios's golden sun climbed the sky above the harbor, warming Tessa's upturned face and heating his own bronze likeness against which she rested. The airy fabric of her chitôn dried quickly, but the heavy cascade of dark ringlets remained damp on her shoulders.

Time without thought passed, flowing unheeded over Tessa. Merchants came to the harbor area, haggled with traders, and left with carts full of goods to sell at market. A new shift of workers relieved those who worked beside the night sea. Unsupervised children, their parents laboring elsewhere in the district, played in the street and pestered all who passed.

The eyes of many strayed to Tessa where she sat at the feet of the colossus. The vague awareness of being ogled did not disturb her. Several times her eyes connected with another's, and she wondered if they could guess her intent.

And yet still she sat there, until she cursed her own slowness. She needed to obtain the means with which to end her life. Perhaps Glaucus's body had been found, and they were looking for her even now. She refused to be at the mercy of men again. She climbed from the pedestal and ventured toward the docks.

She had no illusions of being unnoticed this time. The eyes that turned to her as she walked past held a wary curiosity. Perhaps they had heard about last night and hoped for a similar chance to fill their purses.

Or perhaps the years that had turned her heart to stone had finally worked their way outward to her body, and they only wanted to see what a walking statue looked like.

She passed a sailor who grabbed at her with a leer. She shook him off and moved down the dock, past the trading barges unloading their cargo, toward the end of the quay where fisherman dragged their nets across the beach and separated their catch for the merchants.

Fishermen would have knives, Tessa knew. But she would have to draw close, or she would arouse suspicion. She would have to engage them, to please them, to flatter them.

She once would have felt disgust at such a performance. Today she felt nothing. Nothing at all.

Trying to appear casual, she drifted to the center of the fishermen's sandy beach area, wandered through the wheeled carts waiting for loads of fish. She had no strength to lift her chin, but her eyes trailed over the men, searching for one who might have an unused knife nearby. Raised eyebrows, half-smiles, and elbow jabs into fellow fishermen followed her.

She moved toward a group of five busily pulling fish from nets and slapping them onto carts. One sat on the ground, repairing a tear in the net. His youth still showed even through the dark-tanned skin and muscled arms.

Tessa sighed theatrically and lowered herself to the sand beside him. She lifted her hair from her neck, aware that she still wore it down and using it to her advantage. "It grows warm so early," she said, her eyes on the young man's face.

He grinned at her, then up at his companions. "A bath in the sea would cool us down."

"But you are so busy with repairing your nets. Surely you could not take time to swim with me." The flirtation came easily, came from the stony part of her that needed no thought to act.

"Ah, but there will always be nets to repair," he said and edged toward her. "One does not get to swim with a goddess every day."

Tessa's lips smiled, though her heart had already returned to Helios's feet.

"Will you show me how the nets are repaired?" she asked, still smiling. The knife that lay on the beach beside him had not gone unnoticed. Tessa leaned in, allowing her shoulder to brush against his.

He shrugged, then pushed the net toward her. She accepted the ropes with her left hand, while her right hand slid to the ground. Her fingers circled the knife and pulled it toward her leg.

The young fisherman talked on, about the rough water that tore the nets apart, about the declining quality of rope he had been able to procure. Tessa nodded and smiled and thought of the knife blade against her wrists.

When she was certain that she had worked the knife into the folds of her clothing sufficiently, Tessa leaned into the fisherman's shoulder once more.

"I must return to the city," she whispered. "But perhaps we can meet here again, and you can tell me more of the sea."

He nodded and grinned. "And perhaps we can take that swim."

"Yes," Tessa smiled. "We must do that." She rose to her feet, careful to keep her right hand hidden, and retreated, ignoring the men's laughter and comments behind her.

She was able to lift her eyes now because Helios was before her, calling her forth.

*I am coming. I will keep my vow.*

Tessa did not know if anyone stopped to watch the famous hetaera climb to the base of the legendary statue. She did not care if they whispered, or even if they yelled. It would soon be over. She regained her place at the god's feet, this time facing away from the city, looking out over the sea as Helios did above her.

She leaned her head against the heel again and let her mind drift back over the events of the past several hours, through the series of men whom she had encountered.

Glaucus, demanding and demeaning. Spiro, with his insidious charm. The putrid dockworker in the street, with his foul breath and rough hands. The insolent "hero" who no doubt believed she owed him her life. The ship's captain who had sold her freedom for a few obols. The fisherman, fooled by a shallow smile into believing Tessa favored him.

She had received more attention from men in one night than many women ever did. And yet . . . none of them knew or cared for her heart. She was known, she was admired, she was feared.

*But I am not loved.*

She thought of Simeon. Dear Simeon, he would perhaps be saddened when he heard that she had ended her empty life. But Simeon had his own family in the Jewish quarter. He was kind, yes, but he could not love a woman who had given herself to be used in the way that Tessa had.

Yes, she had given herself, she admitted. She was not simply a victim. The guilt lay at her feet as well. She had hoped for love. She had hoped for someone to uncover her heart and to love what he found.

Love and freedom. Mere illusions, no more substantial than specks of foam on the lip of the sea. And so she would turn her back on her illusions and embrace her truth. She wanted only to be left alone to die. Her heart no longer lived, and it was time for her body and soul to be joined.

She picked up the knife from its place beside her on the pedestal and looked around. Still she drew the notice of passersby. Would someone see what she had done and try to rescue her? She wanted no hero.

She considered her plan. After she made the cuts, she would place her hands between her legs and try to cover them with her clothing. She did not know how much blood must flow before it would be too late for someone to save her. She hoped that it would happen quickly and her fate go unnoticed.

Tessa tilted her head back to gaze up at Helios's chin, proudly lifted to the harbor. Would he approve of the blood spilled at his feet? Would she be an acceptable sacrifice, pleasing the gods and ensuring safe passage to the afterlife?

Tessa blinked away the sun's brightness and returned her gaze to the knife in her hand. The handle was carved from wood and splintered from years of use amidst the salt water and fish. She tested the blade against the tip of her thumb and winced as it bit into her skin.

She moved the cold metal upward to her left wrist. No, she should cut the right wrist first. Her right hand would be more able to make the second cut while injured than her left would.

She switched the knife to her left hand, swallowed, and laid the blade against her right wrist. Blue veins ran across a center ridge. Which of them held the power to pour the life from her? Must she cut them all?

She turned the blade perpendicular to her skin. Her breathing grew rapid. Her heart pounded. She felt some surprise at her body's reaction, surprise that she still had the ability to feel at all.

*You are almost free. Do it. Do it.*

She licked her lips, swallowed, breathed. She closed her eyes and prayed to Helios for strength.

*It will only take a moment. One moment of strength.*

The shouts of children and calling of gulls faded. Her vision tunneled until there was only the faint jumping of her pulse in her wrist, evidence that the blood pumped through her body, crying to be released.

She hesitated. And then the world opened up again, with the sea and the sun and the noisy harbor crowding her vision and the knife blurring.

*I cannot do it. I cannot.*

The realization burst upon her, a massive, crushing blow. Blessed freedom, which a moment ago had been within her grasp, raced away like a retreating wave that would not return.

*I am a coward.*

All of Rhodes knew Tessa of Delos to be the sharp-tongued and fearless companion of one of the island's most powerful men. But Tessa knew the truth. The knife dropped from her numbed fingers and clattered to the stone pedestal. Tears clustered in her eyes and fell on her wrists.

*I am weak.*

The truth rose in her chest, forced itself out in a low moan.

*And I will never be free.*

## Ω

Nikos timed his arrival at Glaucus's home to coincide with the dawn. To appear before first light might require rousing the head servant from bed, and Glaucus had told him two days prior that his head servant had aged beyond usefulness.

Just before dawn, Nikos had slipped through the city's awakening streets and climbed the stony hill that led to the wealthy quarter, where those who wielded power over Rhodes had built their homes. When the sun lit the eastern horizon beyond the sea, he approached a slave carrying a blue, glazed water pot and asked which house belonged to Glaucus. The slave answered in halting Greek, obviously a native of some war-conquered land, and pointed to a peristyle house at the end of the street. Nikos nodded his thanks.

Soon he would be installed in this home as the new head servant, privy to meetings of the powerful, held in secret, gaining knowledge of Rhodian politics. His father expected regular reports, which Nikos would send with sailors headed for other ports. His father had particular interest in the sentiments of several of Rhodes's leaders, most notably Glaucus.

The house was ornate, as Nikos had expected. Glaucus's fortune had come to him on the waves of the Aegean, as with so many other merchants and traders of the island. Intricately carved columns graced the home's front, with several steps leading up to a portico. Nikos paused at the top of the steps and turned to face the sea. The statue of Helios dominated the spectacular view of the harbor.

There was a time, not so long ago, when Nikos would have been awed by the wealth on display here. But a year in his father's home had accustomed him to luxury and taught him how to behave within the circles of pow

He inhaled deeply and enjoyed the air's freshness here above the sea, finally free from the ever-present stench of the docks.

The door stood open, but he knocked on it anyway.

An elderly man emerged from the twilight of the inner hall. His lined face showed the toil of years, and his eyes were shadowed as though he had not slept. "Yes?"

"Glaucus has asked me to come," Nikos said. "May I speak to him, please?"

The older man's eyes shifted. "What is your business?"

Nikos hesitated. No doubt this was the head servant, whom he was to replace. Did this man know of Glaucus's intent to dismiss him? If not, would he welcome the news or fear an uncertain future? Nikos had no desire to be the one to inform him. "I met Glaucus in the agora several days ago," he said. "He asked me to come today, to discuss . . . a possible position within the household."

The man emerged into the morning light, forcing Nikos to retreat onto the portico. "We have no need of additional servants," he said.

Nikos sensed the older servant's desire to get rid of him. He clapped him on the shoulder. "Come, friend. You would not want me to defy his request to come today?"

The man blinked twice, as though attempting to come up with another reason to toss Nikos from the property. "Glaucus has not yet risen. He was meeting with other important men late into the night."

Nikos grinned and shrugged. "I am happy to wait for him, then." He stepped around the servant and pointed into the house. "Shall I wait in the courtyard?"

"No!" His way was again blocked by the older man. "No," he repeated, the man's eyes darting down the hall, then back to Nikos. He motioned toward a nearby doorway. "In here. In the andrôn. I will tell Glaucus you are here when he awakens."

Nikos stepped into the andrôn. He turned to speak to the older servant again, but the man had vanished.

The remains of last night's party still littered the room. In the early morning light, Nikos could see tables sticky with sloshed wine and platters of warming fruit. Several flies buzzed around a tray of figs.

It was no wonder Glaucus sought to replace his head servant. His own father would never have allowed a servant to be so lax in his duties. The room should have been cleaned hours ago, before the servants had bedded down for the night.

Nikos chose a couch and lowered himself onto it, running a finger along a red cushion and appreciating the plush fabric. He propped himself on the cushion and waited, annoyed and frustrated.

Some time passed, and he wondered if he had been forgotten.

He decided to wander the house and seek out the servant. From outside the andrôn, he could hear activity coming from the street as the city awakened and the servants and slaves of other homes began preparing for the day.

In the hall a kitchen slave pushed past Nikos, bumping against him. Nikos raised an eyebrow at the slave's rudeness.

*But you are nothing more than a dockworker, remember?*

Had his former life already fallen away like a discarded remnant? Did he so soon expect to be treated as his father's son? Not here. No, here he would be a servant again, although the head servant commanded much respect in a wealthy household.

The inner courtyard drew him. When he reached the end of the hall and stepped into the open area, the older servant suddenly reappeared, his eyes wide at Nikos's presence. He stood close to Nikos, blocking him from entering the courtyard.

"Where are you going?" he demanded.

"Has Glaucus awakened?"

"I will send for you when he does." The man's lined face seemed etched with fear, his breathing growing rapid. Nikos studied him, wondering if there was more to Glaucus's late night than this servant was telling.

"Please, return—" The man paused and glanced over his shoulder. "I must go down to the harbor," he said. He seemed to reach a decision. "You must come with me."

Nikos frowned. "I am here to see Glaucus."

"Glaucus is not ready for the day! If you are to work in this household, as you say, he would want you to accompany me in my task."

Nikos shrugged. "Very well. What is this task?"

The man's eyes focused over his head, as though envisioning what he must do in the harbor. "We are going to retrieve someone."

# SEVEN

Nikos followed the older servant—Simeon, he had learned—through the city streets, back toward the harbor.

*A slave's errand. I should have refused.*

"We are going to find Tessa," Simeon said, as though Nikos should know the woman.

"Tessa?"

Simeon frowned. "Glaucus's hetaera. Surely you know of her?"

Nikos shook his head. "I am new to Rhodes."

Simeon sighed. "Then you will not be much help to me." He held a hand at his eye level. "She is tall. Very beautiful, dressed in yellow today, I believe."

They turned a corner and Simeon nodded to a slave with a pushcart who greeted him with a smile. Nikos thought perhaps the slave was another Jew.

"And why must Tessa be fetched like a wayward child?" he asked. "Has she run away?"

"Of course not! Tessa is one of the most respected women on this island." Simeon's eyes threw sparks. "Glaucus relies on her wisdom and insight in all matters."

"And yet she cannot find her way back to her patron's house?"

Simeon shook his head. "She was . . . distraught . . . about something this morning. I fear for her well-being."

They gained the harbor district quickly, and Simeon reminded him again what Tessa looked like. "She will be here somewhere, I believe."

They wandered along the street toward the water, navigating the early morning bustle of traders and merchants. Nikos fumed at the delay in securing his new position. This Tessa had better not cause him further problems.

Ahead, the mighty island statue shadowed part of the harbor and formed the hub from which all activity stemmed. Nikos lifted his eyes at the marvel of engineering, as he had many times since arriving in Rhodes. How was such a thing accomplished? From its mighty torch down to its sandals—

Nikos narrowed his eyes and squinted against the morning sun. Was that a woman at the statue's base?

He nudged Simeon and pointed to the woman's back. Simeon followed his gaze and then broke into a run that belied his years. They circled the enormous pedestal until they stood before the statue, peering up at the woman who leaned against the bronze foot, staring out over the sea.

Simeon had been correct: She was startlingly beautiful, though her clothing was dirty and torn.

But it was not her beauty that surprised Nikos.

Though her eyes had grown vacant and her hair tangled since he had seen her hours earlier, there was no mistaking the woman who had let him rescue her and then tongue-lashed him for his effort.

He cursed to himself. *So this is Tessa the hetaera.*

Nikos's plan to embed himself in Glaucus's home and gain information for his father about the political workings of Rhodes began to collapse in upon itself. He saw himself failing his father before he had even begun.

How could he ever become head servant when the influential hetaera viewed him with such disdain?

Ω

*Someone is calling my name.*

Tessa's eyes had long ago grown unfocused as she gazed at the peaks of the underwater mountains cresting the sea's surface. She felt warm and drowsy, as though she drifted alone out over the water. The knife lay unused beside her, a reminder of her cowardice.

"Tessa!"

She sighed deeply but did not drop her gaze from the sea.

A movement in the corner of her eye threatened her peace. She tried to ignore it. But then there were the hands on her. Two men, one on each side, tugging her arms.

Tessa closed her eyes. More men with more demands.

*Do not look at them. Do not resist. They will go away.*

"Tessa, it is time to go back."

She knew it was Simeon's voice. The thought gave her a small comfort, but she felt no desire to respond.

They were dragging her now, pulling her from the safe warmth of Helios's feet, down into the gutter of her life.

*But they cannot make you feel.*

The numbness was complete now, and she welcomed it.

*Feel nothing. Let nothing be important.*

Her feet struck the street, and Tessa opened her eyes to keep her balance. Simeon held her left arm, and another man stood on her right. Familiar, from another lifetime, it seemed.

They walked her toward Glaucus's home. Toward Glaucus's body.

*Soon everyone will know.* And then what? She would be executed for murder. Or passed to the next terrible patron.

*I am too cowardly to end my own life. Now I must pray for execution.*

But she could not pray. Could not feel anything but the stony coldness inside her.

Simeon was whispering in her ear. "We must decide what to do," he said. "We cannot keep it quiet much longer."

Tessa shuffled one foot in front of the other.

Occasionally her trudging slowed to a near stop, but the men would pull her on toward the future.

Up the steps, onto the portico and into the house. They stopped inside the dim hall.

The unknown man spoke for the first time.

"Now I must insist on seeing Glaucus," he said.

Tessa stared at him.

"Now is not the time," Simeon answered.

"But now is the time Glaucus told me to come. Do you intend to defy your master's request?"

Tessa watched Simeon scowl and look at her, as though for direction.

"I will see if he is ready to speak with you," Simeon said at last. "Stay here." He squeezed Tessa's arm and then disappeared toward the inner part of the house.

"I am Nikos," the man beside her said. He stood too near, forced by the hall's narrow confines.

She looked at him, at his close-cut wavy hair and clean-shaven face. At the probing eyes that seemed to seek out her heart.

"I remember you."

He nodded. "Yes, I thought you might." He reached a hand toward her, then let it drop. "You have had a difficult night. Are you in need—"

"Have you come for your reward?"

Nikos shook his head and snorted. "I do not want a reward! I told you that last night." He glanced down the hall, to where Simeon had disappeared. "Listen to me, before he returns. I met Glaucus several days ago, and he engaged my service as his new head servant. He asked me to come today, to replace Simeon. I don't think Simeon knows."

Tessa breathed, the act taking much of her attention to accomplish. "Simeon does not know," she said, "but Glaucus spoke of it to me."

Nikos nodded. "So you must take me to Glaucus."

"Why must I do that?"

"Don't you hold more influence here than Simeon? That is what I've heard."

Tessa blinked her eyes and tilted her head. "You know what I am."

"I know you hold sway in the affairs of this household more than any other." He paused then searched her face again. "Do you not pride yourself on that?"

Tessa frowned. "You think you know me?"

He shrugged. "I know your kind of woman."

A small part of Tessa's heart rebelled at his words. "Do you mean to say beneath you?" she said. "Beneath a fish-smelling dockworker?"

He threw his shoulders back but seemed to bite off his words.

"Say it," she said. "Speak your mind."

He shook his head. "You are Glaucus's hetaera, and I am to be his head servant. I must remember my place."

"You are not head servant yet. Only a dockworker with opinions." She stepped closer and showed him, eye to eye, that her height matched his own. What was it about him that made her angry? "This may be your only chance to voice those opinions. Tell me, what kind of woman am I?"

Nikos leaned in, and his coal-black eyes burned into hers. "I do not know what you once were, but I can see what you have become. Cold, feeling nothing, and caring for no one. And with the coldness comes an arrogance and ingratitude for anything given to you or done for you."

Tessa fingers itched to slap him for his impudence, but he only spoke the truth. She had willingly become all he said, and she would not change.

*But if I am so unfeeling, why does a dockworker anger me enough to strike him?*

She could think of no response to him, and her discomfort enraged her further. Who was he to provoke conflicting emotions in her? He had no right.

Simeon returned, and she turned on him like a tiger ready to pounce. He seemed surprised at her display of emotion.

"Glaucus does not wish to see you," he said to Nikos.

Nikos turned to Tessa. "I insist on hearing from Glaucus that he has no need for my service."

Tessa looked at Simeon, whose eyes begged her to get rid of Nikos. She shook her head. "Join the other servants, then, if you like. Perhaps Glaucus will see you later."

Nikos turned to Simeon, who shrugged and pointed toward the andrôn. "Clean up in there if you must do something."

With that, Simeon grasped Tessa's arm once more and pulled her toward the inner courtyard. "I must speak with you privately."

Tessa looked over her shoulder at Nikos, who stood in the hall, arms folded across his muscular chest. His eyes still held that same intensity, as though he saw the truth and would not let it go so easily.

Simeon pulled her into the sunlit courtyard, across the stones, until they stood in the shadows, beside the fabric-draped bulk of Glaucus's body. In the corner, hidden from the morning light, the sight was even more grotesque. Tessa pulled her arm from Simeon's grasp and turned away.

"We must decide what to do, Tessa."

She looked down at her torn clothing. "There is nothing that can be done, Simeon." She tried to smile and wished she knew how to express her appreciation for him. "You are a good man, and I know you want to protect me. But my fate is already decided. Now we must let the gods do what they will."

From across the courtyard, a quiet footstep scuffled. Tessa turned and looked into the eyes of a girl who had expressed nothing but hatred for the man who lay dead at their feet.

Persephone.

# EIGHT

Persephone's bright blue eyes darted from Simeon and Tessa. She moved to them quickly but stopped when she saw the dark bulk at their feet.

"What is that?"

Simeon held up a hand. "Persephone, it is best if you—"

"What is it?" She strode across the courtyard, her eyes on Tessa, and reached the body in a moment.

Tessa stretched her arms out. "No, child."

Persephone ignored the warning, bent to the fabric, and flipped it away from the body.

A quick intake of breath was her only reaction. But when she looked up at Tessa, her eyes betrayed something Tessa completely understood. Relief.

"Who has done this?" she said.

Simeon glanced at Tessa. "It was an accident."

Persephone studied Tessa, as if to ascertain the truth. "I could never have found the courage," she whispered. "I am in your debt."

Tessa wanted to reach for the girl. "No, Persephone, do not—"

Voices from the front of the house startled them all.

Simeon strode to the hall that connected the courtyard and front rooms.

Tessa bent and covered Glaucus's body again. Beside him she saw a glint of gold and reached to retrieve it. Her gold hairpin, pulled from her head years ago, it seemed.

She inhaled deeply and turned away from Persephone, to the hall. It was time. Three of them knew Glaucus was dead now, and soon the entire island would have the news.

Tessa glided through the hall, always dark in the center where no light reached. Her fingertips traced a path along the walls of the tunnel that she hoped would lead to the end of her pitiful life.

Simeon stood on the portico, conversing with three of the island's ten strategoi, who stood on the white marble steps.

"We must meet with Glaucus immediately," Hermes was saying.

Simeon turned to Tessa as she joined him. "Xenophon is dead," he told her.

She frowned. "How?"

Hermes spoke up. "Poisoned. We were all present. Someone poisoned his figs. Suspicion has fallen on his wife."

Bemus, a smallish man with tiny eyes, looked up at Tessa. "You know the effect this will have on the island. Those of us most trusted need to discuss the immediate future."

The third, Philo, pointed to Simeon. "This servant is refusing to take us to Glaucus."

Tessa smiled sadly at Simeon, who still tried to avoid what must be. "Take them to Glaucus, Simeon," she said. The older man studied her face, and she nodded. "It is time."

A swish of fabric and a sharp voice behind her startled Tessa.

"Who presumes to disrupt the household at such an early hour?" Persephone asked.

Hermes raised amused eyebrows at the girl. "We must speak with your father."

Persephone crossed her delicate arms in front of her. "My father has taken ill," she said, her eyes never leaving the three strategoi. "He does not wish to be seen."

Hermes took a step upward. "We will not disturb him for long."

Persephone held up a hand. "You are aware, Hermes, of what a proud man my father is. This illness is of a violent nature, and he would not be pleased to be visited."

Bemus frowned. "Will he live?"

Persephone smiled. "Of course. It would take more than an angry stomach to bring down a powerful man such as my father."

"Poison?" Philo whispered to Hermes.

Persephone shook her head. "Nothing as sinister as that. Some bad fish, no doubt. That is all." She turned to Tessa.

"While he recovers, my father has instructed Tessa to speak for him. She is the only one he wishes to see, and any questions on matters of state can be directed toward her."

Persephone twirled and exited the portico, leaving Tessa staring after her, eyes wide. Simeon, too, seemed at a loss.

Hermes cleared his throat. "The little girl has grown." He smiled at Tessa. "And she has more of you in her than her mother, I'm afraid."

Tessa stared him down, a challenge in her eyes. The man's penchant for young boys was well-known, and his attention to Persephone disgusted Tessa.

The sun had lifted over their heads now, and they stood with all of Rhodes gleaming behind them, waiting for Tessa to speak.

She silently blessed and cursed Persephone at the same moment. By claiming Glaucus still lived, she had given Tessa temporary freedom—freedom from accusations of murder and freedom from the man who had next paid for her. But the freedom was an illusion.

"Tessa, Glaucus must speak tomorrow morning in the council. With the murder of Xenophon, the people will fear that the leadership is weakened. Glaucus must reassure them."

Something was growing inside Tessa. She could not at first identify it. The feeling was unfamiliar and frightening. She realized in a moment what had been borne within her.

*Hope.*

She swallowed, then turned over the hairpin she still held in her palm. With a practiced hand she swept her hair upward, twisted it once, and secured it with the gold pin. She squared her shoulders, breathed the freshening air, and stepped closer to the three men, accentuating her position above them on the steps.

"I do not believe Glaucus will be well enough to appear in public tomorrow, but we shall see."

Hermes frowned. "Let us hope he is well enough to travel to Crete next week, then. Or perhaps someone will have to replace him."

Tessa ignored his pitiful grasp at power.

She felt a presence behind her and turned slightly to see Nikos standing at her back, closer than appropriate. The heat from his body warmed her. She took in a sharp breath and was surprised to find that he didn't smell of fish at all.

*More like sweet fruit and wine.*

She smiled down at the three strategoi. "Let us all hope for a quick recovery for Glaucus. I will pass on your good wishes."

The men nodded and departed. Simeon turned to her with wide eyes. Nikos didn't move.

"I must be alone," she said to the two men. "I must have time to think."

They disappeared obediently back into the house, and Tessa lifted her eyes to the mighty harbor statue. *Now what?*

Before she had a chance to sort out her thoughts, Persephone was at her side. The girl looked up at her, face framed by the dark hair and the deep blue eyes that captured all who knew her. Tessa attempted a smile. "I do not know whether you have saved me, or made me prisoner of something new, Persephone." The girl clutched Tessa's hand, her eyes large and luminous. "But I know that you have saved me," she said.

"I did not—"

Persephone's hand squeezed hers. "You are brave. I have always known that. But I hated you because you had taken the place of my mother." Tessa remained silent, letting the girl speak the words she had long held back.

"My mother," she said, tears threatening, "my mother cannot fight for herself, so I have thought to fight for her."

Tessa nodded.

"But now . . ." Persephone released Tessa's hand and turned toward the harbor, "now I wish *you* were my mother."

Tessa's breath caught. "No, Persephone. Do not even speak of—"

The girl turned to her again, the tears flowing now. Wisps of hair fell across her eye. "Why not? I heard that awful Hermes. He said I am more like you—"

Tessa brushed the hair from the young woman's face and smiled. "If the gods had made me to be someone else, I should have wished for a daughter like you." She let her hand drop and grew serious. "But such talk is not wise, Persephone. We will be friends, you and I. But we must remember that such a friendship is best kept quiet."

Persephone smiled through her tears, then threw her arms around Tessa with all the impulsiveness of a child. A brief embrace, and she fled from the portico, leaving Tessa with a fierce desire to keep the girl from all harm.

Ω

Nikos had slipped into the house behind Simeon and waited for the man to toss him out into the street, but the older servant seemed to have forgotten him.

Nikos watched him disappear down the hall, and hid himself in the andrôn once more.

*So Glaucus is ill.*

Strange that neither Simeon nor Tessa had told him so, in spite of his insistence on speaking with Glaucus. The daughter had not been reticent to share the information. Very strange.

His resolve to become an integral part of this household hardened. The exchange on the steps had convinced him that this home was indeed a power center of the island. If Nikos were to fulfill his father's charge and gain the necessary information, this was where he needed to be.

Simeon reappeared, frowning. "You have heard that Glaucus cannot speak with you this morning. You must go."

"I will only disturb his rest for a moment—"

"That is not possible. He will see no one but Tessa. You heard his daughter."

Nikos stepped around a table in the center of the room.

"Then I will speak to him through Tessa. She can pass along his decision."

"Stay away from Tessa," Simeon said. "She has enough challenges without concerning herself with staff questions."

Nikos shrugged. "We will let Tessa decide that."

Simeon gripped the doorway with a blue-veined hand. "I am telling you—"

A figure appeared behind Simeon and he turned. Persephone took in Nikos quickly, looked again with the interest of a girl becoming a woman, then lowered her head and smiled.

"What is it, Persephone?"

The girl's smile vanished, and she gripped Simeon's arm. "We must do something," she whispered, as though Nikos could not hear. "We cannot leave—"

Simeon covered her hand with his own and squeezed. "We will speak privately, Persephone." He glanced at Nikos, shook his head in apparent exasperation, and led Persephone from the room.

*Something is not right.*

Nikos surveyed the cluttered room, picked up a tray of half-eaten pheasant, and crept toward the hall. He held back a moment, poked his head through the doorway, and checked for occupants. Simeon and Persephone had disappeared. Tessa must still be on the portico.

*And I am going to find some answers.*

He began to make his way to the kitchen. The hall clearly led toward the inner courtyard, which Nikos was not yet ready to breach. Nikos drifted into a secondary hall, this one darker than the last. House slaves worked silently in the various rooms he passed. At the end of the hall he found the kitchen quarters. Cooking tools and pots cluttered a central table, and *amphorae* lined the walls. Nikos left his tray of pheasant on a table near the door, ignored the questioning glance of a servant, and moved back into the still-silent hallway. Minimizing the scuffle of sandal on stone, he retraced his steps toward the main hall. This time, he turned inward and slipped deeper into the house, toward the sun-bathed courtyard at its center.

Nikos blinked in the brightness and took in the open space. It was the customary layout, with a cistern and fountain as the focal point and a colonnaded walkway at the far edge where the home's inhabitants could stroll or recline in the shade.

The empty courtyard invited him to satisfy his curiosity. He wandered to the center, assessing the lay of the house and the halls that branched from the central hub. Footsteps in the hall from which he had emerged grew close.

He searched for a place to remain unseen, spotted some gardening tools in a dark corner under the walkway, and ran toward them. If he were questioned by anyone, he would claim that he'd been hired to tend to the grounds.

In the shadows he wrapped a hand around a hoe and stepped backward. His foot caught something on the ground, and he nearly lost his balance. He glanced down to step over the obstacle, but his foot lingered in mid-air.

Sandaled feet.

The footsteps in the hall materialized into a servant, and Nikos pulled deeper into the shadows and held fast. When the servant had crossed the courtyard and into the house once more, Nikos moved to examine the bulky form. His hand crept to the fabric's edge, lifted the corner, hesitated, then pulled the fabric away.

He recognized the corpulent face in spite of its ashen color.

Instinct urged him to pull the tile from Glaucus's forehead, but caution stayed his hand. There was no help for Glaucus now, and something told him it was best to leave the body undisturbed.

Perhaps if someone had been able to help immediately . . . but no, it was clear that the tile's corner had penetrated too deeply. Nikos sighed and replaced the makeshift shroud.

*This changes everything.*

Did Tessa know? She must.

Nikos ran back across the courtyard, through the hall, and out on to the portico. The woman stood facing the harbor, exactly where he had left her.

She didn't turn.

He stood behind her and followed her gaze to the harbor. "Glaucus's illness seems to have taken a turn for the worse," he said.

She half-turned her head toward the sound of his voice, then returned her attention to the harbor.

"You should pray to the gods for his recovery," she answered.

Nikos studied her back, saw the tension in her shoulders. *What does this mean for Tessa?*

Nikos moved to within a hand's breadth of her and whispered into her ear. "We both know that no prayers will help him now."

He heard her quick intake of breath.

"Did you kill him?" he asked.

She remained motionless, silent. Then finally, "Does it matter?"

"It matters to me." He studied the set of her jaw, her delicate neck. *She is like a frightened child, pretending to be brave.* "What will happen to you now?"

"I have hope that I will be executed for murder."

Nikos wrapped a hand around her arm, surprised at how cold it was. "You hope for this?"

She yanked her arm from his fingers. A goat wandered onto the street, and they watched it for a moment. "If they do not kill me, I will be given to someone worse than Glaucus. I would rather be dead."

Nikos closed his eyes. *The gods can be cruel.*

A gentle throat-clearing announced Simeon's presence on the portico. Persephone stood beside him. "Tessa," he said, "a private word, please."

Tessa's gaze never wandered from the statue. "You can speak freely, Simeon. Nikos has discovered our secret." She turned, and Nikos thought he saw the trace of tears on her cheeks. "One by one you have all discovered the truth, and soon all will know."

Persephone stepped forward, her eyes flashing. "But I fooled them, Tessa! I made them believe that my father was simply ill. There is no need to—"

Tessa smiled sadly. "We cannot keep this secret. Your father is a very public figure."

Nikos's mind raced. It had taken some time to secure a position in a powerful Rhodian home. He did not have time to begin again, but perhaps there was no need. If Tessa could maintain her position as Glaucus's mouthpiece, he may still gain access to the knowledge he sought.

"We can keep the secret for awhile," Nikos said. Tessa looked at him as though she'd forgotten he stood with them above the city.

"I will help you," he said. "We can keep his death hidden until you make another plan."

Tessa's eyes bore into his own. "Why would you do that?"

He glanced at Simeon, near the door. Beside Simeon, Persephone's attention remained fully on Nikos himself. "Because you will give me a position in this household."

Tessa watched him. Her eyes traveled to Simeon, then back to him. She hesitated.

"You may stay." Tessa tightened her torn chitôn around her body. "But you will work in the kitchen with the slaves. I will not replace anyone in the house."

Nikos thought of his days of poverty, of how far he'd come and his resolve to never return to the past. But his father had charged him with a task, and he would not disappoint him. Was he not willing to do whatever he must to please his father?

He nodded once to Tessa. "I will do it."

# NINE

The sun beat down on the city street, reminding Spiro that the hour grew late, and he had yet to attend the baths, a fitting place to set his plans into motion. His usual practice to take his place among the other strategoi and city leaders in the morning had been delayed by his task in the agora's slave market.

Spiro's steps quickened, both with the effort to reach the baths and the thoughts that had hounded him since Xenophon's murder last night. He reached the baths and passed between the columns into the dim interior. A rectangular pool dominated the low-domed room, with steam curling from the water's surface. The smell of perfumed oils hung in the air and tickled his nose.

A girl approached and helped him shed his himation. The water rippled below him. He wanted to dip deeply into the water today, to pull the heat to himself and let it work its way in.

Across the bath, Orion and Balthasar leaned against the bath's ledge and talked in low tones, their words a hum against the domed roof. Spiro chose to remain apart for now. He needed to think, to plan. No better place than the baths, where his hunger for luxury could nearly be sated.

Another hunger surged, the desire for power that never lay dormant long. *Rhodes can be mine.* The Achaean League represented an important and profitable step away from the outdated concept of democracy. From there it was a small leap from the League to self-rule. *And then I will be monarch.*

In his relentless study of the workings of politics, Spiro had learned much, and one such lesson had been that there was no quicker way to become a dictator than to first become a hero. And in the morning's early watches while Rhodes still slept, largely unaware of Xenophon's death, a plan had begun to take form.

The young attendant approached again, this time with a platter of grapes and honey-sweetened pastries. She bent to Spiro, offering the tray. He chose several succulent purple grapes, full with sweetness. When the girl straightened, Spiro grasped her wrist and pulled her to him again. With a smile he clutched another handful of grapes and ripped them from the stem. The girl's eyes flicked away, as though she feared that Spiro would consume her as well.

Spiro bit into a grape, let the juice fill his mouth, then chewed slowly.

So, first, a hero. It would require several steps, the first of which was to force Glaucus's hand on this ongoing issue of the Jewish population in Rhodes. The Jewish *problem.*

Tomorrow's council meeting would be the perfect opportunity to shine a light on Glaucus's support of the Jews and entrench him in his position so that he could not back down without losing face.

And then the disturbances would begin—Spiro would see to that. When Glaucus had been sufficiently set up to take the blame, Spiro would be well-positioned to take the credit.

He finished the grapes and lowered himself more deeply into the water, until the moist heat reached his chin.

It was an ambitious plan, he knew, one that would require manipulating the desires and concerns of the entire island.

Across the bath, the two men rose, dripping from the bath, and stepped to the benches to be oiled. Spiro followed them out of the water, his smiling eyes on the men as he approached.

"Spiro," Orion nodded. The young man's voice held a bit of disdain. His family had been one of the island's richest for generations, and Orion tended toward boasting.

Spiro lay across a linen-draped bench as the other two did and allowed an attendant slave boy to apply the oils. He gave the boy a moment's attention and pointed to his amphorae of oil. "Do not skimp, boy," he said. The boy nodded, head down, poured more oil into the hollow of his palm, and rubbed firm fingers into Spiro's calf.

Balthasar lay on his stomach, arms folded under his chin, while a boy worked oil into his back. "Were you present at Xenophon's symposium last night, Spiro?" Balthasar asked.

"A terrible sight," Spiro said. He closed his eyes and inhaled the perfumed oil with pleasure. "We began the evening in Glaucus's andrôn, but he was stricken with a headache and we moved to Xenophon's home."

"Pity for Xenophon you did not stay with Glaucus," Orion said.

Balthasar laughed. "I for one would rather spend an evening with Glaucus's headache and Tessa beside him than in any other andrôn on Rhodes."

"Hmmm," Orion agreed. "She makes a man's blood run warm, does she not?"

Spiro turned his head to look at Orion from the corner of his eye. "It is a shame she is wasted on Glaucus, no?"

The warm silence of the bathhouse stretched, like a taut string threatening to snap, but Spiro held, waiting. He must solidify the support of these two. The boy worked the oils into his upper arms.

Orion finally chuckled. "Glaucus is favored by the gods, you must admit. And it is doubtful that any of us will ever be so favored."

"Do not be so sure."

Orion pursed his lips and studied Spiro. "Perhaps someone should warn Glaucus to stay away from the figs."

The boy had begun to scrape the oil and impurities from Spiro's skin with the *strigil*, beginning with his legs, and Spiro felt the muscles tighten under the boy's efforts. But it was not the scraping that made him tense.

Tessa.

Somehow she had come to represent everything he wanted, everything that his father Andreas, ruling from Kalymnos, did not believe he deserved.

But he would surprise his father. He would have it all. Spiro forced himself to relax his hands, which were gripping the bench where he lay with an intensity that made them ache. He would have it all.

"Something other than figs will prove to be Glaucus's downfall," he said. "He may soon regret certain positions he has taken. Perhaps as soon as tomorrow when he speaks at the council meeting. Ask him then about the Jewish problem."

Balthasar turned over on his bench to allow his attendant to work over his back. "We may hear nothing from Glaucus tomorrow."

Spiro lifted his head and frowned. "Why not?"

"He is ill. The headache last night must have been only the start. They say he will not see anyone. He will allow only Tessa to carry messages for him."

Spiro sat up and swung his legs off the bench, throwing the boy off balance. He shoved the attendant away from him and steadied his voice. "Don't you think it is crucial that the people hear from him, given Xenophon's murder?"

Balthasar shrugged. "What can we do? The man is ill."

Spiro stood and grabbed a square of linen. "Perhaps someone should rouse him and insist that he appear."

Orion laughed. "One would think you were Glaucus's strongest supporter, Spiro."

"I support those who will strengthen Rhodes. But it seems to me that Glaucus makes decisions that will pull the island into economic ruin, and no one is asking him to justify his actions. This latest push with the Jews is just one example."

"What of the Jews?" Orion asked.

Spiro shook his head. "I will not elaborate on his position. You must hear the foolishness from him. He must speak tomorrow, while the people still react to Xenophon's death."

Balthasar turned toward Orion. "Perhaps we can use our influence to encourage Glaucus to appear."

"Let us hope your influence is as weighty as you believe it to be," Spiro said. "If Glaucus wants to maintain his position on the island, the people must be convinced that he is a strong and capable leader. If not, we will lose two leaders at once."

Spiro hoped his hyperbole had not overshot its mark.

Orion nodded. "I agree. Glaucus must speak to the council tomorrow. I will collect Hermes and Philo, and we will see what can be done about forcing Glaucus to appear."

Spiro lay back down on the bench and motioned the boy to himself, ready to be perfumed.

Yes, he could do this. He could turn the island toward himself.

And, by the gods, he would.

## Ω

Tessa studied the three who stood before her on the sun-drenched portico in varying degrees of agreement. Simeon, his brow furrowed in doubt that something as momentous as the death of his master could be kept quiet until even sundown. Persephone, in her naiveté believing that their secret would somehow improve her life. Nikos. She narrowed her eyes at the servant. Nikos, with his determination to become a servant in this house and his insistence that he could help her remain free for yet a little while.

The years had taught her she could trust no one. How could she rest her fate in their hands?

She thought back to the interaction with Hermes and the others, to the feeling of power and control she had felt in the role Persephone had handed her, that of Glaucus's voice.

"Yes," she said, in answer to the unspoken question that hung above them all. "For now, we will tell no one that Glaucus has crossed to the afterlife."

"Tessa." Simeon reached a hand across the space between them. She backed away, unwilling to hear him, and wrapped an arm around the column that supported the roof. Simeon dropped his hand to his side. "Tessa, this is impossible. And what good will it accomplish? Whether the island learns now or in a few hours or days, the outcome will be the same."

"Perhaps I can do some good," Tessa said. "Stand against those like Spiro who would destroy democracy."

"But for how long?"

Tessa looked out over the water, at the crests of distant waves that sparkled in the sunlight like jewels from another land. The coast of Anatolia ran along the horizon, leading to rocky islands that littered the Aegean with tiny, uninhabitable rocks and larger, thriving communities. So many islands. She turned back to the others.

"Crete," she said.

The three exchanged puzzled glances.

"In one week, Glaucus's position as strategos will take him to Crete to meet with naval leaders from several city-states. I am to accompany him; this has been planned for some time." She slid her hand up the rough column, welcoming the sharpness that indicated she could still feel something. "Glaucus will make that trip, though no one will see him board the ship. I will be by his side. Neither of us will return."

Nikos raised an eyebrow and gave her a half-smile.

Persephone bounded forward and clutched at Tessa's arm. "You must take me with you."

Tessa would have liked to embrace the girl, but her arm felt wooden. "This is *my* fate, Persephone, not yours."

She did not let go, and Tessa realized she would have to be warned. "Persephone, you must be careful this week. You must be discreet above all. It would be very easy to let something slip—"

"You can trust me, Tessa. I promise."

The girl's eyes were full of hope, and Tessa realized with a start that they probably reflected her own. The hope that had begun to build through the night, that had been crushed when Servia pulled her from the hold of the trading ship and drained away at the feet of Helios, had returned. And in its return it had grown stronger.

She wiped the column's dust from her hands and faced her head servant. "Simeon, I know this is much to ask of you. Will you keep my secret for one week?"

The older man dipped his head. "My greatest wish is for your freedom, Tessa. Body and soul. I will do anything I can to make that happen."

Tessa nodded. "Thank you, Simeon. You are a good man."

*I will try to believe you.*

The sound of slaves shouting to one another filtered from inside the house. Tessa turned to Nikos. "You must help me do something with the body. There is no time to waste. That we have not been discovered thus far is only a gift of the gods."

Nikos nodded. "I await your instructions."

Tessa pushed past them into the house, her thoughts tangled. Could they do this? Could they keep Glaucus's death a secret for seven days? She would have to trust them.

*And then I will be free.*

A shout from the street stopped her. Tessa returned to the doorway as Philo was climbing the steps.

"What is it, Philo? You know Glaucus is not receiving anyone today."

Philo shrugged. "I've returned with a message, Tessa. You may tell him yourself. It has been decided among the strategoi that, ill or not, tomorrow at the council meeting Glaucus must speak."

Tessa struggled to keep her face passive.

"If he cannot, Tessa, there are many who would gladly take his place on the council." Philo smiled. "There are many who would position themselves to replace him as representative to Crete, as well." Philo waved a hand and retreated down the steps. "Tomorrow morning, Tessa. We will hear Glaucus reassure the council of his leadership, or we will give his position to another."

Tessa watched him go and fought to still the panic that clawed at her hope like a wild beast.

Yes, she could do this. And she would do this.

One way or another, she would be free.

# Part II

*Diseased nature oftentimes breaks forth*
*In strange eruptions; oft the teeming earth*
*Is with a kind of colic pinched and vexed*
*By the imprisoning of unruly wind*
*Within her womb, which, for enlargement striving,*
*Shakes the old beldame earth, and topples down*
*Steeples and moss-grown towers.*

William Shakespeare, *Henry IV*

*The LORD Almighty will come with thunder and*
*earthquake and great noise, with windstorm*
*and tempest and flames of a devouring fire.*

Isaiah 29:6 NIV

# TEN

Tessa pushed back into the house, choosing to leave Philo's words outside.

"You see, Tessa," Simeon said. "We cannot—"

She waved a hand at him. "I will deal with tomorrow's problem later. We must remove Glaucus's body from the courtyard now." *Before someone else appears.* She nodded to Persephone who gazed up at Nikos like a puppy with a new master. "Return to the women's quarters. You need not have any part of this."

Persephone opened her mouth as if to argue, then gave Nikos a final smile and fled into the house.

"Simeon, I want you to make certain that no household staff enter the courtyard. Nikos, you and I will move the body."

Simeon's hands twisted into a knot. "Where will you take it?"

"We will find a place."

In the courtyard Tessa crossed to the body, focused on the task and not the grisly reality beneath the fabric.

"He is a large man," Nikos said.

"And I am a strong woman." Tessa reached for Glaucus's feet under the fabric. "We will drag him out of sight, to a storage room for now, and then decide what to do until the two of us leave for Crete."

Nikos smiled. "You speak of both of you leaving for Crete as though he still lived."

Tessa straightened and fixed Nikos with a withering stare. "Glaucus does live," she said, "and I will not hear anyone speak otherwise these next seven days."

Nikos smiled again. "As you wish." He joined Tessa in reaching for Glaucus's ankle.

"Wrath of Poseidon!"

The shout from the courtyard's north side caused them both to release their grip on the body and jump back. Tessa reached to recover Glaucus.

A stick-thin figure flitted into the courtyard, her fingers fluttering at her sides.

Nikos glanced at Tessa, a question in his eyes.

"Daphne," Tessa whispered. "Glaucus's wife."

Daphne's eyes darted to the central fountain, to the potted trees on her left, to the roof of the colonnade, never resting.

The woman's eyes fell on Nikos. "Where is my husband?" she said, one quivering hand at her neck, twisting a string that held a charm bag.

Nikos crossed the courtyard to her. "He has taken ill, mistress."

"Curses of Poseidon!" She lifted the charm bag and held it between them. "We must have more flax."

Nikos turned to Tessa, frowning, but Tessa retreated further into the darkened walkway and wrapped her arms around her waist.

Daphne's green chitôn hung loose on her malnourished frame, and her hair poked from her headband in a manner reminiscent of feathers.

"More flax! More flax!" She shouted now, hands brushing at her clothes, picking at threads only she could see. "We must have more flax!"

Nikos drew close to her. "I am certain more flax will be coming soon," he said. "I believe a ship with flax docks today."

She fixed her gaze on him. "It comes from Egypt, you know."

He smiled. "Egypt has the best flax, I believe."

She laughed, a cackle that raised the hair on the back of Tessa's neck. "Egypt has the best flax!" Her sing-song voice rose in the courtyard and echoed from the stones. She tilted her head back and sang to the sky, "Egypt has the best flax!"

Then her head snapped downward, and her lips tightened. "Where is my husband?"

Nikos touched her arm. "He is ill. He wishes that you be protected from his illness."

Daphne looked at Nikos's hand on her arm, then back into his eyes. Her own hands shot from her sides and clutched his tunic. "Judgment of Poseidon!" she said. "Earth-shaker, sea-god, earth-shaker!"

Nikos gently untangled her hands from his clothing and looked back at Tessa, his eyes wide. Daphne had raised a bony hand to Nikos, and he pulled back as though afraid she would strike him. But she only held her amulet-ring aloft. Tessa knew that the ring was engraved with a crab, Poseidon's emblem and Daphne's fixation.

She kissed the ring, then held it to Nikos for him to kiss. Instead he touched her wrist with a soothing hand and lowered her arm to her side.

"The flax will come," he said. "Perhaps you should return to your quarters and wait for it."

She smiled. "Yes, yes." She seemed to notice Tessa for the first time, and her smile disappeared. Her hands flitted to her neck and face again. Her eyes bulged. "Tessa!" she hissed. In a flash she crossed the courtyard and flew at Tessa, hands curved into claws.

Tessa watched her come and did not move.

And then Nikos was somehow between the two women, his focus on Daphne. Tessa could smell the woman's perfume in the heat. The flowery heaviness of it assaulted her and left her dizzy. A bitter taste rose in her throat, and she took another step backward.

Nikos again lowered Daphne's hands, this time keeping his hands on her upper arms. "It grows warm out here, mistress," he said. "Let us move you to the coolness of your quarters." He deftly turned her away from Tessa and drew her across the courtyard, to the doorway from which she'd entered.

Tessa waited, breathing hard, still in shadows.

Nikos returned a moment later. "I gave her to another servant," he said as he crossed back to Tessa.

Tessa slowly allowed her arms to drop from her waist and tried to ignore Nikos's expression of pity. Did he sense her shame in Daphne's presence? Did he believe that she was responsible for the woman's madness?

She straightened and moved from the shadows. "We must take care of this body," she said.

Nikos hesitated and studied her eyes. She raised her chin and stared back.

His amused half-smile was already growing irritating. She placed her hands on her hips. "Are you going to stand there like a temple statue, or are you going to do my bidding?"

He dipped his head. "I live to do your bidding, of course."

Tessa did not miss the smile that lingered on his lips.

# ELEVEN

The two-wheeled, horse-drawn cart that carried Spiro, and the new slave Ajax who drove him, rolled into the Jewish quarter of Rhodes. Spiro stood slightly behind the bare-chested slave, his head down to avoid notice. They wound through the streets, narrower here amid the run-down homes and businesses. He was conscious of a few eyes on them, but the people largely continued about their business, too occupied with their own survival to take note of his presence.

Spiro could not resist lifting his head when they passed the columned fountain house. Several women stood outside the temple-like structure, large water pots beside them as they chatted stupidly, no doubt about home and family. A smile touched Spiro's lips.

*A few hours from now, this place will be anything but peaceful.*

Within a few minutes they reached the city's outskirts and took a rutted road upward toward the hills. Later, after the deed was accomplished, he would send Ajax back to the Jewish quarter to plant the seeds that he hoped would spring into chaos by tomorrow.

Spiro massaged his stiff left hand with his right, a lingering reminder of a childhood injury that had caused him to suffer ridicule. He looked back to see the city fall away.

It was so simple, really. By tomorrow, when Glaucus stood in the council meeting to support the Jews in their bid for voting rights, Spiro would have given the council members reason to believe that Rhodes would be better off if the Jews were eradicated from the island entirely. And Glaucus would be seen for the fool he was. With Xenophon dead, Glaucus discredited, and several others already supporting inclusion in the Achaean League—if Spiro could sway just one or two others, the island would finally embrace the league.

*And then I will be only one step from my goal.*

"Monarchy." Spiro whispered the word into the air, and it was sweet on his lips. The ever-present self-doubt, spoken in his father's voice, contradicted him, but he ignored it.

First, the water.

He poked the slave's broad back and pointed to an outcropping of stones on the hill above them. Ajax nodded and turned the cart toward the stones. Getting close required leaving the path, and the cart lurched and careened over the rocky field. They drew alongside their destination, and Spiro alighted, Ajax following. Spiro grabbed the pottery lamp and pointed to the tool he had wedged into the cart.

"Bring the blade."

The stone arch seemed out of place on a hillside, but Spiro knew from his dealings with official state spending and planning that through the arch, in the darkness beyond, lay one of the most vital resources of the island.

An aqueduct.

The water that ran to the city's fountain houses was supplied by two separate aqueducts. The system of underground tunnels and clay pipes had its source in the springs above the city. The water ran through a complicated series of settling basins and aqueduct bridges, but when it neared the city, its directional flow became regulated by splitting basins. One such basin lay within this stone archway.

Spiro nudged Ajax. "Let's go."

They pushed into the darkness. The oil lamp's tiny flame flickered shadows onto the rock above their heads. Spiro held the lamp in front of him and, with his other hand, held his himation close to his body to avoid contact with the grimy tunnel walls.

The tunnel narrowed, until Spiro's shoulders nearly brushed the sides, and still they walked on, the dampness penetrating their bones with each step. The silent pressure of the rock on all sides became oppressive, and it was with relief that Spiro detected the sound of water rushing ahead of them.

After several minutes, the channel widened again. Spiro took a deep breath and raised the oil lamp above his head.

They had reached the splitting basin.

To their left, water gushed into a pool, fed by natural springs far above them. To their right, three channels opened at the pool's base and allowed the water to reach the city. Etched above each channel were markings that indicated the city locations fed by each channel.

It was the channel on the far right that held interest for Spiro.

"This is it."

Ajax narrowed his eyes. "It is quite large."

Spiro shrugged. "So it will take some time."

Ajax looked about the chamber. "There is not enough dirt and rock here to block the mouth of the channel."

"Then you will have to bring rocks from outside. It must be done quickly, however. The water must fail by tonight."

Ajax tossed the long-handled blade at Spiro's feet. "Perhaps you could loosen dirt to pack around the stones that I will fetch from outside."

Spiro laughed and stepped back from the blade. "You forget that I purchased a very capable slave."

Ajax shrugged and disappeared back into the tunnel. Spiro found a rocky outcropping in the wall, several hands above his head, and placed the oil lamp on it. Satisfied that it shed enough light to work by, he brushed the dirt from a flat surface of rock beside the basin, then settled himself there to wait.

Except for the dirt, it was almost pleasant sitting there beside the rushing water, contemplating the future. If he closed his eyes, he could imagine that he sat beside a hillside waterfall in the cool of the night. Perhaps with Tessa at his side . . .

In his reverie the time passed quickly, and Ajax returned, carrying several large rocks. He dropped them beside the basin, then gripped the basin's edge and lowered himself into it. He took a moment to plunge beneath the water.

Spiro watched and waited for him to emerge. This was no time for recreation.

Ajax shot out of the water and flung his head back. Spiro pulled back to avoid being splashed.

"The rocks, you brute! There is not much time."

Ajax waded to the edge and took the largest of the rocks. The right-most channel consisted of a wide mouth, half of which yawned empty above the level of the water, half of which was submerged. Ajax plunged under the water again, a rock in his hands, and returned a moment later without the rock. He repeated the process with the other two rocks, then rose, dripping, from the basin.

"Step away!" Spiro snatched at the edges of his himation, now wet from the runoff.

Ajax grabbed the blade and turned on Spiro. "My apologies, master. I would not want you to be muddied."

Spiro narrowed his eyes at the insolence, but Ajax returned his haughty stare. Spiro felt his anger turn to admiration. He laughed. "You do not fear anything, do you, Ajax?"

Ajax grinned and shrugged. "I don't care much for spiders," he said, then disappeared into the tunnel, leaving Spiro alone in the half-darkness, with the earthy smell of water and dirt beginning to make him feel drugged.

Without the sun to mark the passage of time, Spiro could not tell how late it grew. He stopped counting Ajax's trips from the hillside and grew anxious. The pile of rocks crested the level of the water at the channel's mouth, but it needed to be blocked completely, and it must be soon for the water to fail by tonight.

He heard Ajax returning through the tunnel.

"You need to work faster, Ajax," he said. "Time passes quickly, I fear."

A face appeared at the chamber entrance, and Spiro's stomach clenched. It was not his slave.

"Spiro!"

Though he had apparently been recognized, Spiro did not know the man who stood before him. He jumped to his feet. "Who are you?"

The balding man stood a head shorter than he and sweated profusely. He looked in confusion at Spiro, then at the mouth of the half-blocked channel. His brow furrowed, then his eyes widened. "What are you doing?"

"I ask again, who are you?" Spiro drew himself up and scowled down on the man.

"I am Erasmus." He had a pronounced lisp that muffled his speech. "I inspect and maintain the south aqueduct." He looked again at the rock-covered channel. "Why are you blocking water to the Jewish district?"

Spiro groped for a reasonable explanation, but nothing came. There could be no good explanation for depriving a community of its most precious resource.

The man took a step backward.

"Where are you going?" Spiro advanced on him, fists clenched. He could not allow this fool to ruin his plan.

"I—I need to move up the hill to inspect the settling basin," he said, with another glance at the Jews' channel.

A glint in the lamplight behind Erasmus was all the warning Spiro had. A rushing sound of metal slicing air, then the broad *thwack* of the flat side of a blade against the roundness of Erasmus's bald head. The man dropped at Spiro's feet. Behind him stood Ajax, emotionless eyes on Spiro.

Spiro exhaled. "Well done, Ajax. Well done."

"He questioned me outside. I knew he would discover your plan."

Spiro nodded and leaned over the man. Even in the chamber's dim light he could see the blackness of blood that poured from the back of Erasmus's head.

Ajax knelt beside the body and placed a palm on his chest. He looked up at Spiro. "He will not cause you a problem, master."

Spiro smiled slightly. "You will be rewarded, Ajax," he glanced at the water being diverted away from the Jews, "just as soon as our task is finished."

Once the body was out of the way and Ajax had gone for more rocks, Spiro picked up the long-handled blade. He examined the metal, saw the sticky wetness of Erasmus's blood, and nodded. It was an acceptable sacrifice. And there would be more.

He thrust the blade into the dirt beside the basin. The hour grew late. It was time to get his hands dirty.

Ω

Hours later, Spiro reclined on his couch, awaiting his long-overdue evening meal and contemplating the events he had set into motion. After Ajax had returned Spiro to his home, the slave had reentered the Jewish district to begin sowing the seeds of rebellion. *The aqueduct is going to fail,* he had whispered to any who would listen. *The city officials know it will fail, but they have chosen not to repair it. They wish to eliminate the Jewish community.*

The rumors should be enough to cause unrest, though Spiro would not rely solely on the Jews' anger. Ajax would be in the southeast quarter tonight as well. When the water failed in the Jewish fountain house, the people would flee to the nearest alternative, in the southeast section of the city. It was there that Spiro's plans would take root.

His stomach rumbled, and Spiro yelled for a slave. A young man hurried in, head down and platter in hand.

"I am half-starved! Where have you been?"

"My mother, master. She is ill. She has no food, and the lack of it wears her away." He set the platter on the low table.

Spiro eyed the slave, sighed, and picked up a large hunk of roast duck. "Here," he said and flung the meat toward the slave. "Take her this."

The slave bowed out of the room, calling down blessings on Spiro.

*Yes, the gods will favor me. And Father, you shall as well.*

By tomorrow morning all of Rhodes would know that the Jews deserved exile, not citizenship. Spiro tore a piece of bread from a loaf and smiled.

Politically, Glaucus was as good as dead.

# TWELVE

Night fell on Rhodes once more, and still Glaucus's body waited in the storage room. Tessa had stood at a window on the upper floor of his home, watching the last remnants of pink and purple in the sky fade to a deep, dark blue, knowing it would soon be time.

She had spent the afternoon sleeping off the effects of the disastrous night and the decisions of the morning. Simeon had retrieved a sky-blue chitôn from Daphne's quarters to replace Tessa's torn one. She dared not return to her own home yet, not with Glaucus's body hidden below. They waited for darkness to cover the city before they would move him further.

*It is a shame that flesh rots so quickly.*

She pushed away the distasteful thought. Though she and Simeon had informed the rest of the household that Glaucus lay ill in his bedroom, where no one was to disturb him, they could not leave him there for a week, until the ship to Crete sailed. Not with the warm days of Skirophorion upon them.

"Tessa." A soft voice behind her signaled that the time had come. She turned to Simeon and tried to smile.

He nodded. "Nikos is ready. The wagon is in the alley behind the house."

"Thank you, Simeon."

"I will help you."

She shook her head. "No. I know touching the body would render you unclean according to your law. And someone must stand watch for us." She did not add that his age concerned her. As head servant, he had given up the heavy work many years ago.

Tessa followed Simeon through the hall, past the women's quarters, where Daphne probably sat at her loom, spinning more yarn than the household could ever use, from the flax that arrived regularly from Egypt. Tessa held her breath as they passed, praying to the gods that Daphne would not make an appearance. She had no wish to encounter her tonight, especially while dressed in the woman's chitôn.

The hall remained silent, and they descended the steps together. Tessa left Simeon outside the doorway of Glaucus's interment chamber. She pushed the curtain aside and found Nikos waiting. He turned from the covered body stretched on a cushion and studied her eyes. "Are you certain you want to do this?"

"Do you want his head or his feet?" she answered.

After some maneuvering, they pulled the body from the cushion and decided that working side-by-side, each pulling the body from under one arm, was best. They were careful that the blanket did not slip too far and reveal their burden, in case someone got past Simeon.

They dragged the body across the storage room, their progress slow.

*Glaucus's penchant for pastries has made our job harder.*

She pulled the curtain away from the doorway and leaned her head out.

Simeon nodded. "No one is about. But you must hurry!"

Nikos touched her arm and said again, "Are you certain you can do this?"

Tessa jerked away from his touch. "We are wasting time!"

They bent to the task again, and Tessa felt her lower back cramp with the effort. Nikos's shoulder rubbed against her own as they dragged the body through the back hall, and she tried to ignore the contact and focus on the task.

The night had grown cool, but they both were sweating by the time they reached the outer door. Nikos propped the door open with a nearby urn and returned to Tessa's side. Glaucus's body was half into the alley, with both of them bent over it, when a night breeze snaked between the houses. The wind snatched at the corner of the linen that covered Glaucus and tore it from his body.

Dead eyes stared up at Tessa, the terra-cotta tile still wedged between them like an axe left buried in a chopping block. Bile rose in her throat. She dropped the arm she held and backed away.

Nikos grabbed at the fabric that blew into the street. He covered the body and this time wrapped the linen securely around it.

He turned to Tessa with concern in his eyes. "Let me get Simeon to help," he said. "You can return home."

Tessa swallowed and lifted her chin. "I am not as weak as you seem to think."

He shook his head. "I didn't say you were weak. But even the strongest woman would find this task distasteful."

"I have grown impervious to distasteful tasks."

Nikos's eyes connected with her own in the way that always disturbed her. "Maybe it is time that you remembered what it is like to feel something."

"Maybe you should remember that you are nothing more than a hired hand."

Nikos raised an eyebrow, an unspoken reminder of her own position.

Footsteps at the mouth of the narrow alley froze them both. The sound faded into the night, and they bent again to Glaucus's body. The wagon lay only a few feet away, but after the effort expended to bring Glaucus from inside the house, Tessa could not imagine how they would possibly lift his body onto it.

When the body lay at the wagon's base, Nikos pulled a flat length of board from the wagon bed and propped it against the lip, a ramp to haul their cargo aboard. They had pulled him halfway up the ramp when the board slipped. It dropped away from the wagon, leaving Glaucus's shoulders and upper body on the wagon. His legs flopped to the ground. Tessa and Nikos grunted and tugged harder from within the wagon. One final pull and the legs came up and over the edge. The momentum knocked them both backward onto the wooden-slatted bed. They lay for a moment, breathing hard. Tessa looked at Nikos in triumph, daring him to call her weak now.

Instead he reached across and pushed a damp curl out of her eyes.

She scrambled to her feet. "It grows late and we have a journey ahead."

Nikos stood beside her and frowned. "I still do not think this is a good idea, Tessa. Let me do it alone."

"No. I will see this through."

"But even you must be horrified at what you must do now."

*Even a woman made of stone, you mean?*

"I do what I must." She looked down at the body at her feet, then lowered herself to the wagon floor. "You brought another blanket, did you not?"

Nikos reached behind the front seat of the wagon. "I will cover you both with this."

Tessa inhaled, closed her eyes, and lay down next to Glaucus's body. She felt the slight swish of the dark fabric moving air overhead, and then the cloth settled about her like a shroud. She turned her head away from the body so that her mouth and nose would be free. The darkness pressed around her. She realized for the first time that a body dead these twenty-some hours would begin to smell. Again, she fought back nausea at the vile stench and focused on breathing through her mouth.

It had to be this way, she knew. Nikos could drive a wagon from the city in the night, but not with the city's most recognizable hetaera at his side. She had considered letting him take Glaucus out of the city by himself, but this was her fight, and she intended to make certain it was done right. Besides, who was this stranger that she should trust him with her only chance at freedom?

The wagon rocked slightly, and Tessa knew that Nikos had climbed into the front seat. He gave a soft command to the single ox he had harnessed, and the wagon lurched forward.

Tessa had come up with the plan earlier in the day. The festival of Skira had passed only ten days ago. Outside the city, on a road lined with graves and tombs cut from the rock, a certain pit had been designated for the entrails of swine that the women brought there during the festival. She herself had participated in the ritual, tossing the remains of animals into the pit and then pushing dirt over them. The entrails would rot there through the warm months of Skirophorion and Hekatombaion. When the festival of Thesmophoria arrived in Pyanopsion, the women again would travel to the pit and dig up the decomposed remains, then place them on altars in a fertility rite that had always been the way of the Greeks.

*What will remain of Glaucus when the entrails are dug up?*

Certainly the bones would tell the story that more than pigs had been buried there. But would anyone be able to recognize the swine Glaucus? She had no idea how long it took for death to render someone unknown.

The wagon turned a corner. The wheels jumped from one set of ruts to those in the next road, and the wagon rocked, rolling Glaucus's body into Tessa.

Her breathing grew rapid. She pushed against the bulk but was unable to budge it. The body's weight pressed her against the wagon's side, and she felt her chest begin to convulse.

It took a moment for her to realize what was happening: She was crying. A deep, silent heaving that gathered ten years of fear and hatred and revulsion and compressed it into something that threatened to crush her completely.

The wagon bumped along the rutted limestone road, and the splintered wood of the wagon's sideboard roughened her face, but she barely noticed.

Crushed between the wagon, Glaucus's bulk, and the weight on her chest, Tessa fought to retain a hold on her sanity. She felt it slipping, floating away on a dark breeze, and feared she would scream. She desired to scream. Desired it above all else.

Then it would be over. All of it.

The panic rose higher in her chest, overran her mind, and nearly escaped when the wagon suddenly stopped. Tessa thrashed her head to either side. *Why did we stop?*

A moment later the fabric was ripped away from her. Nikos stood above her. "Where are we?" The words came out as a croak.

Nikos braced himself against the wagon's side and shoved against Glaucus. "We are outside the city. I saw that the body had rolled against you, so I stopped."

She looked up at him, unable to voice her gratitude. He kneeled at her side and touched her face. She was aware that her cheeks were dry, as though no amount of sobbing could call up tears from her heart.

"Tessa," he said.

She only stared, wishing she had the strength to pull away.

"Keep driving," she finally whispered.

The pity in his eyes was unbearable, so she closed her own. The fabric was replaced, and she felt Nikos jump down, then climb to the seat above her head and urge the ox forward.

The remaining minutes were not as terrible. Though Tessa studied the underside of the dark blanket that covered her, the only thing she saw was the look of compassion in Nikos's eyes.

By the time she felt the wagon leave the road and roll into the grassy field of the entrails pit, Tessa had successfully replaced Nikos's kind face with Glaucus's dead one and steeled herself for the next horrifying task.

$$\Omega$$

Nikos brought the wagon to a stop off the road, near the marker Tessa had told him of, and jumped down into the grass. He moved to the back of the wagon and found Tessa already out from under her shroud and sitting up. He offered his hand, but she ignored it and climbed out.

*There's the Tessa I know.* The return of her self-reliance relieved him, strangely. He had no time for distractions.

He stood beside her in the field for a moment and searched the moonlit road in both directions to be sure they were alone. Along the roadside, scattered tombs lay in various degrees of grassy neglect, some having long since exhausted the money set aside for their upkeep. The roadway was empty and silence deep. If not for the pit's overwhelming stench, it would have been a restful sort of place.

Nikos turned to Tessa and studied her face, flushed even in the moonlight. "Are you well?"

She tossed her head. "Of course. Let's finish this."

They pulled from the ankles this time. Nikos was amazed that Tessa was still able to summon the strength she did.

Their respect for the dead had long since given way to expedience. Nikos made no effort to keep Glaucus's body from tumbling from the wagon to the ground. The sheet remained tucked around the body even as it fell.

"Do you wish to recite?" he asked Tessa.

Her eyes widened. "Do you think I care if the rites are performed?"

*She's been mistreated. And she bears the marks.*

"Ready?" he asked. She nodded, and they bent to the body.

It took several strenuous pushes to roll the body, then a final shove. The pit was not deep, perhaps the height of man. Nikos heard the body hit bottom, then heard the slither and hiss of snakes that had found a feeding ground in the pit.

"We must cover him," Tessa said. "Someone may happen to look before Thesmophoria."

Nikos retrieved the broad-bladed hoe he had brought. He motioned Tessa away from the edge of the pit and dug.

Under his breath, as he tossed dirt into the pit, he whispered the rites as best he could remember.

"Stop." Tessa's icy voice pierced the darkness. "He doesn't deserve a proper burial."

Nikos paused and leaned on the hoe. "Do you call this a proper burial?"

She snorted. "To be covered in dirt is to pass to the afterlife. It is still more than he deserves."

"You have been hurt by him, Tessa, I know, but—"

"You know nothing!"

Nikos bent to his task again. By Zeus, she was cold. Beautiful and cold, like one of the marble statues in the Temple of Athena Polias.

The blackness of the pit would not reveal whether Glaucus's body was well-covered. Only daylight could tell them that, and they could not afford to remain that long. Nikos wiped sweat from his brow and took a deep breath, remembering too late about the stench. His hands felt gritty with dirt.

"I think it is enough," he said.

Tessa waved a hand as if it did not matter. "He must remain buried for only a week. After that, I will be gone."

*Let us hope so.*

Nikos tossed the hoe back onto the wagon and came to stand beside Tessa. She had wrapped her arms around herself as though she had grown cold.

"Do you think it safe to ride beside me until we reach the edge of the city?"

Tessa stared into the pit, then up at the lightening sky. "Glaucus is expected to speak in council this morning," she said. "We must get back quickly."

"What will you tell them?"

She turned to him and half-smiled. "I will tell them what Glaucus has sent me to tell them."

A melody that sounded strange for a birdcall floated to them. Nikos turned toward the sound. "What is that?"

They waited, listening. The melody came again.

"A flute," Tessa said.

Nikos looked at her in confusion. The music grew closer. "Who would be playing a flute?"

Tessa's eyes grew wide. "A funeral."

At that moment a procession of mourners rounded the corner, torches lighting the way. The soft wails of women's laments floated toward them.

They would be seen.

Nikos saw the panic in Tessa's eyes and did the first thing he thought of. He reached for her, pulled her to the ground, and half-covered her body with his own.

She beat his arms with her fists. "Stop! What are you doing?"

"Shhh. They will think we have come out here to be alone." The procession grew closer, the wailing louder. "Keep your head down," Nikos said. "They may recognize you."

She stopped pummeling him but shifted her body and pushed against his chest with her hands, creating an unbreachable space between them. He countered by pulling her against himself, and there they remained motionless. Nikos could feel the tension of her arms holding them apart. He turned his head away from the road and leaned his face into her hair, hoping the mourners would pass by without noticing them.

Tessa's strength failed and her arms buckled. Her body slid toward his.

Her face was only a hand's breadth from his. She smelled of hyacinth, and he could feel the warmth of her body along his own.

*So . . . she is not so cold after all.*

Her eyes held terror, and Nikos sensed that it was directed as much at him as at those who passed on the road. The flutes and the laments drew alongside them, and he expected her to pull away again, but she did not. He put his lips next to her ear.

"Don't be afraid, Tessa," he whispered. "You are safe with me."

Her eyes turned to his, and he felt a change. As tentative as the flutter of a bird's wing, but the tension in her body eased. Her lips parted, and she looked at him with a desperation that cut to his heart. He felt a surge of anger toward Glaucus and all the other men who had hurt her.

*Would that every one of them lay in a pit of rotting flesh.*

She turned her head away, toward the torches in the road.

"It is Xenophon's funeral," she whispered.

Nikos followed her gaze and saw the wooden coffin being drawn on a wagon toward its final stone rest. A few heads turned their way, but they continued on, uncaring of a tryst between unknown lovers.

"They have almost passed," Nikos said. "We will be safe."

Tessa began to breathe evenly. Nikos looked back to her. She had grown cold again, as though she had sailed away from him in the moment that he had looked to the funeral.

Perhaps Tessa was unchanged, Nikos thought, but he could not make such a claim for himself. It had only lasted a moment, but he had seen through to her heart, and the truth there changed everything.

*I believe parts of you are made of bronze, Tessa of Delos.*

*But even bronze can be melted.*

# THIRTEEN

## ✦ *Five Days before the Great Quake* ✦

Tessa turned her head away from Nikos and buried her face in the blades of green grass. She breathed in deeply, hoping the earthy smell of grass would erase the vulgar stench of the pit. And the smell of Nikos.

The funeral's sounds faded into the darkness. She shoved Nikos away from her and sat up. He still reclined, leaning on one elbow and watching her.

"We must hurry," she said, looking to the sky. "It is nearly dawn."

"I am sorry." Nikos reached for her face. "I know that was hard for you."

She swatted him away. "It was nothing." She would not tell him how much she hated the feel of his body near hers.

*Yes, hated it.* But the word had a hollow sound, even in her mind.

She pushed to her feet. "I will ride in the back. We cannot take chances." She ignored his protest and climbed into the back of the wagon. The ride back to the city would be pleasurable compared to riding next to Glaucus's body. She pulled the scratchy blanket over her head, lay down, and tried to block all thoughts of both Glaucus and Nikos from her mind.

*I need to focus on the next challenge. The speech.*

Philo had insisted that Glaucus speak, and he seemed to have the support of the other strategoi. Would they accept her as a replacement? Could she stand before them and speak as though she had Glaucus's authority behind her?

Tessa peeked from beneath her covering several times and watched the coming dawn with anxiety. She could not be late, and she still needed to wash and change. The night's events had not been kind to her clothing.

*Daphne's clothing.*

"Hurry!" she called. "Can't you get that ox to move faster?"

Nikos laughed, something she'd noticed came easily for him. "Do not speak to me. Speak to the ox."

Tessa growled in frustration, and Nikos laughed again.

She felt the difference in the road when they entered the city, and dared not risk another look outside the blanket. There would be slaves in the street, and women carrying jugs for water. She tried to remain unmoving, focused on pressing her body into the roughened floor of the wagon.

The wagon jolted to a stop, but she remained still.

Only when Nikos pulled the fabric from her did she open her eyes. "Come," he whispered. "There is no one about. We will reenter the house the way we came out."

He took her hand to help her from the wagon, and she was unable to wrest it from him. A moment later they were in the house.

Simeon stood in the hall, his face creased with concern. "Is it done?"

Tessa nodded. "We were not seen."

He eyed her clothing, and she looked down at herself. She had stood near enough to Nikos while he dug that she, too, was covered in dirt. The wagon ride and time on the ground had taken a toll as well. She wondered in passing if her face and hair were as grimy and looked away from Nikos in embarrassment.

"I must wash," she said to Simeon, "and have clothes for the council meeting."

Simeon's usual placid nod was his only reaction. "I have water and clothing ready."

*Always thoughtful, Simeon.*

Tessa turned to Nikos for only a moment before following Simeon. She could not meet his eyes but said, "Thank you."

She felt, rather than saw, his easy smile upon her, like a warm robe falling on her shoulders. "It is my pleasure to serve you, Tessa."

Simeon cleared his throat. "The council meeting draws nigh, Tessa. We must hurry."

Tessa raised her eyes for only a moment to Nikos. He nodded and smiled. "You will do well."

As she turned toward the women's quarters, Tessa wondered how one smile could fill her with the confidence needed to face the ordeal to come.

## Ω

Spiro had intended to spend the morning after his aqueduct excursion at home. He truly had. But when the sun rose over Rhodes and he contemplated the events he had orchestrated to take place that morning, his usual restraint was defeated by curiosity.

By the time the women of the Jewish district were rising to their morning tasks, Spiro had positioned himself near the fountain house. He cared little if a few peasant women noticed him. Spiro rubbed at his left hand and waited.

The fountain house resembled a temple in some ways. And rightly so, for water was even more important than the gods, if one were to be honest. The square, white building in the Jewish quarter boasted only four columns on the front side, though many had more. Inside, a large basin, fed by the aqueduct running down from the hillside, bubbled water in a steady stream. *Usually.*

A thin woman meandered out of a doorway down the street, an orange pot in her arms. She was clearly enjoying one of her only times outside her home, in no hurry to shorten her task. Her eyes swept the doorways of other homes on the narrow street, and Spiro watched her break into a smile when another woman emerged and crossed the street to join her.

Together the two wandered past Spiro on the opposite side.

The two disappeared into the fountain house. Spiro eyed the door.

*One. Two. Three . . .*

And then it was Spiro's turn to smile. Both women ran from the fountain house, their pots abandoned. They separated only feet from him and flew into their own houses. Moments later, their husbands emerged and the four ran again to the fountain house, shouting to each other. Several other women entered the street, also with pots. They saw the men running for water, and the confusion on their faces satisfied Spiro.

It took only a few minutes more before the disaster had roused the entire street from their homes. They scuttled about in front of the fountain house like ants whose hill had been trampled. Angry shouts were heard above the buzz of conversation. People began pouring into the street.

"They've known for some time," one man shouted above the noise. "I heard that the officials have chosen to ignore the problem! It is only water for the Jews, they say!"

Spiro smiled, amazed once more at how easily men were manipulated.

Ω

It was a half-hour walk to the nearest fountain house in Rhodes. Since the angry horde of Jews would probably be moving faster than he, Spiro knew that he would not have long to wait.

Ajax stood outside the fountain house, his back against the wall, arms folded across his chest. He saw Spiro and pushed away from the wall.

"All has been accomplished?" Spiro asked.

Ajax gave a sharp nod of his head. "Rumors are rampant that the Jews will come and attack this district and take over its water supply."

"And what of the guard?"

Ajax looked toward the entrance to the fountain house. "Dead."

"Witnesses?"

"Only one, of course. Who will swear that he saw a Jew sneak in during the night and murder the man."

Spiro patted the slave's shoulder, an unfamiliar affection washing over him. "Well done."

In the street behind them, several women chatted and strolled toward the fountain house. Spiro and Ajax moved away from the entrance and into the street.

A distant hum grew. Spiro lifted his eyes. The Jews were coming.

He began to distinguish individual voices, shouting to one another. Then a group of Jews, larger than Spiro could have hoped for, spilled into the street like water from a pot.

Ajax's work of the previous night had its effect. The southeast district was ready. Men sprang from houses along the street and emerged from alleys. The women of the district disappeared, though many Jewish women streamed toward the fountain house with pots.

Several of the locals carried large sticks. Spiro nodded to himself.

*Always violence. The only way.*

The stick-wielding men rushed into the Jewish horde. Several women screamed, the high-pitched shrieking fanning the flames of fear and fury.

A man rushed from the fountain house. "Feodore is dead," he shouted above the crowd. "His throat has been cut!"

An older man with squinty eyes jumped up and down. "I saw a Jew enter the fountain house during the night! A Jew! A Jew!"

The riot sprang to life. A writhing and twisting mass of flesh. Pots breaking. More screams. More sticks. Men on the ground. Women on the ground. The wail of a child.

Spiro's heartbeat matched the pulse of the crowd.

*Whatever it takes.*

Ajax drew up beside him. Spiro gripped the man's arm.

A nearby group of men beating each other shifted toward Spiro. Ajax pulled him back.

"We should return home, Spiro."

"Not yet. Not yet."

Ajax pulled him away. "We are finished here. It is accomplished. You are not safe."

Spiro allowed Ajax to lead him away, but he could not tear his eyes away from the chaos.

*They do my will without knowledge of it.*

He rubbed at his left hand and turned toward home. And for a moment the crushing desire to achieve something his father would respect seemed to ease its interminable grip on his heart.

*You shall see.*

# FOURTEEN

In Glaucus's empty bedroom, Tessa took care to wash every trace of the night's doings from her body.

She smiled at Simeon's thoughtfulness. Along with the water pot, he had placed clothing for her on the bed's cushion. On the table were also the cosmetics she would require if she were to appear before the council as Glaucus's mouthpiece.

She studied her reflection in a plate of polished bronze and applied whitening powder to her skin. The tiny vessel of powder was precious, formed by scraping corrosion off lead. She rouged her cheeks and lips with mulberry, lined her eyes with charcoal, and fastened her hair atop her head with a jeweled headband. The chitôn Simeon had laid out was a deep purple with gold stitching.

The color of royalty.

But no amount of clothing and face paint could make Tessa feel like a queen.

*It should be me in that pit outside the city.*

She shook off the black thoughts. The hour grew late, and her next performance was required.

Across the courtyard, Simeon stood with Nikos, talking softly. The two looked up at her as one, and she tried to ignore the admiration in the eyes of both.

"Is the cart ready?"

Nikos extended a hand toward the front of the house. "In the street."

She nodded and walked past, but Nikos followed.

"I do not need a driver," she said without turning.

"I know you do not need one. But a woman such as yourself is rarely unaccompanied."

*A woman such as myself.*

A gilded two-wheeled cart and a black horse waited below the steps of the house. Tessa allowed Nikos to step into the cart in front of her. He reached back and took her hand to pull her in.

Her narrowed eyes told him what she thought of his help. He lifted the reins, clucked at the horse, and they started for the agora. Nikos looked back at her. "After the night's horrors, the morning is beautiful, is it not?"

"Do not feel you must make conversation. I require only a driver."

He laughed. "Yes, Nikos," he said in a mocking voice. "It is a stunning morning. I was just contemplating the beauty of the world, as I often do."

Tessa frowned. Her attempt to regain appropriate distance between them did not seem effective.

All roads seemed to lead to the agora, and the press of people heading to market increased as they grew closer.

The central area of the city boasted the most open space in Rhodes, with dozens of statues scattered across the paving stones, surrounded by a shrine, a small temple, and the long *stoa*, or portico, along the east side. Beside the stoa stood the bouleuterion, where the council met regularly and where the strategoi were often called to speak.

Nikos drove the cart into the agora, and they passed between market stalls already clustered with shoppers seeking bargains and slow to move. Tables and wagons were loaded with wines, olive oil, honey, and cheeses. Tessa's stomach rumbled, reminding her that she hadn't eaten since the night before.

"Stand aside," Nikos shouted.

Several shoppers responded with angry gestures. The haggling calls of merchants and shoppers filled the agora like the bleating of sheep, and it occurred to Tessa how, like sheep, they needed strong leadership.

They passed tanners and potters and drove through the pungent smells of those who sold fish or duck or hares, the day's catch hanging in the sun to be admired and purchased. Heads turned toward Tessa, but she acknowledged no one. They would not expect it.

The sun beat hot on her back, and she felt her chitôn grow damp. Her nervous energy didn't help.

Nikos slowed the cart at the table of a cheese merchant, a burly man with an unkempt beard and long hair. From under his tunic, Nikos pulled an obol and pointed to a small package.

The merchant held up a hand, his face the picture of disbelief. "Ah, the lady will be wanting more than such a small amount of this fine cheese."

Nikos pressed the coin into the man's hand. "Perhaps later," he said. "But for now, the lady is hungry."

The large man shrugged, threw up his hands in surrender, and gave over the package to Nikos.

When he passed the package to Tessa, he never met her eyes.

They continued through the agora, and Tessa ate the soft cheese hastily, the sharpness of it watering her eyes for a moment.

They arrived at the bouleuterion, and Tessa took a deep breath to steady herself. Nikos turned to her.

"I will be here when you emerge," he said.

She nodded absently and stared at the council house. Inside, she knew, she would find fifty men and probably eight strategoi, all of them wanting to hear Glaucus's opinion on the Jewish matter.

*And I shall give it to them.*

She stepped from the cart and ascended the steps. She paused at the bouleuterion's entrance and closed her eyes.

A scream behind her chilled her blood.

"Tessa!"

She spun on the steps. Daphne ran toward her through the agora below, arms extended as though she would fly away. "Where is my husband?" she yelled.

Tessa bolted down the steps to face Daphne. The eyes of many shifted their direction. How did the woman even get here? Tessa kept her voice low and even. "He is at home, Daphne. He is unwell."

Nikos was there a moment later, his presence like a balm. Daphne lowered her arms and turned to him.

"You will take me to him?"

Nikos eyed Tessa, then nodded. "I will take you home."

He whispered to Tessa as they turned. "I will be back for you."

Tessa exhaled, nodded to those whose curiosity had not yet been satisfied, then ascended the steps again and entered the bouleuterion, the place where the island's democratic way of life was defended and upheld.

The room buzzed with the earnest conversation of dozens of men. The single large chamber, with tiers of marble seats around three sides and an open central area supported by columns, allowed all who sat inside to observe Tessa's entrance. The room fell silent, as though a heavy lid were clamped over a boiling pot. All eyes fixed on her. When had a woman ever entered this room?

Tessa raised her chin, threw her shoulders back, and marched into the room. She scanned the seats and decided on an empty one near the entrance. Her footfalls on the steps echoed in the silence. She took her seat and turned her attention to the front of the room and the door she had passed through.

Conversations began again, this time low and ominous, with heads inclined together about the room and eyes straying toward Tessa.

*This is only the beginning.*

The council of fifty men had been chosen by lot to serve the island for one-tenth of the year, then they would be replaced by the next group, also chosen by lot. Though the Assembly was the ultimate ruling body in Rhodes, made up of all male citizens of qualifying age and wealth, the Council was charged with preparing proposals for the Assembly, as well as implementing its decisions and seeing to everyday matters of state, such as public finances and the use and maintenance of public buildings. It was the Assembly that annually elected the ten strategoi, and these ten men held powerful sway over both the Assembly and the Council.

The meeting began and several necessary matters of state were addressed before any major issues could be raised. Tessa tried to focus on the matters being discussed, but her mind strayed to the comments she must deliver. The discussion then turned to Xenophon's murder and the necessity of the Assembly's election of someone to fill his place. A debate erupted as to whether a special meeting of the Assembly must be called, or if the matter could wait until the next regular meeting. Tessa tapped a sandaled foot on the floor and tried to steady her breathing.

She did not have long to wait. Spiro rose from his seat and waited until all attention was focused on him.

"In light of Xenophon's death and his well-known position in support of the Jews, I feel we must turn our attention to the matter. Without Xenophon, it falls on Glaucus to speak." He inclined his head toward Tessa. "But Glaucus has failed to appear before the council, and I move that—"

Tessa rose and lifted her voice above Spiro's.

"I am here to speak for Glaucus."

Spiro stopped in mid-sentence, and the buzz filled the room again, louder than before.

"Glaucus has fallen ill," Tessa announced. "The illness does not threaten his life, but it keeps him from attendance. He has given me his authority to speak for him on this matter."

The *epistates* of the council, in charge of the proceedings, held up a hand, as though he could think of no response to such an outlandish statement. Tessa took advantage of his silence.

"Glaucus has made his position clear on the matter of the Jewish population in Rhodes, and I know that many of you stand in support of him. He is confident that if the Jews were to be accepted as citizens of Rhodes, they would only enhance our position as a strong trading nation. The Jews have brothers in nations with whom we trade, and they have skills that can be better put to use. If they are able to rise above the poverty imposed on them by their status as non-citizens, they will contribute to the wealth of Rhodes through the payment of taxes and the purchase of goods in our marketplace. It serves no one to keep the Jews living among us in poverty."

Tessa concluded her passionate prepared speech but did not sit. She expected derision, even argument, but the council members seemed more confused than anything.

Spiro stood again, his smile almost tender. "It would seem that Tessa fights to retain her position as Rhodes's most political hetaera, in spite of Berenice's growing popularity." The crowd murmured in amusement. "But while Tessa is clearly an eloquent speaker, it is also clear that neither she nor her patron have kept abreast of current events in Rhodes. That she has no knowledge of this morning's murder and destruction perpetrated by the Jews should not surprise us. One often finds Glaucus's head buried in the sand. Or perhaps in his wine."

Murmurs of agreement spiraled around the room.

Murder? Destruction? Tessa's heart pounded. How was she to answer accusations she knew nothing about?

Vasilios called out, "What say you, Tessa? How can we support the Jews' citizenship when they violate our laws and murder our people?"

"Yes," Balthasar called from the other side of the chamber. "Perhaps it is time for those foolish enough to support the Jews to relinquish their positions of influence."

Tessa's headband chose this inopportune moment to begin to slip. She would not take the time to fix her hair with the eyes of the entire council upon her, so she reached for the band and pulled it out. Her hair cascaded to her shoulders, and somehow in the freeing of her hair, the panic fled. Tessa was left with a strengthened resolve. She looked Balthasar in the eyes, letting him grow uncomfortable under her gaze. The room quieted.

"Glaucus has served you well," she said. "Has served Rhodes well. He has been elected to his position by the will of the people, who respect his leadership and admire his intellect. The insolence of men chosen simply by lot will not be tolerated."

She tossed her hair back over one shoulder, scanned the room with a stony glare, then stepped from her seat and left the silence of the bouleuterion for the sights and sounds of the agora.

*The Jews.*

Anger surged through her veins. So little stood between her and freedom. Only a few days more until she sailed for Crete. But the tiny flame of hope she had allowed to flicker since Glaucus's death was a fragile thing—one that could easily be snuffed out by a community of people she knew nothing about.

# FIFTEEN

On their way back to Glaucus's home, Nikos told Tessa what he had learned of the riot in the southeast district. He concluded, frowning, "I don't understand why the district's people were so quick to react with violence against the Jews. It's almost as if they were lying in wait."

Tessa drew alongside him at the front of the cart. "If we had not been so long in our night's errand, I might have heard of all this before making a fool of myself in the council meeting."

The city rushed past them, oblivious to her anger, and the wind caught her loosened hair and tangled it about her face.

"I am sure no one thinks you a fool, Tessa."

"Well, it does not matter, does it?" She slapped the cart's side. "If they think Glaucus is unable to fulfill his position as strategos, they will replace him as emissary to Crete, and I will never leave this island!"

Nikos directed the horse to the front of Glaucus's house, and suddenly Tessa could think of nothing but sleep, as though the wind that had filled her sails through the long night and all morning had dropped away, leaving her muscles slack. She gripped the edge of the cart. The steps leading to the portico swam before her.

"Tessa, are you ill?"

She heard the question, but from a great distance, hazy and indistinct. She fought to regain control.

"Tessa!"

The house floated away, and blue sky filled her vision. Had she fallen?

*No. He carries me.*

Her fatigue overtook her desire to rebel against his familiarity. She closed her eyes and, a moment later, welcomed the softness of one of the andrôn's couches.

Nikos knelt beside her.

*Move away, Nikos. I am not strong enough to fight you today.*

"Do you need water?"

"I am tired. That is all. Leave me. Please."

He reached for her hair, splayed across a cushion, but seemed to think better of it and dropped his hand.

"Sleep, Tessa. You will be safe."

He disappeared from the room, and Tessa waited for sleep to overwhelm her, but it did not come.

Instead her mind traced back to the council meeting, to the critical mistake she had made in voicing Glaucus's former opinion on the Jews without knowledge of the morning's violence.

*I must recover his reputation.*

She struggled to think of an answer, but the softness of the couch, the day's drowsy warmth, and the lazy buzz of a fat fly circling the room weighted her eyes and her mind. Her thoughts spun and twirled without coherence. She closed her eyes, no solution yet discovered, and succumbed to exhaustion.

## Ω

Nikos left Tessa in the andrôn, hoping she would rest for awhile. Two nearly sleepless nights were beginning to take their toll on him as well, but he would not rest yet. He had gained almost nothing thus far, and he did not know how long he had before his father would demand answers.

He found Simeon in the hearth room. The older servant tended the charcoal fire in the center of the room. Beside the fire a freshly killed pheasant awaited plucking. Simeon looked up when Nikos entered, then returned his attention to the fire.

The smoky hearth room was where the family generally took their meals, and where time was spent relaxing. Adjacent to the kitchen, it was also where most of the cooking was accomplished. Pottery and bronze containers for storing and serving food lined the room's perimeter.

Nikos pulled a chest from its location near the wall, placed it next to the fire, and sat upon it.

"What do you hear of your fellow Jews this morning, Simeon?"

The old man did not answer immediately. He rearranged the charcoal within the flames, then sat back on his haunches and regarded Nikos.

"I hear the people of Rhodes are quick to accuse."

Nikos nodded, sensing the man's suspicion of him. He needed to push past it to get the information he sought. The situation had grown considerably more complicated since he had first arrived in Glaucus's home.

"I find it surprising that the water problem would so quickly erupt into violence."

Simeon poked at the fire. "What does a Greek care about the Jews?"

Nikos reached for the pheasant and pulled soft feathers from the body.

"It is Tessa I am worried about," he said. "In the council meeting this morning she proclaimed Glaucus's support for the Jews without knowing of the morning's events. The council was not pleased."

"Still, I do not see how this concerns you," Simeon said. "Tessa does not need your protection."

"Because she has yours?" The words were not said unkindly, but Nikos could see that his words had struck like a well-aimed arrow. "Simeon, let me help you care for her. I do not want to see harm come to her any more than you do."

Simeon rubbed his eyes with gnarled fingers. "The only way she will not be harmed is if she escapes this island."

"Then we will make that happen."

He felt Simeon studying him and continued his plucking. When the pheasant was naked, he handed it to Simeon, who threaded it onto a spit and swung it over the fire.

"Simeon, tell me what you know of this morning's violence."

The man gathered the feathers into a mound and nodded slightly. "Before the water failed late last night, there were rumors in the Jewish district that it would fail."

"But how could anyone have known?"

Simeon waved away the smoke wafting toward him. "My daughter could not tell me where the news came from. Only that yesterday was the first she had heard it, and that it was being said that city officials knew the water would fail but had refused to repair the aqueduct because they did not care if the Jews perished."

Nikos crossed his arms and contemplated this news. The pheasant sizzled, its juices dripping into the flames.

"There is more," Simeon said. "The fountain house guard in the southeast district was murdered in the night, and there is a witness who claims he saw a Jew enter the fountain house there. It is assumed that the Jew came for water or somehow threatened the guard, and then killed him."

"But why? Killing the guard serves no purpose."

"Well, it incited the district's people to meet my people in the streets."

Nikos sighed. "Was your daughter harmed, Simeon?"

The older servant shook his head. "No, she is well, and her husband besides. God was merciful."

"I am glad."

Simeon looked up at him and gave him a sad smile. "I am praying that God will be as merciful to Tessa."

Nikos nodded. "She can use help from all the gods."

Simeon gave the spit a quarter-turn. "There is only one true God, Nikos. One God who is Deliverer."

Nikos shrugged. "I have never cared much for any gods. They did not seem to care for me for many years."

"Yahweh cares for the affairs of all men, even those who are not children of Israel."

"A god who is interested in the people of another race? He must be a greedy god."

Simeon smiled. "He is jealous for all people to cast down their false gods and call on Him alone."

"I will leave you to deal with your god, Simeon. My concerns lie elsewhere."

"Our history tells of many outsiders who chose to turn and bow before Yahweh. Perhaps you will be one of them."

"Hmm. We shall see."

The pheasant popped and sizzled, and Nikos stood to leave Simeon to his cooking. Tessa was safe for now. And across the city lay a district that suddenly held much interest for him.

## Ω

Tessa awoke on the couch, aware that the sun had passed overhead and the afternoon grew late. She shot upright, took a moment to steady herself, then jumped from the couch.

*I have wasted time.*

She chafed at the moment of weakness in the street with Nikos. She had been momentarily wearied by the events of the night and the disaster of the morning.

*And I must undo the disaster.*

Her speech this morning had given Spiro and his colleagues an advantage over her. *Over Glaucus*, she reminded herself. If she were to maintain the appearance of Glaucus's authority in the city, she needed to better understand the Jewish problem.

She went in search of Simeon and found him in the kitchen. He stepped away from the slaves he had been instructing and motioned her to follow him into the hearth room.

The fire's warmth assailed her, and the smoke caused her eyes to water.

"Tessa, the slaves are asking questions about Glaucus. I fear that I cannot keep them and the master's wife from entering his room and finding him missing." He glanced toward the hall and further lowered his voice. "I believe you should take up residence here, rather than return to your own home."

Tessa ran a hand through her hair. "The people of the city will be shocked."

Simeon reached for a bird roasting over the coals in the center of the room and turned it. "I know," he said, "but you must be here to speak for Glaucus if he is needed—and to keep the curious from learning the truth."

Tessa lifted her chin. "You are right. And why should I care what they think? They will expect nothing less from me anyway," she said. "I have already defied every convention. What is one more?" She strode to the doorway. "I will move into Glaucus's room. Tell the slaves that I alone will take food to him and see to his needs." She looked down at her borrowed clothing. "But I must return to my home for my clothes. I cannot continue to appear in his wife's wardrobe."

"Let me send Nikos—"

Tessa thought of the house where Servia trained her girls.

"No. I will go myself."

## Ω

By the time the sun had started its descent over the city, Tessa had returned with a large bag filled with clothing and trinkets. It had occurred to her that she might not enter that house again before sailing for Crete, and so she had brought with her everything she had of value, though it took no more than one bag. She hauled it up the steps and into the house of Glaucus.

The house was quiet, and she was grateful to be left alone. She crossed the courtyard and headed for the back of the house. Beside the column where Glaucus had fallen, a flash of memory placed him again there on the ground. She paused, drawn to relive the moment.

What was that on the ground?

She leaned closer to the dark spot and realized with horror that the stones at the column's base were stained with blood. It had dried to a dark sheen on the paving stones and pooled in the cracks between them, a silent accusation waiting for someone to give heed.

Tessa hurried to Glaucus's room, deposited her bag, and searched out Simeon in the hearth room. She ran into the room, and his eyes registered fear.

"What is it?"

"Blood!" she whispered. "Glaucus's blood remains in the courtyard."

He released the handle of a cooking pot. "I will be there in a moment."

Tessa returned to the courtyard and sat on the edge of a bench. She gripped the edges and waited. Simeon appeared with white rags, and she joined him at the fountain in the center, dipped a rag in the stone basin, and squeezed the cool water through her fingers.

A moment later they were both bent over the stones, scrubbing at the evidence of Tessa's guilt. The rags reddened with Glaucus's blood. Tessa's knees scraped against the stones, and the roughness tore skin from her knuckles. She did not pause.

*How could we have not thought of the blood?*

She was nearly satisfied with their efforts when a tuneless singing filtered into the courtyard. Tessa's eyes shot to Simeon's. The voice was unmistakable.

Simeon grabbed the rags from her. "Go to his room. I will distract her."

But it was too late. Daphne wandered into the courtyard, her eyes unfocused, and her melody high and shrill.

She smiled at Simeon, but the smile faded when she saw Tessa.

"Why are you here?"

The words were spoken with clarity, and chill ran through Tessa.

"I—I am tending to Glaucus," she said.

Daphne frowned. "Glaucus is ill."

"Yes. He—he requested that I care for him until he recovers."

"You are staying here?"

Tessa swallowed and tossed her hair over her shoulders. "Yes. I am."

"I see." Daphne's gaze traveled to Tessa's unbound hair, her borrowed clothes, and back to her whitened skin. Her eyes grew dark. "Then may the gods deal with you as you have dealt with me."

With that she was gone, and Tessa exhaled in relief.

A young slave passed through the courtyard toward the back of the house, carrying a platter. Tessa watched him for a moment, then called out to him, "Where are you going?"

He slowed and turned. "I am taking Glaucus his evening meal."

Tessa shook her head. "I am to do that." She glanced at Simeon.

*Can we do this, Simeon?*

He smiled and nodded as if to answer her question. She ran to the slave, took the platter of thick lentil soup and bread, and headed for Glaucus's bedroom.

Behind the curtain, she was alone with the meal and realized she hadn't eaten anything since the cheese Nikos had purchased for her in the agora. The lentil soup smelled of garlic. She scooped some on a chunk of dark bread and consumed it eagerly.

With only the linen curtain separating her from the rest of the household, Tessa felt vulnerable to prying eyes. There was nothing to be done, however.

*Four more days. Only four more days, and I will be in Crete.*

# SIXTEEN

Evening fell and Tessa found she could not remain in Glaucus's bedroom for another moment. She longed to feel the wind on her face, the night breezes she knew would be flowing through the city, whisking away the dust and grime of the day. She had spent the past several hours sitting on the bed, reviewing recent events and considering whether the ruse was worth the effort. Should she simply put an end to all of it now? Her afternoon nap had erased her fatigue, and the room's walls closed in upon her. Nothing like the walls of a coffin, however.

*If this is to be my home for these four days, I need to make some changes.*

The bedroom in which Glaucus had taken residence was larger than most, just as Glaucus himself had been. Rich tapestries covered one wall, and statues of the grain goddess guarded either side of the doorway, indicating the importance Glaucus placed on the harvest.

If she were to leave the room, first she must make it appear that Glaucus resided in his bed, in case any prying eyes looked past the curtain. Tessa rose from the bed and crossed to a large chest against the wall opposite the door. She pulled a woolen blanket from it, folded it lengthwise several times and placed it on the bed. Given the girth of her former master, she would need more blankets.

She found extra blankets in the storage room and arranged them on the bed. When she was satisfied she had approximated Glaucus's mass, she spread one single blanket over the mound and stepped back to judge her work.

*Believable for a moment at least. Hopefully, that is all I will need.*

With a last look at "Glaucus," she left the confines of the room for the relative freedom of the courtyard. She pushed some fruit she'd saved from Glaucus's meal through the bars of Mynah's cage and cooed softly to the sweet bird. Mynah cocked her head to the side and studied Tessa, as if she too wondered at her presence in the house. Tessa smiled, then headed for the stairs. Halfway up, she heard Simeon call her name.

"Tessa, where are you going?"

She looked down at Simeon's concerned face. "I am only step-ping onto the balcony for a few moments."

He frowned but nodded.

Tessa smiled and resumed her climb. *Is this what it would have been like to have a father?* But then she thought of poor Persephone and was glad that she had not been forced to deal with yet another man in her life.

On the balcony the sky was beginning to deepen from lavender to indigo. Tessa raised her face. The city slowed beneath her, and the breeze picked up, lifting her hair and cooling her neck. If she closed her eyes and inhaled, she could feel the sea, smell its salti-ness. Several night birds called from nearby. She indulged a favorite pastime and focused on the calls, trying to identify them. One swooped past, a nightjar, with its white patches on velvety gray. She held out a hand, wishing it would settle there on the balcony with her. Wishing she could fly away with the bird to its home at the edge of a woodland somewhere.

Her mind returned to her speech and the disaster she'd made of it. Certainly by tomorrow Hermes or Spiro or one of the others would force a vote to remove Glaucus from his position because of his illness.

There had to be a way out.

A footstep shuffled on the balcony behind her. She turned.

"Nikos. Do you not have tasks that need attending?"

"My work is done for the day. I wanted to speak to you."

Tessa returned her gaze to the city.

"Tessa, I have been speaking to Simeon about the violence among the Jews this morning."

Tessa listened carefully but did not turn her head. Nikos did not seem bothered by her silence. He drew alongside her at the balcony's stone wall and looked out at the sky. He brushed at some loose rocks on the wall's edge.

"Something is not right with all of it. It makes no sense. Rumors were whispered yesterday that the city officials knew the aqueduct would fail—"

"The officials knew no such thing! I would have heard—"

Nikos held up his hand. "I know. That is what I am saying. These rumors sprung up only yesterday. How could anyone know it would fail, if the strategoi and the council did not know?"

Tessa frowned. "They could not."

"And the guard whose throat was cut in the fountain house— why was that done? Other than inciting the people of the district to meet the Jews with violence, what purpose did it serve?"

"You think this was all arranged."

Nikos turned to face her. "Perhaps it was all done to make the Jews appear dangerous. And in the process, ruin Glaucus for his support of them."

"Who would—" Tessa broke off, her stomach churning. "Spiro."

Nikos flung some pebbles into the street below, and she heard them plink against the ground. His voice was low. "Spiro?"

"He hates Glaucus. He is always trying to undermine him before the other strategoi, just as he did in the council meeting this morning. He would like to rip democracy from our hands. You should have seen him, gloating over the information he used against me." She caught herself. "Against Glaucus."

"What will you do?" Nikos asked.

*What can I do?* She drew herself up. "Do not concern yourself—"

"Stop, Tessa."

She tensed at his presumption. "Excuse me?"

"You heard me. Stop telling me to ignore the danger you are in."

"You are a servant—"

Nikos gripped the wall. "It is not my status that concerns you, and you know that. You are afraid to let anyone care about you, afraid to care about anyone else."

Tessa wrapped her arms around herself, suddenly chilled by the breeze. "I am not afraid of anything, as all who know me will tell you."

"I don't care what they say!" Nikos pounded a fist against the lip of the wall, loosening more stones. "You are terrified by even the thought of trusting anyone."

*And what if I am?* "Life has been my tutor, Nikos. And I have learned my lessons well."

He turned to her and grabbed her wrist. "I thought you wanted to be free."

She pulled away, but he did not let her go. "I seek freedom for my *body*, Nikos. Leave my heart alone."

Nikos released her wrist. "Tell me what you are going to do. Try to let me in, if only a little."

*Very well.* "Proof," she said. "I need proof of Spiro's duplicity. Something to take to the council." Her voice rose, and she fought to control it. "If I can show them that Spiro set all of this in motion to discredit Glaucus, then he will be held accountable for the fountain house guard's murder, he will be removed from the strategoi, and Glaucus's reputation will be saved. As will our trip to Crete."

Nikos nodded in agreement.

Tessa exhaled and looked down over the city. A man walked in the street below them, his head down and his steps purposeful. A woman followed. Tessa watched them for a moment, until recognition flashed on her and panic set in.

"Hermes!"

Nikos looked at her in confusion.

She pointed and whispered, "Hermes!"

She fled the balcony, ran down the stairs and into the courtyard. Hermes was already in the house. She could hear Simeon's protestations at the lateness of his call. She braced a hand against the door into the hall.

"Send him to the courtyard, Simeon. I will see him here." She crossed back to the bench and sat, arranging her body in a way that felt casual.

Hermes strode into the courtyard, followed by Berenice, the hetaera everyone was recently talking about. He stopped when he saw her.

"What can I do for you, Hermes? It is certainly past the hour for a social visit."

Hermes pursed his lips. "I had hoped to hear that Glaucus was well."

"Not yet, I am afraid. Though he does appear to be improving."

The woman behind him tugged on his arm. He pulled her forward. "Tessa, you know Berenice, I am sure."

Berenice curled her lip into a smile. "Tessa is spoken of practically as a goddess in Servia's house," she said. "Though even goddesses can be toppled."

Tessa scowled at Berenice, then at Hermes. The man's appetites were clearly unlimited. "You have acquired an amusing new toy, Hermes?"

Hermes laughed. "Jealousy does not become you, Tessa."

Berenice left Hermes's side and strolled across the courtyard. Tessa kept an eye on her but spoke to Hermes.

"Was there some message you wanted me to pass along to Glaucus?"

"What is his position on the Jewish issue given this morning's events?"

"Glaucus is confident that the truth will come to light." She turned back to him and smiled. "Perhaps all is not as it seems."

Hermes plucked at a leaf on a potted fig, then his gaze rested on Tessa like a prosecutor before the accused. "That is exactly what I was thinking."

Tessa's heart missed a beat, but her smile never faded. She pressed her shoulders into the bench. "Then I will beseech the gods that truth will be revealed."

He nodded, never taking his eyes from her. The leaf fell from his fingers, crushed and broken. "And I will join you in that prayer."

"Glaucus is also wondering what is being done about the water problem in the Jewish district."

"Being done?"

She snorted. "The people cannot survive without water. Is the aqueduct being repaired?"

Hermes shrugged and dusted his hands against each other. "With the morning's events and Xenophon's murder, the council

had enough issues to discuss. We have placed soldiers at the fountain house in the southeast district, to control any violence. The
aqueduct inspector is being located."

Aware that Berenice had disappeared, Tessa rose from her bench
and tossed her hair behind her. "Perhaps the Jews were right in their
belief that the magistrates of Rhodes do not care if they live or die!"

Hermes opened his mouth to speak, but suddenly Persephone
was in the courtyard.

*Not now child, not now.*

"Get him out of here! He is not welcome here." Persephone
twisted her chitôn between her fingers.

Tessa stepped in front of her, dismissing Hermes. "Good night,
then, Hermes. I will tell Glaucus you inquired after his health." She
called toward the back of the house. "Berenice, it is time to return
to your pen."

Berenice appeared, sneering, and joined Hermes.

The man said nothing, only shuffled two steps backward, his
eyes on Persephone, then turned and departed.

Nikos appeared a moment later at Persephone's side. "I was
listening from above."

"Does he know anything?" Persephone asked. She clutched
Nikos's arm and looked up at him, wide-eyed. He patted her hand
with his own, and she seemed to relax against him.

"Something must be done," Tessa sighed. "Hermes will not
leave this alone until he knows everything."

Ω

The darkness of night did not fully obscure the figure of Helios
looming over the harbor, though it did serve to cloak the movements
of rats in the street off the docks. Nikos stepped over the street's
gutter and stayed close to the rotting buildings. The day's events

had given him little confidence that Tessa's plan would work, and so he was determined to find a way to release Tessa from her chains himself.

A single inquiry had given him the location of Servia's home and training center, though his new street-friend had also told Nikos, with a wink and a jab, that he'd have better luck finding what he wanted at the taverna where he'd first encountered the woman.

The taverna was dimly lit, not much brighter than the alleyway outside. The unconscious remains of tonight's customers littered the couches along the walls, and the smell of cheap wine and dirty bodies melded to turn Nikos's stomach.

The barman hailed him and held up a cup, presumably already filled with the stuff that had rendered his other patrons dead to the world and its cares. He was an absurdly short man, balding on top, with long hair that began just above his ears. Nikos crossed the sticky floor and took the cup. He held it at arm's length and paid the man, who seemed to be partially blind.

*From living his life in darkness, no doubt.*

Nikos's entrance had drawn the attention of another. Servia eyed him from a corner and slithered across the darkness to greet him.

She smiled, the gold tooth glinting like another eye in the meager lamplight. "Didn't I say you'd regret passing up my girls?" Her gaze traveled from his face down to his sandals, as though calculating how much money she could extort from him.

*Far more than you'd guess.*

Behind them, two men broke into cackling laughter, no doubt a joke that would not even bring a smile in the sober light of morning.

Servia leaned in and caressed his arm. "Come with me," she whispered. "I have something you will like."

In spite of himself, Nikos gulped the bitter contents of his cup. He stepped back from Servia's shrewd gaze.

"I am interested in only one girl."

Her eyebrows shot up. "A man who knows what he wants." She touched his arm again. "So refreshing."

"How much for Tessa of Delos?"

Servia's fingers seemed to grow icy. She pulled her hand away.

Nikos stared her down.

"She is Glaucus's hetaera."

"I will pay you more."

She laughed. "More tonight, or more every week?"

"One payment. Tonight. And then she belongs to me, completely."

Servia's face grew passive. Nikos tried to read her expression but could not.

"How much?" she said.

Ah, finally.

Nikos pulled a money pouch from under his tunic and shook two talents into his own palm, perhaps twenty years' wages for most of the unskilled laborers in the room. The coins caught the lamplight and winked at them both. He glanced up at Servia and caught her look of amusement. Quickly he dumped the rest of the coins into his hand.

Servia started to chuckle, a deep-throated laugh that shook her bulky frame and built to a roar. Nikos scowled and returned the coins to his pouch.

"Oh, do not be hasty," Servia laughed, clutching his tunic. "We can still find some place to put all of that." Servia could not seem to control the laughter. "Are you sure we are speaking of the same Tessa?"

Nikos buried the pouch under his tunic again and flung Servia's hand from him. The pouch contained all the money he had brought to Rhodes. He could obtain more from his father, but not anytime soon.

Servia's voice rose to include anyone who would listen. "Tessa will earn me more in my lifetime than any other girl I have ever bought," she said, her tone changing from amusement to that of a patient instructor. "She has been an investment, one that has paid off well, and will continue to pay off even after Glaucus is dead. Even now, others have paid me to be on a list of future patrons." She poked at his waist where the pouch was tied. "I could not part with her for twice that sum."

Nikos pulled away and turned for the door.

"She is all you want?" Servia called after him.

*She is all I want.*

Ω

The sea was restless tonight. Nikos watched from the base of Helios's statue, considering the ships that lay in the harbor, their sails rigged and set for distant ports. Somewhere out there must be a ship that would take Tessa far from Rhodes—and a captain who would be willing to trade the safe passage of one haughty woman for all the drachmas Nikos could muster.

After the taverna, the money pouch felt conspicuous, and he was on his guard for ambush. A group of sailors passed him, calling to each other as they gathered to board their ship. Nikos followed and merged into the group.

"Is your captain on land?" he asked one sailor, taller and thinner than he, with a crop of strangely orange hair.

The younger man pursed his lips. "He comes ashore for wine and women, but he has staggered aboard by now." The sailor took in Nikos from head to toe and gave him a languid smile. "Looking for entertainment?" he asked with a lifted eyebrow.

Nikos put distance between them. "Looking for the captain."

They approached the quay and the sailor pointed. "You found him."

Nikos looked to where the sailors scrambled up the side of a mid-sized boat. A weather-beaten seaman stood on the dock, directing them with muttered curses and unmistakable authority.

"May I speak to you?" Nikos asked and inclined his head away from the ship.

The captain's expression grew wary, but he followed Nikos a few paces from the sailors, a significant limp slowing his progress.

"Where are you headed?" Nikos asked.

The captain's leathery skin made it difficult to guess his country of origin. "Halki," he grunted.

"Room for a passenger?"

The captain scowled. "Who are you running from?"

"Not me. A woman."

Nikos checked his anger at the captain's half-smile.

"A woman might have—difficulty—on a ship full of men."

"I'm willing to take that chance. She needs to get off this island."

"Whose is she?"

Nikos frowned. "What do you mean?"

The captain snorted. "Who *owns* her, man? You would not be paying to put her on my ship if she were free."

"A woman named Servia."

The captain laughed. "We'd all do well to stay on Servia's good side. Not a woman to make angry."

Nikos held up one talent. "How much?"

The captain licked his lips and studied Nikos's coin, then looked back at his face. "What's the girl's name?"

Nikos hesitated but decided Tessa would probably be recognized anyway. Better to have the details worked out in advance.

"Tessa."

The captain's hands flew up between them, an unbreachable wall.

"The hetaera?"

Nikos rubbed the coin. "Yes. She needs to—"

"No." The captain shuffled backward toward the barge, one hand still separating them. "No. Helping an unknown slave escape is one thing. Giving passage to Servia's prize hetaera is quite another. You won't find a ship's captain in all the Aegean stupid enough to do it. Servia would never rest until the penalty for helping a slave escape had been fully executed."

Nikos held out a second talent. "No one need know—"

The captain shook his head and pushed past Nikos toward the barge that would carry him to his ship and the open sea. "Keep your money. And I'll keep my life." He rejoined his sailors and they pushed away from the dock, away from Nikos, who still held a great deal of money that would do no good here.

*This is not an island. It's a cage.*

# SEVENTEEN

## ✦ *Four Days before the Great Quake* ✦

The winding climb to the Acropolis of Rhodes would take more time than Spiro could afford. But he had a dual reason for visiting the goddess this morning. It had been weeks since he had left a votive offering in the temple—and he had learned that Philo and Bemus, the two strategoi who joined Hermes and Glaucus in opposing the Achaean League, would also make the climb today.

The morning grew hot, and Spiro's neck grew damp with perspiration beneath his untraditionally long hair. An unimposing dirt road led to the Acropolis, which dominated the western and highest part of the city of Rhodes. From his position below the hill, Spiro could already see the columned stoa that bordered the temple complex. Soon the Temple of Athena Polias—Athena of the city—would come into view.

Spiro's stomach rumbled, and he fingered the knotted string on the linen package of olives and dried fish strapped beneath his tunic. No, he would wait until after he had placed his offering in the temple.

*And after I have placed a few well-chosen words in the ears of those who must hear them.*

The lush vegetation on either side of the road deepened as he climbed. Above him lay fields and groves that hid subterranean cave-like structures used for recreation and worship. As the road flattened and Spiro topped the ridge, a full view of the temple on the hill and the sea beyond welcomed him. He paused to drink it in.

*Exhilarating.*

The Acropolis, though not fortified like those of Athens and Thebes, was nearly a city unto itself. To his left a library, a stadium and a gymnasium, as well as the Temple of Apollo, stretched across the crest of the hill. Columns bordered all sides of the Temple of Athena Polias, and palms overhung its gleaming marble. Inside lay the texts of treaties with other states, as well as the sacred chamber where the statue of Athena resided.

Spiro entered the temple quietly and approached the west wall where votive offerings were placed in cuttings in the rock. He pulled a sack of barley from the pouch under his tunic and poured it into one such indentation.

From the corner of his eye, he saw that Philo and Bemus whispered at the temple's north side, near the *cella* where the statue of Athena demanded obeisance. Spiro moved toward them, head down in a posture of worship, until Philo's feet appeared near his own.

"Spiro." Philo acknowledged his presence, and Spiro looked up, feigning surprise.

"Philo. Bemus. Come to give the goddess her due?"

"What do you hear of Glaucus and yesterday's council meeting?" Philo asked.

Spiro looked around at the few other worshippers who dotted the temple. "Let us adjourn outdoors, out of respect for the goddess," he said. "Have you taken your lunch yet?"

Philo extended a hand toward the exit. "As you wish."

Outside Spiro led the way across a grassy field at the edge of a grove to a knee-high cluster of rocks. "Shall we sit?"

The three men each retrieved a package and began unpacking their lunch.

Spiro looked out to the water. "It is pleasant here above the sea, is it not?"

Bemus grunted. "The temperature is—"

"Philo, you asked about the Jews, I believe," Spiro said.

Philo took a bite of his bread and chewed slowly. "I spoke only of yesterday's meeting. But this situation with the Jews does grow tiresome."

Spiro lounged back against his rocky seat and shrugged. "If not for Xenophon and Glaucus, we would not even be discussing it. The Jews would have been dealt with long ago."

"But Xenophon is dead," Bemus said.

Spiro pulled apart a dried fish. "And Glaucus is incompetent." He let the statement ride awhile, and they ate in silence.

*Only you two and Hermes remain.*

Philo finally spoke. "I take no pleasure in seeing violence in our city, even if it strengthens our position."

"I agree," Bemus said. "I abhor violence of any sort."

Spiro chewed the last bite of his fish and swallowed. "But when left to rule themselves, men will always descend to violence, will they not?"

"It is an age of enlightenment," Philo answered. "Our philosophy instructs us in self-rule."

Spiro smiled. "And yet you both retain your positions of leadership. Why do so if the people are better left to rule themselves?"

Bemus sighed. "Xenophon's murder, Jews rioting. It would seem some days that democracy is not the answer."

"A wise man thinks for himself, Bemus," Spiro said. "I commend you on going your own way." Bemus looked confused, and

Spiro pressed on. "It appears that Xenophon's murderer will soon come to justice. Let us hope that a quick resolution to the Jewish problem will be found as well."

His companions nodded.

The arduous climb up the hill had been worthwhile, Spiro decided. The days to come would indeed bring resolution; he would make sure of it.

Ω

Tessa's plan to reveal that Spiro was behind the Jewish violence came to her, fully formed, when she opened her eyes to the sunlight streaming over Glaucus's bed. She lay beside the mound of blankets, fearful of leaving Glaucus's room in case another ambitious slave took it upon himself to earn favor with some task done for Glaucus.

She rose from the bed, distaste washing over her in spite of Glaucus's physical absence. Within an hour she had explained her plan to Simeon, found Nikos, and was ready to set out.

Simeon met her in the courtyard.

"Nikos is bringing the cart to the front," he said, handing her a string-tied scroll.

"Thank you, Simeon. Are you certain you will be able to—"

"I will keep your secret safe, Tessa." Simeon took her hand and squeezed. "You must trust me."

His words chilled her. *Again, someone asks the impossible.*

For the first time, Tessa wondered what would become of Simeon after she was gone to Crete and Glaucus did not return. Would he go on serving Daphne? How long before it was discovered that Glaucus was dead? But Simeon was old. Perhaps it was indeed time for his service to end.

"And you are certain your daughter will receive us?"

"She is a good girl." He pointed to the scroll and smiled. "She will do as her father says."

Tessa lifted the scroll. "Thank you, again."

"You had better go."

Tessa found Nikos in the front street with the cart that had carried them to the agora. Persephone stood beside him, and Tessa paused to listen.

"Another time, Persephone," Nikos said. "This trip must be for Tessa alone. But I will take you for a ride soon."

The girl seemed satisfied. She turned to the house and gave Tessa a self-conscious smile. As she passed Tessa on the steps, she squeezed her arm as though sharing a secret.

Tessa waited until the girl was inside, then hurried down the steps.

"The child has much to learn, Nikos," she said. "Do not toy with her."

He frowned. "I've done nothing to encourage her."

"See that you don't."

He turned to the ox, a smile on his lips. "You sound jealous."

"Jealous of a child?"

"She is not a child, Tessa. It seems everyone can see that but you."

Tessa tossed her untied hair behind her shoulders in a manner that was becoming habit. Nikos smiled and raised his eyebrows.

"What?"

He shrugged. "Nothing."

"Then move this thing!"

"As you wish, mistress."

*How is it your deference always sounds mocking, Nikos?*

The Jewish district lay less than an hour away. Simeon had given Nikos instructions on how to find his daughter's home. Once there, Tessa would question Marta and her neighbors about the rumors that had circulated before the water failed. If they could learn how the rumors were started, perhaps they could trace the source back to Spiro and discover how he had manipulated the situation to his own ends.

The morning was cloudless with a light breeze, the kind of morning to revel in, but Tessa's thoughts were of Spiro's duplicity and she barely noticed her surroundings.

"Try to feel it, Tessa."

Nikos's words shook her from her thoughts.

"I am not in the mood for riddles."

"No riddles. I am simply asking you to feel the sun, feel the morning, feel even the danger of our task."

"You speak like an actor in a theater comedy."

He smiled. "Do I? Perhaps the comedies have much to teach us."

Tessa scowled. "And would you have me laugh in the face of my destruction?"

He turned to face her. "I would have you *live* in the face of it, Tessa. *Live.*"

They rode the rest of the way in silence.

In the Jewish quarter the narrow streets drew the homes closer together here than in other sections of the city, as though they could not bear to be separated. Ahead of them Tessa saw a cluster of children playing some kind of game in the street, their laughter and shouts echoing off the homes and into a chorus. As the ox pulling their cart clopped toward the children, they ceased their game and opened a path between them, pressing themselves against the homes on either side, their eyes wide with curiosity at the beast and the strange people who approached.

Nikos drew the cart slowly through the midst of the children. One of them found the courage to reach out to touch the ox. Suddenly there were more than a dozen hands reaching for the ox, the cart, and for Tessa and Nikos. They all spoke at once, their chatter largely unintelligible to Tessa. She drew back from the dirty hands that reached for her. Nikos slowed the cart to almost a stop, apparently fearful that the ox would tread on bare toes.

"Let us pass, children," he said laughing.

One little boy, perhaps six or seven years, smiled up at Tessa, his face smudged and several teeth missing in front. He reached two small fingers toward her arm reverently, as though he had never seen such finery. Tessa swallowed, her ability to pull away stolen by the innocent brown eyes that studied her. She looked down on the fingers that touched her chitôn and pressed into her arm. The boy's touch sent a jolt to her heart. She felt tears spring to her eyes, and the sensation shocked her like nothing had these past few days. She reached for his hand, closed her fingers over his small ones, and held on.

Nikos reached out to one of the oldest boys and laid a hand on his shoulder. "You look like a leader, son. Can you have your friends let us pass? Follow us to our destination, and I will give you all some hay to feed the ox."

The boy seemed to grow several inches at Nikos's words. "Let them pass, everyone," he said. "Step away. Follow me."

Tessa released her admirer's little hand, though she followed his smile with her eyes, and they set out again, this time with the pack of children trailing them like hungry sheep.

Nikos found Marta's home in the next street. He pulled the ox cart as far to the side as possible, then helped Tessa down. The children waited behind the cart, the tallest boy holding them back with an authoritative arm. Nikos reached for the bundle of hay he had brought and handed it to the boy. "What is your name, son?"

"Matthias."

"Give everyone a little bit, Matthias. And make certain they keep their fingers clear of his teeth."

Matthias nodded solemnly.

Tessa watched the joy spread over the children's faces, and it seemed to her that the sun had grown brighter.

"Are you ready?" Nikos asked.

"What?"

"Ready to go inside?"

"Oh. Yes." Tessa gripped the scroll Simeon had sent and followed Nikos to the door. He knocked and it opened a moment later to reveal a lovely woman not much older than Tessa. Her hair was covered with a blue cloth, and her hands and dark blue tunic were dusted with something white. Flour, perhaps. Her eyes roamed back and forth between the two strangers at her door. Tessa was aware how out of place the two of them must look.

She stepped out from behind Nikos. "Are you Marta?"

"Yes. Have we met?"

Tessa shook her head and thrust the letter toward the woman. "No. I am Tessa, a—friend—of your father's." She did not miss the wide-eyed recognition of her name. "This is Nikos, another servant in our household. Your father sends his greetings and this message."

Marta took the scroll, her forehead creasing. "Is my father unwell?"

"No, no. He is—wonderful. But we need your help."

Marta's eyes conveyed her confusion, and she opened the letter quickly and scanned the words. A quick smile passed over her features.

"Come in," she said. She wiped her hands on her tunic, then reached for Tessa. "Come in." Marta slipped an arm around Tessa and pulled her into the house as though her sister had come for a visit. Again Tessa marveled at her inability to resist, a sudden longing for a family threatening to shake her apart.

Tessa's eyes remained sun-blind, and in the darkness her first impression of Marta's home was one of standing in a noisy cage of puppies.

"Children!" Marta said. "We have guests. Quiet down!"

Tessa could make out several figures bobbing and weaving around the room, and moments later could count them. Five. And another on the way, she suspected.

The house was built in the Greek fashion but on a smaller scale. Marta led them to the kitchen, where her half-finished bread waited on a table. She looked down at her flour-dusted tunic. "I am cooking for this evening," she said. "I am sorry for the mess."

Tessa held up a hand. "No, we are sorry for the interruption."

Marta laughed. "In this house, I stopped noticing interruptions years ago."

Several children bounded up to their mother, and an older girl followed, attempting to quiet them. Tessa watched the girl, about Persephone's age, until she turned and smiled at Tessa.

"Sit," Marta said, indicating a chair near the wall. "Please sit. I must set this bread to baking, but then we can talk." She waved a hand at the oldest daughter. "Give them some fruit, Sarah. They must eat."

Tessa shook her head. "That is not—"

Marta made a scolding sound. "Of course you must eat. Sarah—the fruit!"

The oldest daughter shooed the other children from the kitchen and brought them plates of peaches with honey. Tessa lowered herself to the chair and laid the plate on her lap. Nikos leaned one shoulder against the wall and held his plate with one hand.

Marta pounded her dough flat, as though she did not want it to rise, something Tessa had never seen. She smiled at Tessa. "My father cares for you very much. Do you know that?"

Tessa returned her smile. "He is a good man."

Marta nodded, as though satisfied with Tessa's answer. "He is much respected here. It is a different life from that in the house of Glaucus."

"All who serve under him do so with respect."

Marta peeled the dough from the table and laid it across a flat stone. "I am certain you are right. But it is not the same. Here he is a leader of his people." She picked up the stone. "Will you come to the hearth room? We can talk there."

They followed her to the fire, where she placed the stone over the coals. Several other pots simmered on the heat. The aroma of garlic in a bubbling broth made Tessa's mouth water.

Marta pointed to a long-handled spoon beside the fire. "Will you stir the soup?"

Never having stirred soup in her lifetime, Tessa picked up the spoon with care and placed it into the pot. She knew Marta's amused smile meant her inexperience was showing.

"Marta, we came to ask you about the water—"

"Mother!" Two children skidded into the room, grabbing at each other. "Daniel has taken my sword and hidden it!"

Marta sighed. "Daniel, give back Levi's sword."

"But he took my bow!"

"Boys!" Marta rose to her feet, hands on her hips. "Both of you return the other's things." She pointed to the doorway. "Now go!"

The two left and she smiled in apology. "Boys and their weapons. They learn to battle much too young, do they not?" Marta took the spoon from Tessa and patted her hand as if to thank her. "Is the aqueduct being repaired?"

"I am sure that it will be soon. But I came to ask you about it."

"I do not know anything about it."

Tessa moved to a low couch near the fire. "Simeon says that you were told the water would fail before it actually did."

Marta nodded. "Not long before, but yes. Sometime in the afternoon I heard Nathaniel speaking of it in the market. Early the next morning, Amos came to our door to tell us that the basin in the fountain house was dry."

"You said that Nathaniel told you. Do you know where Nathaniel heard this?"

"Nathaniel did not actually tell me. I only overheard him talking with someone else in the market. I thought it was just foolish talk at the time. But then later . . ."

Nikos leaned toward Marta. "Were others talking of it, also, do you think? Other than Nathaniel and this other person?"

Marta smiled and laid the spoon aside. "It is hard to say. News travels very quickly here. I only know that by morning, everyone was talking of how the city magistrates knew the water would fail and did not care."

Tessa turned to Nikos. "I think we should speak to this Nathaniel. Find out where he obtained this information."

Marta moved to Tessa's couch, sat beside her, and touched her arm. "I do not think—" She put an arm around Tessa's shoulder. "I do not think Nathaniel will speak with you."

"Then I will have Nikos—"

Marta shook her head and pulled Tessa to her. "It is not simply because you are a woman," she said. "It is because you are Greek. And you are—" Her eyes betrayed her embarrassment.

Tessa lowered her head. "Because I am a hetaera."

Marta squeezed her shoulders again. "I know you are a good woman because my father says so. Not all the Jewish people will share that opinion."

"Then Nikos—"

"He is Greek. He is from your household." She smiled sadly. "I know that not very far from here you are a woman of influence, one who is greatly respected. But in many ways, this is not Rhodes; this is Israel. And your influence means nothing here."

A door slammed and a figure appeared in the doorway. "Marta?"

"Jacob." Marta stood and held out a hand. Her husband entered the room and grasped her hand. "We have guests."

Tessa watched the man's expression go from curious to displeased as he took in his visitors. His eyes lingered for a moment on Tessa's hair, not only lacking the acceptable Jewish covering but hanging below her shoulders.

"This is Tessa," Marta said.

Jacob's eyes, wide with embarrassment, shifted immediately to the plank floor. "Why are they here?"

"They are trying to find answers about the water problem. My father—"

"Leave."

The word was spoken in the quiet undertone of veiled anger.

Marta put a hand on his arm. "Jacob—"

"They must leave, Marta! We cannot have—her—in this house. Especially not today!"

Tessa stood. "I am sorry to have bothered you, Marta. You have a lovely family, Jacob."

The man still would not meet her eyes, but his words were for her. "Do not even speak of our family."

*I do not blame him.*

Marta walked with them to the door. "Jacob is—"

Tessa held up a hand. "You do not need to explain, Marta." She lowered her voice. "Will you tell us where to find Nathaniel?"

Marta looked over her shoulder. "In the market, selling meat," she whispered. "But wait outside for a few moments. I will send Sarah out with something for you that might be of help."

The warmth that had begun to fill Tessa was evaporating. She nodded, wanting to escape the shame of Jacob's downcast eyes as soon as possible.

"If you need anything," Marta said, "return here. I will talk to Jacob. It will be fine."

Tessa moved to the door, but Marta pulled her back and into an embrace. "God be with you," she whispered and hugged her.

"Thank you," Tessa managed.

They waited outside for only a few minutes. Sarah came out of the house, a bundle in her hands. "Mother says you will do better with these," she said, and thrust the bundle toward Tessa. She smiled shyly, then disappeared back into the house.

Tessa examined the gift. Clothing. Traditional Jewish clothing for both her and Nikos.

Nikos nodded. "It is a good idea," he said.

Tessa inhaled and looked back at the doorway. "She is a good woman." She balled the clothing in her fists.

*Now I must pretend to be one.*

# EIGHTEEN

In a narrow alley between homes Nikos shed the white tunic that marked him as a Greek servant. He donned the earth-brown tunic Marta had given him, then changed places with Tessa at the head of the alley, to stand watch while she slipped off her linen chitôn and exchanged it for a scratchy woolen tunic and head covering.

A few minutes later he felt her presence at his back and turned to find her transformed. He couldn't identify the look in her eye. A challenge, perhaps, to say the right thing. But he had learned that women were complicated that way, and it was often impossible to say the right thing. He chose to simply nod his head and let her interpret this however she chose. He took her chitôn from her hands, ran back to the cart, and placed their clothes in it.

They had entered the Jewish district to the fanfare of children, and Nikos had little hope that they would remain anonymous as they strolled to the market. But perhaps the change of clothing would help them find the answers they sought.

Nikos led the way to the street Marta had indicated. A small square opened before them, a fraction of the size of the agora at the center of Rhodes but with the usual tables and stalls.

Tessa held back. "Do you think they will speak to us?"

"We can only try."

The crowd in the market had thinned by this hour, the heat having risen. They ambled past tables of oil and wine, neat piles of fruits in reds and yellows, and wilting leafy greens. Merchants called out to them as they passed.

"Five obols! Five obols for the finest grain in Rhodes."

Nikos shook his head and held up a hand.

"Four obols! Only four! You will not be disappointed."

Another merchant claimed to have the best figs in Rhodes, and Nikos bought a handful, hoping it would make them appear more casual. He handed one of the dark fruits to Tessa and chewed on one himself.

Ahead, a cluster of people at one stall blocked their view of the merchant's specialty. Nikos tried to get a better view.

"I think this is it," he said, swallowing the sweet fruit. "The meat seller."

Nathaniel was younger than Nikos had expected, with the build of an athlete and a generous smile for every customer.

They lingered at the back of the small crowd, listening to him deal with customers. Lamb seemed to be the item in demand today. The meat merchant hacked pieces from a hanging carcass with a cleaver.

Two women reached an agreement on a price with Nathaniel, then moved on, satisfied with their purchase. Nikos and Tessa inched forward. Now they had a better view. A variety of carcasses hung above the table. Flies buzzed around the meat where it hung, and also on the ground where drops of blood pooled in a line of dark circles in the dirt. The peculiar smell of meat hanging in the sun hovered about the stall like a heavy mist.

When they had worked their way to the front of the group, Nathaniel turned his attention to them. "Lamb?" His eyes took stock of them, the smile now absent.

Nikos shook his head, and Tessa stepped beside him. "We have questions."

Nathaniel scowled. "I sell meat, not answers."

"It's about the water," Tessa said.

Nathaniel's gaze flicked between the two of them. "Who are you? I know most everyone in this district, and I have never seen you."

Nikos felt the eyes of the remaining meat buyers on them. His gaze strayed to Nathaniel's knife, its blade buried in a chopping block.

"We were told that you knew about the water failing before it happened," Tessa said, ignoring the man's suspicion.

Nathaniel's answer took in the whole crowd. "We have curious strangers among us," he said. "Does anyone want to speak to them?"

Nikos watched the heads of nearly everyone in the crowd turn away, look at the packed earth, the blue sky—anywhere but at the two of them. He wrapped his fingers around Tessa's upper arm, and her muscles tightened to stone beneath his grip.

"My wife sometimes speaks before she thinks," he said to Nathaniel. "Accept my apologies."

Nathaniel's expression remained hard. "You should teach your wife to remain silent."

Nikos smiled. "If you can tell me how, friend, I would be most grateful."

Nathaniel's eyes narrowed for a moment. Then a grin broke over his features and he bellowed out a laugh. "Now that is a question I will never have the answer for!"

Nikos laughed with him and slapped his arm. "We are new to Rhodes," he said. "Friends of Marta and Jacob—you know them?"

Nathaniel nodded. "Of course, of course."

Nikos sighed and looked at the people. "The situation is disturbing for us. We came to Rhodes in hopes of a better life for our family." He put an arm around Tessa's shoulder. "But to find that the city does not even care enough to keep the water flowing—we begin to wonder if we made a mistake."

The crowd around them murmured agreement.

Nathaniel fingered the knife in the block. "Yes, they knew about the problem, that much is certain."

Tessa leaned forward. "How—"

Nikos squeezed her against himself. "How do you know?"

Nathaniel noticed Nikos's silencing of Tessa and gave him a wink. "I heard it from a Greek slave," he said. "Someone who had come to the market for the peacock. We have the best peacock here, you know. Better than any you can get in the agora."

Nikos eyed a hanging bird. "Perhaps we will take some home," he said. "So this slave who told you about the water, whose slave was he?"

"I do not know. Whoever owns him, he must be worth much. A huge man."

"Huge?"

Nathaniel held up a hand, nearly a foot above his own head. "With a bald head and arms like a bull." He laughed. "A fine piece of meat!"

The customers in line behind them laughed as well.

Nikos pointed to the peacock. "How much?"

Nathaniel's eyes took on the glint of business. "One drachma."

Nikos knew better than to agree easily, but he had no wish to linger. "You rob me, Nathaniel. But since we are new and you have been so friendly, we will agree to your price today." He pulled a drachma from his purse and held the coin out to Nathaniel. The man reached to snatch it, but Nikos held it for another moment.

"But only today, friend," he said with a smile. "Next time we will not be so generous."

Nathaniel gave him a half-smile. "Of course."

A shout at the market's end caused them all to turn their heads. Two Jews were in the dirt. Above them, three men stared down the market. Greek soldiers.

Nathaniel growled. "Dogs. Come scrounging for a fight."

Nikos saw the fear on the faces of the crowd. "Why are they here?"

A woman behind him spoke. "They keep coming, since the water failed. As though they are waiting for us to rise up and take over Rhodes." Her voice dripped bitterness.

Nathaniel's hand gripped the handle of his knife. "Return to your homes," he said. "They do not like more than a few Jews together at once."

The soldiers had already covered most of the distance from the end of the market.

One of them called out. "What are you doing there?"

"Minding our business," Nathaniel called back. "And you should do the same!"

The soldier's hand went to his sword, and the crowd backed away as one.

Nikos stepped in front of Tessa. "I will tell them who you are," he whispered.

He felt her breath on the back of his neck. "No! We have not learned all we need here."

He half-turned his head to look at her determined eyes. Beneath the head covering, she was the same Tessa.

The crowd dispersed behind them, and the commanding soldier seemed provoked by Nikos's defiant stance. He yelled at Nikos, though he was only a few feet away, "Are you the leader of this revolt?"

Nikos held up a hand. "There is no revolt here. Only people hungry for some meat." He extended a hand toward Nathaniel's stall. "Finest peacock in the city, you know."

The soldier stepped up to Nikos and sneered in his face. "Are you implying that Jewish poultry is better than Greek?"

Nikos leaned closer, their noses almost touching. He hoped that the rest of the crowd had disappeared by now. He sniffed at the soldier. "There does not seem to be the same stench about Jewish birds," he said.

The Greek's eyes widened. His sword glinted in the sunlight, and Nikos cursed his passion for justice that always surfaced at the wrong moment.

Ω

Nathaniel stepped up beside Nikos to face the soldiers with him and pushed Tessa backward. The knife rested expertly in his hand.

"We want no trouble here," he said.

From behind him, Tessa grabbed Nikos's tunic and pulled him toward her. "We are leaving, Nikos," she hissed.

He took a few steps backward, watching Nathaniel and the soldiers to be certain that there would be no trouble. Tessa turned Nikos around.

The soldiers shouted to the small cluster of people that remained at the edge of the market, "Back to your homes, all of you!"

Nathaniel returned to his stall, his eyes never leaving the soldiers. He pressed a package of meat into Nikos's hand and nodded his approval.

Tessa led Nikos out of the market square, back toward the street where they had left the ox cart. The soldiers followed discreetly at a distance.

An older woman in gray scurried alongside Tessa, her sun-weathered forehead creased. "I do not like this," she whispered. "Ever since that Greek came here and started talking about the water, there has been nothing but trouble."

Tessa looked to Nikos. He gave a slight nod, as if to say, *Talk to her, Tessa.*

"You heard him?"

"Ha! I would not speak to a Greek if I lay dying in the street." She jabbed a bony finger toward a house. "My husband. He said the giant Greek brought bad news, though no one believed it at first."

They reached Marta's street. Tessa had no doubt that the soldiers would notice the two of them climb into the cart and ride away from the district. Their older companion disappeared into her home.

"We cannot leave yet," Nikos said.

She nodded her understanding. They walked the half-block to Marta and Jacob's home on the narrow street. Nikos could not seem to resist a sneer in the soldiers' direction before he pushed Tessa through the doorway.

"Tessa!" Marta met them inside the door and grasped her hands. "Is there trouble?"

"No," Tessa said. "Not much. Some soldiers followed us. We thought it best to come inside before leaving." She glanced around down the hall. "Is Jacob—"

Marta squeezed her hand and pulled her deeper into the house. "Jacob will be fine. He read Father's letter and he understands." She led them both back to the hearth room. In their absence a table had been set and the beginning of the meal already placed on it.

Nikos cleared his throat and handed Nathaniel's meat to Marta. "We do not want to interrupt your meal."

Marta smiled. "It is almost dusk. Do you not know what is about to begin?"

Tessa looked at Nikos, but he only shrugged.

Marta still held Tessa's hand. "It is nearly Passover. And you must stay."

"Passover?" Tessa had never heard the word.

Jacob entered the room, and though he still would not look at Tessa, he seemed agreeable to her presence.

"Has he arrived yet?" Marta asked.

Jacob shook his head. "I am sure he will be here before the sun sets."

Marta nodded. "Will you bring more cushions, Jacob?"

Her husband left silently, and Marta bustled about the table and began shifting plates and cups to make room for two more. "Passover is a holy day and is celebrated every year. No one in the district will be about the streets this evening. Any Greek soldier would know that you are not Jewish if you are seen out. But perhaps you don't mind being seen?"

Tessa bit her lip. The information about the big Greek spreading information about the water had further convinced her that Spiro was behind the trouble. She would rather he not find out that she had been in the Jewish district asking questions. Besides, they still had no proof.

"There is more we need to learn here, Marta," she said. "But I do not wish to presume—"

Marta clapped her hands in delight, then gave Tessa a quick hug. "You will stay for the Passover meal and then for the night. In the morning you can finish your business."

"Thank you."

*I will accept your hospitality, but don't expect friendship from me, Marta. I'm not capable of it.*

Jacob returned with cushions and with the children. Behind them a familiar face appeared.

"Simeon!" Tessa's surprise turned to panic. "You left the house—"

Simeon smiled and held up a hand. "Do not fret, Tessa." He came close and spoke softly to her and Nikos. "Persephone is standing guard, and the servants have been instructed not to disturb Glaucus for any reason."

Tessa frowned. "What about Daphne?"

Simeon's eyes shifted down to the floor. "She often requests a certain herb to help her sleep," he said quietly.

"And she asked for it tonight?"

His gaze still on his feet, Simeon smiled. "Not tonight. But I thought perhaps she would appreciate it anyway."

Nikos chuckled, and Tessa tried to trust in Simeon's judgment. "What are you doing here?"

The older man beamed at Marta. "I came to celebrate this special night with my family." He turned to Tessa. "And with you."

Tessa swallowed. *Don't, Simeon.*

Marta lit the candles on the table, and they all sat, with Jacob at the head and Simeon at the foot of the table. Tessa and Nikos sat side by side, and the youngest son, Daniel, plopped down beside Tessa.

The candlelit table, with its white linen cloth running down the center, glowed with happy faces and steaming food. Tessa eyed the roasted lamb hungrily and wondered at the dishes she did not recognize. Jacob stood and all eyes turned to him.

"We are—pleased—to have guests at our Passover table this evening," he said. He managed to look at Nikos. "May you be blessed by the meal and its meaning."

Nikos nodded his thanks, and Tessa smiled.

Jacob raised a hand over the table and began a haunting recitation of something in Hebrew that sounded to Tessa like it must be a prayer. When he sat, the meal began.

The roasted lamb was as succulent as it looked, and from the way the children dug into it, she suspected that they did not often have such a meal. Even so, Marta was careful that her guests each received a hearty portion.

There were unusual dishes, including a mixture of apples and chopped nuts. A plate of bitter herbs was passed, and when Tessa saw that each of the children took some, she felt she should as well. When the bread circled the table, Tessa felt some pity for Marta, for the bread had not risen as it should. No one else seemed to notice, however.

Through the meal, several cups of wine were poured, and at various times, Jacob stood and spoke of the meaning of each cup.

"*Kos Rishon*," he said. "To remember God's promise to bring us out of Egypt." And the second cup, "*Kos Sheni*," in remembrance of God's promise to deliver the Jews from slavery. It was a recounting of their people's history.

Beside her, Daniel grinned up at her.

When the family dipped the bitter herbs in what appeared to be salt water, she followed along. Her eyes watered as she chewed the mouthful of herbs, and she looked down at Daniel. When he scrunched up his nose at the taste, she nearly laughed.

She looked up at Jacob, wondering if she were ruining his Passover. But his eyes were on Marta, and the look that passed between them was so full of adoration it threatened to close Tessa's throat with a longing she had no desire to experience.

She glanced around the table at the children, serious about their meal, and at Simeon, smiling down on his brood. And at Nikos, whose smile was only for her.

Without warning, Daniel jumped to his feet and stood beside her. Raising his chin and squaring his shoulders, he spoke in Hebrew. "*Ma Nishtana ha-lahylah ha-zeh mi-kol ha-layloht?*" Everyone smiled, as though his question were not unexpected.

Simeon spoke to Jacob. "Perhaps since we are blessed with guests at this year's Passover, you will allow me to explain some of our customs?"

Jacob dipped his head in agreement, and Simeon turned to Tessa and Nikos. "Daniel asks, 'Why is this night different from all other nights?' It is a question meant to prompt curiosity in the children." He smiled. "But perhaps others are curious as well." He patted Daniel on the arm and the boy sat.

"It is a night to remember the slavery we experienced at the hands of Egypt, a night to remember the freedom we were given by the living God. But most of all it is a night for understanding redemption." His eyes lingered on Tessa. "And the message of redemption is one for all people, not only the Jews."

He nodded at Daniel, and the boy asked another question, this time in Greek with a shy smile at Tessa. "Why is it that on all other nights we eat either bread or *matzah*, but on this night we eat only matzah?"

Jacob nodded and spoke to all of them. "We eat only matzah because on the night we were delivered from the hand of Pharaoh, our fathers could not wait for their breads to rise, and so they took the breads out of their ovens while they were still flat, which was matzah."

Daniel then asked, "Why is that on all other nights we eat all kinds of herbs, but on this night we eat only bitter herbs?"

Tessa listened in fascination. Jacob answered, "We eat only *maror*, a bitter herb, to remind us of the bitterness of slavery that our ancestors endured while in Egypt."

"Why is that on all other nights we do not dip our herbs even once, but tonight we dip twice?" Daniel asked.

"The bitterness of our forced labor has been replaced by tears of gratefulness. The *charoset* of nuts and apples symbolizes the mortar used by the Israelites in their forced labor."

A question about the roasted lamb was followed by a third and fourth cup of wine that symbolized the Jews' God redeeming them with a demonstration of His power and calling them as a nation. Tessa's eyes filled with tears more than once at the beauty of all the symbols, and her desire to remain aloof from the family's tradition grew hazy.

When a fifth cup of wine was poured, Simeon stood and looked inquiringly at Jacob, who nodded his approval.

Tessa reached for the fifth cup and waited for Simeon's explanation.

"The fifth cup we do not drink," he said.

Tessa returned the cup to the table in embarrassment, but all eyes were on Simeon.

"This night commemorates a most important night in our history. The sun set on our people in slavery, and when it rose, we were a free nation. This was a physical deliverance, but it points also to a deeper truth."

Simeon turned to Tessa, and she felt in some strange way that this entire meal was meant for her.

"The God of Israel is the only true God," he said. "And though He is the God of Israel, throughout the ages He has been the God of Melchizedek, of Ruth the Moabite and Naaman the Syrian, of Nebuchadnezzar and of Rahab the harlot, and so many others outside of the family of Israel whom God has chosen to redeem unto Himself."

Tessa could not take her eyes from Simeon.

"He is the God of Redemption," he continued. "He gives us the sacrifices to cover our sin, but there will come a day when the Messiah will come and be our Redeemer for all time." Simeon smiled and his hand reached for Tessa. "For all time, and for all people. This is what we remember at Passover, but it is also what we look forward to." He indicated the fifth cup. "This is the cup of our redemption yet to come, reminding us that the God of Israel can free those who once were in bondage, not only in physical chains but chains of the spirit as well. Redemption and forgiveness are found only in Him."

Simeon sat and the table was silent. Tessa studied her plate, the remains of lamb and herbs and fruit calling out their message to her heart. She battled a desire to cry out her desperation for the redemption of which Simeon spoke.

Another prayer was sung and the family moved about the table, but Tessa could not take her eyes from her plate. She sensed the table being cleared around her. Several times she was aware that Nikos brushed against her, and once his fingers even gripped her shoulder briefly. It was too much. All of it, too much.

Marta whispered in her ear, "It grows late. Let me show you where you can sleep."

Tessa stumbled to her feet. Marta led her to a small bedroom, with only a bed and a wooden chest.

"Jacob will share a room with Nikos and my father. You can sleep here with me."

"No, I can't—"

Marta laughed and touched Tessa's hair. "Yes. Yes, you can."

Marta disappeared, and Tessa looked at the bed. She still wore the tunic that Marta had given her, and it seemed best to simply sleep in it. She climbed into the bed and covered herself with the blanket, wondering if Marta had woven it herself. The soft bed welcomed her tired muscles, and she sighed deeply.

*Why do I feel so strange?*

Sleep did not come at first, and Tessa lay in the darkness listening to the family's laughter. With every part of her, she wanted to return to the hearth room, to pretend they were her children, that she had erased the past by proving herself a better mother than her own.

"Someday," she dared whisper into the night.

Some time later, Marta slipped into the room and crawled under the blanket. "Are you asleep?" she whispered almost silently.

"No."

"Thank you for sharing Passover with us, Tessa."

Tessa's eyes filled once more with unwelcome tears. "It is I who owe you thanks, Marta."

"We welcome you into our home, just as Yahweh welcomes you into His fold."

"I do not know much of your God, Marta."

"But He knows much of you."

Tessa sighed and turned her head away from Marta's voice. "If He knows me as you say, He has not kept me from heartache."

"My father has told me of your life, Tessa. And I know that God does not always keep us from heartache. But He is good. And so He uses the pain to make us more beautiful."

In the darkness, Tessa felt brave enough to whisper her heart to this woman. "I do not want to feel the pain anymore, Marta."

"And that is why you must, Tessa. That is why He will not rest in His work on your behalf. He will allow more pain. He will bring people who will not allow you to turn to stone."

"But I cannot trust anyone, don't you see? I cannot believe that they will not hurt me."

Marta found her hand and squeezed it. "None of us can fully trust another, Tessa. But we risk the pain, because we trust Yahweh to hold us in spite of others' failures."

Her soft hand stroked Tessa's cheek. "My father was right to send you to us tonight."

Tessa smiled, finding she was not surprised that her sharing the Passover with his family had been Simeon's intent since he wrote the letter to his daughter this morning. It was a message he had been trying to give her for a long time.

*Redemption and forgiveness are found only in Him.*

Redemption, forgiveness, and *life*.

Somewhere deep within her, in the place Tessa had long ago given over as stone, she sensed that a deep and dangerous shift had begun. In the faces of Marta and Simeon, of Nikos and Daniel, and even of Jacob, Tessa was finding that love and forgiveness perhaps had the power to break apart stone.

Yes, a shift had begun. But Tessa suspected she had not yet seen what fears such a tremor could bring on.

# NINETEEN

## ✦ *Three Days before the Great Quake* ✦

Tessa awoke disoriented. It took a moment to recognize that she lay in Marta and Jacob's home in the Jewish district—and to remember the dangerous feelings of the night before.

*Not today. Today we will find out how Spiro caused the water to fail. Today I will not think of anything else.*

Marta had risen already. Tessa flung the blanket from her and raked fingers through her hair. The morning still held coolness, but Tessa sensed that the hour grew late.

She expected to find Marta preparing the morning meal and was surprised to find the kitchen empty. A search revealed most of the family and Nikos in the hearth room, sharing bread and honey and wine around their large table.

Nikos jumped to his feet when she entered the room. "Did you rest well?" He was dressed again in his own clothes and seemed out of place in this Jewish home.

She remained in the doorway. "Thank you again, Marta. And Jacob." The man actually met her eyes for a brief moment.

Marta's bright eyes and warm smile threatened to undo her resolve. "Please sit, Tessa. Have some food. I've cooked nothing hot, I'm afraid, since it is the Sabbath."

Tessa shook her head. "Nikos and I must be going."

Nikos stepped in front of her, blocking her from the family's view. "Eat something first, Tessa," he growled.

She exhaled her impatience. "Very well." She found a seat at the table between Daniel and Sarah, the oldest daughter. "Is Simeon still here?"

Marta pushed the bread in her direction. "He left at daybreak to return to Glaucus's home. He said he had some important business to attend."

Jacob addressed Nikos, still chewing a hunk of bread. "Will you return to Glaucus today as well?"

Tessa responded, "No. We are trying to find answers about the aqueduct's failure. Someone spread the news here that the water would fail before it happened. The only way anyone could have known is if he sabotaged the water himself. Nikos and I will travel the length of the aqueduct to find the source of the failure. We will begin with the splitting basin and continue up the channel to the distribution basin if we must."

All eyes at the table turned to her. She shrugged. "I have been part of the workings of this city for many years."

When the bread had disappeared, Nikos stood. "I will feed the ox and ready the cart," he said to Tessa.

"Bring my clothes to me," she said. "I will return Marta's and wear my own today."

Marta cleared the basket and honey pot from the table. "That is not necessary, Tessa."

"It is time to go back to being myself, I'm afraid."

Marta's long look caused Tessa to shift in her seat. She stood and retrieved a sticky spoon from the table. Nikos disappeared outside, and Tessa followed Marta to the kitchen. She placed the spoon beside a washing pot. Nikos was at her side a moment later, her chitôn in his hands. She took it from him and waited until he left the kitchen again.

"May I change my clothes in your room, Marta?"

Marta smiled. "Of course. And you probably only have a moment before that man is back."

Tessa frowned. "It will take him awhile to tend to the ox."

"He does not seem able to stay away from you for very long."

Tessa stared at Marta, the chitôn tangling in her stiff fingers.

Marta gently pulled the fabric from her and smoothed it. "Come, Tessa. You must have noticed."

Tessa straightened. "I have noticed that he is the most insolent servant I have ever encountered."

Marta laughed and laid the chitôn over Tessa's arm. "Go change your clothes. I will pack food for your journey."

Within the hour they were back on the cart, with Nikos holding the reins and Tessa trying to forget Marta's words and her smile. Marta and Jacob both emerged from the house to see them off.

Marta held her fingers for several moments after the cart had begun to pull away. She studied Tessa's face and spoke quietly. "Come back to us, Tessa."

The heavy feeling in Tessa's chest returned, and she pulled her hand from Marta's warm grasp.

The Sabbath streets were quiet as Nikos followed a well-worn path out of town. A grassy hill and a narrow dirt road rose ahead of them. Within minutes the ox was grunting its protest.

Nikos snorted in response. "Should have brought a horse."

The hill's incline had them both fighting to remain upright. Nikos turned to Tessa. "Come up here and stand beside me where you can hold on better."

She shook her head. "I'll stay back here." She planted her feet firmly on the floor of the cart, but still needed to spread her arms wide to grip the paneled sides. The stony path up the hillside rocked the cart from side to side until Tessa's stomach roiled.

The sun rose overhead and Nikos's neck beaded with sweat. "Are you sure this is the way?" he asked for what seemed the hundredth time.

"Yes!" Tessa resisted the urge to smack his shoulder. "I have looked at the aqueduct maps many times."

"How will we know when we reach it? Isn't it underground?"

"I will know."

"Wonderful."

"You're in a foul mood today."

Nikos's jaw tightened and a vein on his neck bulged. "And what does it matter to you?"

"What does that mean?"

"Do you really concern yourself with the moods of servants anymore than the mood of this ox?"

Tessa tightened her lips. The call of a bird drew her gaze upward, and she recognized a pygmy cormorant, black and full-bodied. She followed the bird's flight until it disappeared over the horizon. "That was not kind," she finally said.

Nikos inclined his head toward her, but then looked away. "I shouldn't think you cared."

She bit her lip. "Why are you being cruel, Nikos?"

"I am tired. That's all. Too tired to disbelieve the things that are said about you."

A large rock tipped the cart to the side and Tessa gasped. The cart righted and continued. "And what is said about me?"

Nikos was silent for a moment. "That you are a marble Athena, thinly covered in flesh." He shifted the reins in his hand. "A goddess of love who cannot love anyone."

*That shouldn't hurt. Don't let it hurt.* She studied the road ahead. The rocks. The wind-blown grasses. Struggled to think of something else. But Nikos's words irritated like a pebble in her sandal.

A loud crack sounded and the cart lurched to the left. Tessa cried out and clutched at Nikos. He cursed and pushed past her, off the back of the cart.

"A spoke splintered," he said, examining the damage. Nikos untied the rope sash from his waist. "I will do what I can."

While he worked, Tessa wandered up the hill a little way. She had not gone far when she saw a stone entryway into the hill. She called down to where Nikos knelt beside the cart. "The entrance is here!"

He stood. "Good. We may be able to ride down, but I don't think we should go up any farther." He pulled the reins from the cart, wrapped them around a large rock and tucked the ends under. With a pat to the ox's rump, he said, "I don't think he's motivated to go very far anyway."

He retrieved the small lamp they had brought, and they approached the tunnel entrance. Tessa hung back from the yawning blackness.

"Stay with the ox," Nikos said. "I'll check the basin."

"I can do it."

"Of course you can. Tessa can do anything."

The sarcasm in his voice stung for only a moment. She pushed past him and entered the tunnel. The lamp's murky light revealed a greenish mold on the tunnel walls. The brackish smell of wet dirt repulsed her, but she pushed on. It was as though they had entered the underworld, and Tessa felt the growing pressure of the earth above them. The sound of rushing water led her on.

A chamber opened before her. The light from the lamp Nikos held behind her barely penetrated the chamber, but she knew they had reached the basin. Ahead, she could make out three clay pipes that led from the basin. She rushed forward, and her feet jammed something soft. Momentum carried her upper body and she fell, hands in front of her, with a grunt. Her hands, then elbows squished into the mud, and she lay astride something on the ground.

Nikos bent at once and brought the lamp to her side.

She half-turned to see what had tripped her up.

Beneath her lay the body of a man, his unseeing eyes wide and fixed on Tessa's face.

# TWENTY

Tessa scrambled to her feet, trying not to touch the body. Nikos set the lamp into the mud and kneeled beside it. He felt the man's neck with his hands.

"What are you doing?"

"I am seeing if his heart still beats."

"He's dead, Nikos."

A moment later he sat back and picked up the lamp again. "Who is he?"

"I have never seen him before. He is Greek."

Nikos leaned over the man's body. A thin line of blood traced a path from his mouth to his ear. Nikos half-turned him over and waved the lamp over the back of the body. "Here," he said, indicating the head. "He was struck with something."

Tessa inhaled, then coughed, covering her mouth with the back of her hand. "Murdered, then?"

He laid the body on its back again. "Whoever he was, he got in the way of something."

Tessa pointed to the far-right channel at the foot of the splitting basin. "He got in the way of that."

Water lapped at the mouth of the channel but could do little more than trickle around the edges of the man-made blockage. Rocks had been piled in the opening, and debris plugged whatever crevices existed between the rocks. The water had been completely diverted.

Tessa looked across the body at Nikos, feeling some satisfaction in having solved part of the mystery.

"Spiro sent someone to tell the Jews that the water would fail. Then he blocked the aqueduct so that it would," she said. "And murdered this man in the process."

"And when the Jews went to the southeast district to get water, the people there were already incited by the guard's murder to believe that the Jews meant them harm."

Tessa waved a hand at the channel, then the body. "All of this to discredit Glaucus?"

Nikos stood. "It seems extreme. But perhaps there is more to his plan than we yet see."

"More importantly," Tessa sighed, "we have no proof that it is Spiro who is behind all of this."

"There is one person who may have spoken to Spiro."

Tessa waited.

"The man who says he saw a Jew murder the guard."

"We must go to the southeast district and find him."

Nikos retrieved the lamp from the mud and deposited it in a crevice in the rock wall. He crossed to the edge of the basin, placed one hand in the mud at the side of the stone wall, then swung his body over and splashed into the water.

Tessa jumped back from the splash. "What are you doing?" she yelled.

"Clearing the channel." He looked up at her in confusion. "What did you expect?"

*By the gods. Do you have to fix everything you see?*

"We don't have time for this! We need to find that witness, then return to Glaucus's house before someone discovers that he—and I—are not there!"

Nikos waded to the mouth of the channel, his arms held above the chest-high water. "How long do you think it will take for the magistrates to send someone to repair the water problem?"

"I do not know! But it's not our concern."

Nikos glanced her way, his eyes saying more than he seemed willing to speak. Tessa growled.

"As you wish, then. Don't be long about it, though."

"It shouldn't take us very long."

"Us!" Tessa stepped back from the basin, careful to avoid the body on the ground. "I'm not getting in there!"

"No, you're not. You're going to stay at the edge, and I'm going to hand the stones to you." He pulled the first rock, the size of a man's head, from the top of the basin and waded back to Tessa. "Put them over there, beside the wall."

She struggled to take the dripping boulder from his hands. "This is madness."

Nikos laughed. "Stop pretending you don't care that Marta and Jacob have no water, Tessa."

"I thought you said I was incapable of caring about anyone."

"Hmmm." Nikos's back was to her, but she was sure he was still laughing at her. "That is what others say."

An unfamiliar ache weighted her chest and she turned away until Nikos called for her. He brought her the rocks one-by-one, some of them quite heavy. They worked in silence. The blockage was now cleared above the water level, but Tessa's thoughts were on Nikos's earlier comments about her heart, closed off to everything.

He handed her two smaller rocks. "It won't be long before it all breaks through, you know."

*That's what I'm afraid of.*

She watched him chip away at the blocked channel, envisioning the coming rush of water. "When you get to a certain point, there will be no controlling it," she said.

He turned in the water and smiled slightly. "It's dangerous to release it all, yes. But without water, there is no life."

Tessa studied the growing pile of rocks, then looked back to Nikos. "How much longer will it take?" She spoke only of opening the channel now, but Nikos eyed her carefully.

"I wish I knew."

She turned from his gaze, and a moment later he dove under the water's surface to continue removing the stones. They worked in silence again for some time. Tessa's clothes muddied and her hands burned from scraping rocks. The water level in the basin dropped significantly, as it resumed its three-way flow out of the chamber. The current became swifter toward the third channel and Nikos fought to retain his footing on the floor of the slippery basin.

He came up from a dive empty-handed, hoisted the upper half of his body onto the edge of the basin, and rested his elbows in the mud. "There is one huge stone at the base," he said, breathing hard. "I can feel it. Must have been dropped in. Moved into place."

"Can you bring it up?"

He shook his head, and water ran down from his dark curls, between his eyes. "Too heavy to lift. Going to try to shift it to the left, between the channels."

"Be careful."

He grinned, then dove beneath the water.

Tessa watched the surface, waiting.

Waiting.

*Come back up, Nikos. It's too heavy.*

The water level dropped suddenly. Water gushed toward the third channel. Nikos shot above the surface and gasped. He dragged air into his lungs but then disappeared again.

"Nikos!"

Tessa leaned out over the basin. His head bobbed above the water. More than an arm's length away. Eyes closed.

"Nikos!"

The current rushed three ways now, any one of them strong enough to carry a man away. She spotted Nikos, arms floating at his sides. The third channel yawned, ready to swallow him.

# TWENTY-ONE

Tessa did not stop to remove her sandals. She leaped over the side, and the water surged to her chin.

"Nikos!"

She clutched at him. The fingers of her right hand grasped his hair and she pulled. Her other hand wrapped around his tunic. She released his hair and hooked her arm around his neck.

He floated face-up, his head near her shoulder. The current pulled them both toward the channel. She kicked her legs furiously to push them away from it. Nikos coughed once, thrashed in her arms, and they both went under. Tessa's mouth filled with water. She pushed off the bottom of the basin, back into the air. She spit water from her mouth, tasting the dirt. Nikos continued to struggle in her arms. Should she release him?

He made the decision for her. With a twist, he wriggled from her grasp. His arm circled her waist, and he pulled them both toward the edge. Gasping and choking, they scratched at the mud at the basin's edge. A moment later they both lay in the dirt, panting.

"I told you it was dangerous," she said.

He laughed. "But it is good." He grasped her hand. "Thank you."

She lacked the strength to pull away. They rested for several minutes, until Tessa grew uncomfortable lying next to a dead body.

"We must keep moving," she said, rising to a sitting position.

"What of him?"

"We will inform the magistrates when we return to the city. Someone will be sent for him."

The trek back to the hillside seemed less ominous than the journey into the basin. Tessa could see light ahead and welcomed the hot sun on her wet skin.

The ox was placidly eating grass where they had left him. Tessa hoped Nikos's repair to the wheel would hold until they reached their destination, but she was prepared to walk if necessary. Nikos climbed into the cart and turned it downhill.

Tessa resumed her position behind him. "We must find the witness to the murder of the fountain house guard as quickly as possible, then return to the house. I fear that the strategoi may come, demanding to speak with Glaucus."

Nikos clucked at the ox and the cart lurched forward. "We cannot ask questions in the city looking like this." He tipped his chin to his own mud-soaked tunic and the dirty chitôn that clung to her.

Tessa wrapped her arms about her waist.

"We will be passing by Marta and Jacob's home," he said. "We can clean up there."

Tessa fumed at the delay. "If you had not insisted on fixing the aqueduct yourself—"

He shook his head. "You never stop, do you?"

Marta met them at the door, an expression of shock at their muddy appearance. She pulled Tessa in, and Nikos followed.

"Jacob!" Marta wiped at Tessa's face and shook her head. "Bring water!"

"Oh, Marta. The water—you don't have enough for us—"

Nikos interrupted. "She soon will."

Jacob appeared in the hall behind his wife. "What's that?"

"The water. It should be trickling down even now. By nightfall it will return in full."

Marta clapped her hands. "Do you hear that, Jacob?"

Jacob grunted, but his approval was unmistakable.

"Come, wash," Marta said. "I will fetch clean clothing."

Marta put Tessa in her bedroom yet again and led Nikos to another. She was back in a moment with a basin of water and a tunic draped over her arm.

"I do not know what to say, Tessa." She placed the basin on a low table. "You risked your safety for us."

Tessa looked at the floor. "It was Nikos, Marta. Not me."

Marta looked at Tessa's bedraggled chitôn. "You did more than simply watch."

"The water—Nikos was nearly swept away—"

"Ah," Marta smiled and laid the tunic on the bed, "I see."

Tessa ignored the amusement in the woman's voice.

"I will leave you to wash and dress."

Tessa emerged from the bedroom a few minutes later and went in search of Nikos. She found Marta in the hearth room, talking with another woman who held a baby. They both looked up at Tessa's entrance.

"Where is Nikos?" Tessa asked, anxious to be leaving.

Marta motioned for Tessa to follow and led her to a nearby room off the front hall. On a small cot in the center of the room, dressed in clean clothes, Nikos lay face-down, sleeping.

"He is exhausted," Marta whispered.

Tessa chafed at yet another delay, but she could not bear to wake him. Marta intertwined her fingers in Tessa's. "Come and visit with Rachel and her baby."

Tessa followed Marta back to the hearth room and met her friend, a fair-skinned woman who could not meet Tessa's eyes when introduced. A baby girl slept in her arms, wrapped in a blanket the color of pink hibiscus, her tiny lips forming a pout. Tessa sat beside Rachel, her eyes on the baby.

A look passed between Rachel and Marta. Rachel turned to Tessa, and raised her chin slightly. "Would you like to hold her?"

*No. No.*

*Oh, yes.*

Tessa reached with her hands and found them shaking. Rachel placed the bundle in her arms.

*What am I doing?*

She could feel the soft breath of the sleeping child and touched her cheek with one finger. The petal-soft skin was the most amazing thing. She breathed in the baby's scent and felt again that most dangerous shift deep within.

"Marta tells me that you have restored the water."

Tessa still gazed at the baby. "Not me, really. Nikos did it."

"A servant in the household of Glaucus," Marta explained.

"Ah, a friend of your father?"

Marta nodded and touched Tessa's arm. "Yes. Another friend."

The two women talked quietly of their children and husbands, of the water and of the recent violence in the southeast district. Tessa watched the baby sleep, knowing that time was passing but forgetting why it mattered.

*This is what I fight for. She gave me to Servia without a backward look. But I am not her. Would I not be a good mother?* She rocked the baby slowly.

The sun dipped below the city's rooflines. Tessa looked up to see Nikos standing in the hearth room doorway, his eyes on her and the baby.

*Don't look at me, Nikos. Not like that.*

A knock on the door startled them, and Marta went to open it.

"Is he still here?" Tessa heard a man ask.

She saw Nikos look at the front door from where he stood in the hall. He was frowning. Tessa turned to Rachel and held the baby to her. "Thank you," she whispered, resisting the pull to kiss those soft cheeks before she stood.

A shout went up from street, as though a small crowd stood outside the door. Tessa joined Nikos in the hall and saw that a crowd indeed had formed.

"The Sabbath ends," a man shouted. "And the water flows!"

A woman grabbed Marta's wrist. "They are saying the Greek restored the water."

Marta smiled. "That is true." A cheer went up from the assemblage.

Tessa eyed Nikos in concern. They had managed to remain unidentified until now. It had been a mistake to return here.

"We must leave," she said. Nikos nodded.

"Marta, thank you once again," Tessa said. "We will return your clothing, but we must go."

Marta hugged her. "God be with you, Tessa. And you, Nikos."

An instant later their names traveled through the crowd like a flame through dry tinder. "Tessa! Nikos!"

Tessa fled into the street, her eyes on the ground. Hands grasped at them as they passed, their names on the lips of each. The press of bodies, their faces turned to them in gratitude, frightened Tessa. She pushed through the crowd, trying to reach the ox cart.

She had been recognized. Nikos was being hailed as a hero. Spiro would hear of it. And still, they had no proof of his guilt.

They reached the cart, climbed aboard, and rolled into the street, the crowd following.

Tessa closed her eyes and beseeched the gods that no one had yet discovered that Glaucus's room lay empty and that his hetaera was a fraud.

# TWENTY-TWO

By the time they gained the southeast district, darkness had fully fallen. Tessa chafed at the passing hours. She had been away two full days, relying on Simeon and Persephone to keep her secret.

The night was warm and men still stood on street corners, talking and laughing. Tessa and Nikos rolled through the streets without notice. Tessa kept her head down, though she was tempted to search the face of each man they passed. The darkness reminded her of the aqueduct tunnel, and she felt her shoulders tighten at thoughts of what Spiro had done. People had been hurt, and for what? His political aspirations?

*I will find a way to bring you down, Spiro.*

Nikos brought the cart to a stop in the square that lay central to the district. At the end of the square, the fountain house was still crowded with extra traffic from the Jewish district, people who had not yet heard that the water flowed closer to home. Soldiers patrolled, their hands on swords, as if expecting trouble to break out at any moment. Nikos told her to wait in the cart. She considered ignoring him, but she did not wish to repeat the scene they had left. Better to remain unseen, unknown.

Nikos worked his way through the crowd in the square, his head bent to various men. She watched them shake their heads, gesture, and sometimes turn away. He did not seem to be having much success. Several pairs of eyes traveled to her. She met their stares in spite of herself.

Their presence in the square gradually took effect, and before long she had become the central character, with whispers and fingers pointed subtly in her direction. She flung her hair back behind her shoulders and dared them with her eyes to approach her. Why should she care if Spiro heard she had been here? It was he who should be afraid, not her.

An argument between a Greek and a Jew broke out near the fountain house, and the attention of all in the square turned that direction. Tessa took advantage of the distraction to step from the cart and catch up to Nikos, who stood alone at the moment.

"What have you learned?" she asked.

He shielded her from the crowd with his body. "None of these people know who it was who claimed to have seen the fountain house guard killed. Either that or they don't want to get involved."

Tessa exhaled in frustration. "Someone had to have heard."

"I will keep trying. You stay out of sight."

"No. I'm coming with you."

Nikos looked at her for a moment, then moved on as if he knew he could not stop her. A group of women carrying water pots strolled up the street toward them. Nikos looked at Tessa and nodded toward the women. She approached them, while he held back.

One of the women whispered to the others, wide-eyed, as she neared. The others turned to her in surprise.

*How is it that so many know my face?*

She explained her quest to the women in low tones. "I am trying to help the city magistrates bring his murderer to justice," she concluded, "but we must have the killer's description."

One of the women stepped close, a tiny woman who had probably sacrificed her childhood toys to Artemis within the year past. "I was there that morning," she said, her voice low. "It was Cadmus who saw the Jew kill Feodore."

"Cadmus? Where will I find him?"

The young woman spent another moment pointing and giving instructions. Tessa returned to Nikos.

"Well?"

She pointed to the left. "The man lives on this street. His name is Cadmus."

Nikos moved in that direction, stepping over the gutter.

"Slow down!" Tessa said and hurried to draw up beside him.

"I am tired of moving slowly!"

*Ah, finally we are in a hurry.*

## Ω

Nikos knocked on the first door and asked for Cadmus. The man who answered shook his head and closed the door without a word. They moved down the street and knocked again.

A woman answered their knock this time. She was broadly built, with black eyes. Her hair hung in greasy strands below her shoulders, and her chitôn was frayed and dirty.

"We are looking for Cadmus," Nikos said.

"What do you want?"

Tessa pushed past Nikos. "Is he here?"

The woman's face scrunched into something resembling anger. "Who are you?"

"We have been sent by the magistrates," Tessa said, "to find the Jew responsible for killing the guard."

"Ha!" The woman's laugh was like the squawk of a chicken. "They sent a woman?"

Nikos pushed into the house. "It is none of your concern whom they sent. We need to see Cadmus."

"He is not here. He works at night."

"Where?"

She shrugged. "If you find out, you can tell me."

She moved to shut the door, but Nikos pushed back and entered the house. Tessa followed. The house stunk of cooking cabbage, and Nikos was glad there was no chance of their being offered the hospitality of a meal.

"Cadmus!" he shouted.

"He's not here, I tell you!" The woman was all elbows, trying to shove him out of the house.

A shadow lurched into the hall. "Who's here, woman?" The words were slurred, and when the speaker appeared, his eyes were cloudy and red-rimmed. His hair had grayed in odd places, and his pock-marked face bore the evidence of hard living.

Nikos pushed the woman aside. "You are Cadmus?"

Cadmus's eyes widened. He glanced at his wife, then spun in the hall and disappeared into the darkness.

Nikos followed, Tessa at his heels, but Cadmus had already gained the back of the house. The two ran out the back and saw the man fleeing through the alley, into the darkness beyond.

Nikos outpaced Tessa through the alley, but he chose not to slow down. *She should have stayed in the square,* he thought. Her involvement in every part of this quest left him fearful for her safety.

His quarry's footsteps echoed from the homes that lined the streets. The sound led Nikos on, but within moments the echoes ceased. Cadmus had reached the outskirts of the district and was running toward the Acropolis hill. Nikos pumped his arms and sprinted. It would be harder to find Cadmus in the darkness beyond the lights of the residential district.

An indistinct shadow blurred on the hill. Nikos followed, his calves burning with the day's exertion.

*Why did you have to run, fool?*

He feared that Cadmus might be the key to the answers they sought. He must reach him.

"Cadmus!" Nikos shouted. "Stop! You are in no danger!"

The shadow above did not slow.

Nikos's blood pounded in his ears. The rhythmic crunch of the gravel path beneath his sandals kept time. Stars pierced the sky above the Acropolis, and Nikos ran on.

"Cadmus!"

Had Tessa followed?

Cadmus crested the hill and ran along the ridge. Nikos kept his eyes on the silhouette, grateful for the risen moon that outlined his prey for him.

And then Cadmus was gone.

*He leaped over the cliff!*

*To his death? To avoid a few questions?*

Nikos ran for the spot where Cadmus had disappeared. Sparse grass tangled among small rocks at the cliff's edge. Far below, the sea crashed into boulders and retreated from a stony beach. Nikos slid to a stop at the cliff and leaned over.

Eight feet below, a ledge ran along the cliff.

*Cadmus knows this hill better than I.*

Nikos leaped over the edge. He could not be far behind Cadmus.

He hit the ground and his ankle twisted. He righted himself and took to the ledge's path with a limp.

The path led along the cliff for several hundred paces, then faded away into the side. In the darkness Nikos picked his way with care, unsure of the path's width.

The roar of waves below drowned all other sound.

His foot slipped over the edge. One leg shot downward. The other knee dug into the dirt path. Nikos grabbed at anything, everything. Weeds, vines. His weight shifted and carried him over the edge. The vines held. He hung between the waves and the stars, breathing hard.

The vines cut into his hands. One ripped from its roots. It gave way and Nikos dropped half the length of his body.

With clenched fingers and chest heaving, he pulled upward. The vines held still.

*A little farther. Just a little farther.*

With a groan, he heaved his upper body onto the ledge. His legs swung easily then, and he was back on his feet, ankle still throbbing, but anger now propelling him forward.

Cadmus had disappeared off the end of the path. There had to be a way up or down.

Nikos slowed when he reached the end, then smiled.

A cave.

Cadmus must have counted on Nikos not seeing him drop over the cliff's side. He had trapped himself in the cave.

Nikos braced himself for the unknown. He pushed into the cave, fists at shoulder level.

A shifting movement to his left. He pivoted. Stepped that way. He was at a disadvantage with the light behind him. Cadmus would see him first. There would be only one chance.

He felt the man's lunge before he saw it. And he was ready.

They scuffled for a moment, then Nikos had him on the ground. He dragged Cadmus to the cave's mouth and straddled his chest. A scattering of small bones crunched beneath them.

"Why did you run?"

Cadmus thrashed, his eyes wild.

"Stop!" Nikos pinned his arms to the ground. "I do not want to hurt you."

"Leave me alone!" Cadmus drove a knee into Nikos's back.

"I only want to ask you what you saw."

"I saw nothing!" Cadmus bucked again. The moonlight threw their shadows against the cave wall.

Nikos squeezed his chest. "You told the others you saw a Jew murder the guard. Is that not the truth?"

"I want no part of it now!"

"No part of what?"

The man's lips clamped shut. Nikos felt his anger building again. "I said I don't want to hurt you," he growled, "but I will. Who killed the guard?" His shout echoed back to him. He dug his knees into Cadmus' paunchy middle and tightened his hold.

"No one! I saw nothing!"

"Then why did you say you saw—"

"For the twenty obols!"

Nikos relaxed his knees a bit. "Someone paid you."

"I don't know anything more!"

"Who?"

Cadmus said nothing. Nikos shook him. "Who?" A frightening urge to leave Cadmus's bones here to dry out with the others washed over him.

"The huge Greek! I do not know him. Hairless and as tall as Apollo. That is all I know."

Nikos jumped off the man's body, lifted him from the ground, and dragged him to the ledge outside the cave. He pushed Cadmus's upper body over. Prickly weeds tore at his arms.

"Please!" Cadmus begged. "I have told you all I know! The giant Greek paid me twenty obols to say it was a Jew who murdered Feodore. Think of my wife and children!"

Nikos exhaled and stared at the man's eyes. Satisfied, he pulled him back from the edge and released him. "Get out of here."

Cadmus scurried along the ledge, past where he had dropped off the cliff. A moment later Nikos saw him outlined on the cliff above again.

Only then did it occur to him that Tessa might still be coming this way. He ran after Cadmus, climbed up to the top. Cadmus ran downhill toward the city.

*And there she is. Of course.*

Cadmus didn't slow. He ran past Tessa without incident, and Nikos nearly laughed at her expression as the man passed.

"Let him go," Nikos called.

His ankle gave a sharp reminder that it was injured. He dropped to a large rock on the cliff's edge. Tessa reached him quickly.

"What did you do to him?"

"It doesn't matter."

"Did you find out—"

Nikos unstrapped the ankle ties from his sandal. "The same Greek spreading the news about the water in the Jewish district paid Cadmus to lie about the guard's murder. Probably killed this Feodore himself."

Tessa pounded a fist against her thigh. "But still we do not know who the bald Greek is. And we have no proof that Spiro is involved."

Nikos rubbed at his ankle.

"Let's go," Tessa said. "We have been gone far too long. We must get back to the house."

Nikos didn't move.

"Come, Nikos!"

He laughed. "You are going to have to wait, Tessa the Great."

"What is wrong?"

"I have just chased a man through a city, up a hill, over a cliff, and into a cave. I need a moment to rest."

Tessa huffed and plopped herself down on the rock beside him.

"A moment, that is all."

He shook his head. "You are too kind."

They looked over the water in silence. The frothy surf formed a thin line along the white beach, advancing and retreating like the forward guard of an uncertain army.

"It grows late now, Tessa. The city leaders will be attending symposia, or heading to their beds. I don't think we need to hurry back."

She slapped at the rock.

He sighed. "We will find the answers, Tessa. But for now we will sit together and admire the night." He smiled and pointed to the spangled sky.

And that, Nikos knew, might be the most dangerous thing they had done thus far.

## Ω

The night breeze caught Tessa's hair and blew it across her face. She sat down beside Nikos, then considered moving to another rock or even the ground. The moon seemed to offer a path of escape across the water, a lighted road she could travel beyond the dark horizon. Beyond everything.

Nikos worked at the muscles in his lower leg. The silence lengthened, though she sensed his desire to speak and wondered what kept him from it.

He finally inhaled and broke the silence. "I am sorry for what I said."

She waved the comment away. "I understand you need to rest."

"No. I meant earlier. About what others say about you. That you are made of marble—"

Tessa shrugged. "They speak the truth. It doesn't bother me."

Nikos looked out over the sea. "It is not the truth."

"Well, then I wish it were."

"I know."

The waves crashed below them. Tessa tried to think of something else to talk about.

"When did you give up hope, Tessa?"

She pulled a long blade of grass from the ground beside her and rolled the tip around her finger. "It was too long ago to remember."

"The day you gave up hope, you stopped living."

"I had to."

Nikos shifted on the rock to face her. He said nothing, but she felt his eyes on her, waiting. She told him then of the long years that had come before. Of her mother. Of her training. Of her life with Glaucus. He listened without speaking.

"Do you know what it's like to keep hoping and being disappointed?"

"No," he admitted. "But I would rather be alive and disappointed than made of stone."

"Well, I would not! I would rather be made of stone!"

"Would you? Really? It doesn't seem to be working. No matter how hard you try, you cannot stop feeling."

*I am trying. The gods know I am trying.*

"Then perhaps it would be best if I were dead."

"Because that is the only way to truly stop the pain."

She shrugged and wrapped her arms about her waist. "Soon I will leave Rhodes and none of that will matter."

"Once you are off this island, away from Servia and your master, do you think you will start to live again, Tessa? Do you suppose you ever can?"

"Don't ask me that."

"I must ask. I want to help you, but I am not convinced a change in your circumstances will change your heart."

"What do you know of my heart?" The words spilled out in anger, but oh, how much she wanted to hear the answer.

His answer was quiet, as though he were afraid to frighten her. "I know that someone, perhaps many people, hurt you grievously, in a place you keep well-hidden. And I know that you are terrified of being hurt again. You believe that everyone you meet will fail you, reject you, or disappoint you. And so you will not trust anyone, and you will not feel anything."

*Oh, Nikos. Leave me alone. Leave me alone.*

He shifted on the rock again and it seemed to Tessa that he moved closer, but perhaps it was only the feeling that he was surrounding her, like a heavy blanket that would either warm her or smother her, she could not be certain which.

The tide swept in below them, tossing the waves onto the rocks with a hissing upward spray.

"Tessa," he whispered. "To be alive to love and alive to joy is to risk being hurt, to risk people failing you and disappointing you."

"Then I do not wish to be alive to those things."

He reached for her hand, intertwined her fingers with his own. "But can't you see that your philosophy is not working?"

Tessa swallowed, fighting the heaviness in her chest.

"It does not work, this trying to become stone. You are left refusing the joys of life in order to refuse the pain. Yet the pain remains even when joy has been denied. You have rejected the best of life to avoid the worst, and still you are unhappy."

She closed her eyes. *Do not make me feel. Please, stop.*

"You are not a marble Athena, thinly veiled in flesh, Tessa. In truth, you are the opposite—a passionate, spirited woman trying to encase yourself in stone." He squeezed her hand. "You will never be made of stone. And death is the coward's way out. You must live. And to live, you must risk. You must trust."

"I cannot," she whispered. "I do not know how."

His fingers still clutched her own. Nikos reached his free hand to her cheek and turned her face toward his. He smiled. "Your skin is so much warmer than marble."

Tessa drank in his smile, his eyes, his warmth, and responded with only a whisper, spoken from a place of such fear it was barely audible. "I think somehow, Nikos, the marble dissolves under your touch."

# TWENTY-THREE

When the message came, Spiro reclined in his andrôn alone, watching the young dancer whom Ajax had brought him perform the intricate steps of the *emmeleia*. A boy accompanied her from the corner of the room, piping a mournful melody on a wooden flute and beating slow time with high wooden shoes.

It had been a long day, moving about the city and working conversations among council and Assembly members to his advantage. The tide was turning in his favor. With the night upon him, Spiro indulged himself in an hour of private entertainment and a bowl of wine he planned to consume alone.

The boy's music crescendoed, and the girl's steps picked up tempo. She swung her head from side to side, and her waist-length hair swirled around her face, covering her eyes and mouth.

Spiro was mesmerized by her hair, her body, her delicate fingers.

*I should have my own hetaera.*

No, patience was called for. A short time more. Though he had gained much support, he still faced the opposition of four strategoi. Although he had planted seeds of doubt, they held firm.

*Do you have what it takes to prove yourself to your father?*

They must be removed—Hermes, Glaucus, Philo, Bemus. When these four were eliminated, Rhodes would join the Achaean League, and his considerable influence would be transformed into raw power.

*And then, Tessa.*

An image of her floated in his mind, a goddess for the taking.

Ajax entered on soundless bare feet. Spiro sensed the news was not good. The slave bent to where he reclined on the couch.

"What has happened?"

"There is news from the Jewish district."

"More violence?"

Ajax shook his head. "It seems a hero has appeared among them."

Spiro sat up. "What hero?" He flicked a hand at the dancer and boy. The music cut off mid-note and the two slipped from the room.

Ajax straightened. "Someone was asking questions in the district. This morning he traveled to the splitting basin to inspect the aqueduct. When he returned later in the day, he reported that he had cleared the blockage. The water is already flowing."

Spiro slammed a fist on the table beside him, toppling the bowl of wine. "Who is this Jew?"

Ajax scowled. "Not a Jew."

"What? Who else would make the Jewish problem their concern?"

"The talk I hear is that it was a Greek servant by the name of Nikos. From the house of Glaucus."

"Glaucus!" Spiro jumped to his feet. The couch's cushions spilled to the floor. "What—why would he—?"

"There was a woman with the servant."

Spiro eyed Ajax. "Don't tell me—"

The bald giant nodded. "Tessa."

Spiro growled and threw a pillow across the room.

*Everywhere I turn, Tessa.*

But in his anger, he couldn't hold back admiration.

*She is a woman worthy of the gods.*

"Is there more?"

"The Jews are hailing this Nikos as a hero. He has told them that the water failure was not due to the magistrates' neglect but deliberate sabotage by someone who wished to incite violence. The mood in the district has turned."

Spiro threw himself onto the cushions. "Have the Jews gone mad? They would make a hero of a Greek slave?" He threw a sharp look at Ajax. "Has this servant named the responsible party?"

"It does not appear that he knows who is responsible."

"Then we must make certain his inquiries end before he gets any closer to the truth."

"Give me the word, and I will do your bidding."

Spiro returned to a sitting position. "You are loyal, Ajax. But, no. You have been too visible already. I need someone who cannot be tied to me." He stood. "Come. We go to the gymnasium."

Ω

Spiro spoke not at all during the walk through the night to the Acropolis. His thoughts consumed with the potential destruction of all he had worked for.

*I will not fail, Father. You shall see. I will rule this island one day.*

He entered the gymnasium from the northern side. Even at this late hour, men and boys were hard at their training. Torches burned at the edges of the open court and the covered running track that bordered it.

Located off the track were the bath rooms, more rooms where one could be oiled and dusted, and a series of lecture rooms to satisfy the Greek passion for combining intellectual training with the physical. During the day the greatest Greek minds spoke there of philosophy and literature, of music, mathematics, and science.

But Spiro would not find what he needed in the quiet lecture rooms.

He strode into the open court, Ajax trailing, and planted himself where he could observe the wrestlers. They trained in groups of two, wrestling naked, until one succeeded in pinning the other. Spiro scanned the court, his gaze resting briefly on each pair of bodies, their oiled skin reflecting the torchlight. Seven matches were currently engaged. One by one, participants were pinned, until Spiro had found what he was looking for.

He approached one of the victors, a man who looked to have passed the age of eighteen, when his military training would have ceased, and who had been particularly vicious in his method. His opponent slunk off to bathe.

Spiro clapped his hands together three times in appreciation for the man's victory. The wrestler lifted his chin in acknowledgment. His braided beard reached to his chest, and a scar angled across it, from shoulder to waist.

"You fight well," Spiro said, "but angry."

The man laughed, a short bark of amusement. "Sometimes anger is useful."

Spiro raised an eyebrow. "I fully agree." He glanced at the other wrestlers, all occupied with moving to another match. "What is your name?"

"Calisto."

"Do you know who I am, Calisto?"

His wrestler shrugged. "I do not concern myself much with those outside the gymnasium."

Spiro nodded. "Do you concern yourself with money?"

The barking laugh again. "I train for the prize."

"I offer a prize, and it requires but one night to win."

Spiro turned and walked toward the running track, wanting to be less conspicuous. He knew Calisto would follow; he had seen greed in the man's eyes. Ajax tagged along but kept his distance.

Spiro stepped into the shadows and turned to find the wrestler beside him. Calisto had grabbed a tunic from a basket they passed and flung it over himself.

"What does this one night require?" the man asked.

"Your excellent talent only. I will name your opponent, and you will leave him with worse than only fatigued muscles."

Calisto's eyes flicked to Ajax. "Why me?"

"The task requires a certain amount of . . . anonymity," Spiro said, watching the eyes and judging how far to push. "You are military trained?"

He nodded and his chest lifted slightly.

"Then you know how to do more than wrestle."

"I can kill a man in less than a minute."

Spiro laughed. "Then I have chosen wisely." He leaned in close and whispered, "Eighty drachmas."

Calisto's lips parted slightly.

"We are agreed?" Spiro asked.

"We are agreed."

Spiro pulled him deeper into the shadows and whispered all the details his new hired beast would need to find this servant Nikos and discourage further interference.

## Ω

Nikos had made a mistake, and he knew it. He had pushed Tessa too far, tried too hard to show her the truth. As the ox cart rumbled over the rutted stones, Nikos could not entice Tessa to speak of even trivial matters. She had set her alabaster face forward, her lips a hard line. He was beginning to know that look, to understand what it meant, if not where it came from.

Nikos had not lived a life of ease before his father acknowledged him and brought him into the family, but for all his hardship he had not encountered anything that had threatened to harden his heart like Tessa's.

Thoughts of his father's generosity stabbed Nikos with apprehension. He had not yet learned what his father had sent him for, and the time spent helping Tessa had not brought him much closer.

*I have allowed myself to be distracted.*

The moon had risen and threw their shadows before them. Nikos urged the ox forward, anxious to get Tessa back to the house. Her anxiety was palpable. When they rounded the last corner, he thought he heard her exhale in relief.

"All seems quiet," he said, watching her silent profile.

They drew up to the front steps and Nikos tugged on the reins. He jumped from the cart, offered his hand as usual, and was surprised when she took it. Her eyes were on the front of the house, however.

"There are lights burning still," Tessa said.

Her feet touched the street, and Nikos held her hand a moment longer. "Perhaps Simeon left a torch burning for you."

Tessa took a deep breath. "I wish we could go back to the Jewish district."

Nikos squeezed her hand, then released it. "There *was* something there."

Tessa searched his eyes, but he did not have an answer for her.

Behind her, the darkness shifted with a flutter of white. Nikos pushed her behind him and stepped forward.

A slave, still a boy, emerged from the night.

"What are you doing in the streets at this hour?"

The boy's face hardened. "I have a message."

Tessa stepped from behind him. "What is your message?"

"I am to give it to the servant Nikos alone."

Nikos studied the boy.

"Tessa, go on to bed. I will deal with this."

She watched him for a moment, her expression a mixture of curiosity and suspicion. Finally, she turned toward the stairs, lifted the hem of her chitôn, and glided up the steps.

Nikos turned to the boy. "Go on, deliver your message."

"It is from your father."

Nikos glanced up at the door to Glaucus's house, but Tessa was already inside.

"Your father is here. In Rhodes."

Nikos turned to the ox and retrieved its reins. *So soon?*

"He requests that you meet him in the bouleuterion immediately."

"At this hour?"

"I have been waiting since sunset. He said I should not come back until I have found you, and you should come no matter the hour. He has been waiting long."

*And not happy, I am certain.*

"He also wants his presence here to remain unknown at this time. He bid me tell you to come alone and be certain that no one knows where you're going."

Nikos almost smiled. That sounded like his father. Always looking over his shoulder for the knife blade he expected to be slipped into his back by one of a thousand would-be rulers.

"I must take care of the ox," he said. "Then I will come."

The boy shrugged. "He does not seem a patient man. But I will tell him you come quickly."

Nikos nodded and the boy disappeared into the night.

Nikos climbed onto the cart once more and directed the ox into the alley along the house. The ox's stall adjoined Glaucus's home at the back. Nikos navigated the darkness to restore both the animal and the vehicle to their designated stalls, his mind barely on the task.

*It is too soon. He comes too soon.*

*Why did he not give me time to learn what he needed?*

Nikos left the stall and thought he saw a shadow waver at the corner of the house. He slowed and waited, but no one appeared.

He crept through the streets, using alleys to traverse the city, remembering the boy's warning to come unseen. The bouleuterion would be empty at this hour, though the agora was never entirely deserted. Nevertheless, Nikos was not surprised that his father would choose the island's seat of power for even a clandestine meeting with his son.

Though the moon loomed overhead, its light did not filter down into the narrow alleys. Nikos wished for a torch. More than once he had the prickly sensation that footsteps followed him.

A menacing growl cut through the street's dark silence. Nikos slowed, his eyes on movement ahead. Two dogs, their coats mangy and patched, were circling one another.

*Not my fight.*

Nikos crossed to the alley's other side and watched from a safe distance as he passed. Between the dogs lay the discarded bone of someone's dinner, chunks of meat still clinging to it. Another low rumble in the chest of one of the animals, then it pounced on the bone. The other dog would not give up its dinner easily, however, and rushed forward, its yellow teeth flashing before they sank into the throat of its opponent. Nikos hurried along.

He was near the agora when the footsteps behind him sounded again. This time he did not believe he imagined the sound. Someone was following him.

He ducked into another alley, away from the agora and the bouleuterion.

Twenty steps down the alley he pressed himself into a doorway and waited. His follower walked lightly, as though trying to remain unheard. The footfalls paused, scuffled a moment. Confused perhaps. Then moved forward again.

*Come on. A little farther.*

Nikos counted out the follower's pace, timing his attack.

*Now.*

He leaped from the doorway, thrust his arms outward, grabbed and spun the slight figure, pressing himself into his attacker's back.

A flowery perfume was the strongest thing to assail him.

"Persephone!"

The girl's fear relaxed at once, and she leaned backward into his chest.

Nikos twirled the girl to face him and held her at arm's length.

"What in the name of Zeus are you doing here?"

She looked up at him, her tiny lips forming a pout at the anger in his voice. She opened her mouth to speak, but then froze. Even in the darkness, Nikos could see the whites of her eyes widen in fear.

"Nikos!" she said, looking past him, toward the entrance to the alley.

He had no time even to turn.

A well-muscled and oiled arm snaked around his neck and squeezed.

# TWENTY-FOUR

The house's solitude was a relief to Tessa after the long and silent ride back from the Acropolis hill with Nikos. Truly, the man frightened her.

A single torch burned still in the courtyard, throwing off a small amount of light, and Tessa silently thanked Simeon for his thoughtfulness. She entered the open space from the hall and moved toward the back of the house where Glaucus's room lay, hopefully undisturbed since she had left.

Halfway across the courtyard, the shadows shifted.

"Tessa."

She jumped. "Who is there?"

A face drew close to the torch, and the flame danced shadows across it.

"Hermes." Tessa swallowed. "What do you mean, skulking about in the shadows?"

He remained several feet away but raised a goblet to her with an amused smile. "Good evening, Tessa."

"It is late, Hermes. If you will excuse me . . ."

"Late, indeed. Late to be roaming about the city while Glaucus lies too ill to speak for himself."

Tessa tossed her hair behind her and stared him down. "Did you have a reason for calling, Hermes, or did you simply need a cup of decent wine?"

Hermes smiled again. He swirled the contents of his cup, threw it back, then raised the cup again to Tessa. When he spoke, his voice was low, seductive.

"Glaucus always did have the best wine."

*I am too tired to play games.*

"What do you want, Hermes?"

Beside him the torch sizzled and danced. Within their pool of firelight, they seemed the only two people in the night. Even Mynah appeared to be asleep in her cage. Hermes shrugged one shoulder. "To spend time with the great Tessa, of course. As it seems others are favored to do."

"I should see if Glaucus needs me."

"Something tells me he has not missed you."

Tessa fought to keep her expression passive.

"Come, Tessa," Hermes said. "Sit with me for a time." He blurred into the shadows behind the torch. Tessa could see that he retrieved an amphorae and refilled his cup. He turned and watched her.

Her feet seemed rooted to the courtyard stones.

Hermes slipped to the nearby bench and lowered himself onto one side of it. He held the cup aloft and patted the seat beside him.

"Hermes, I do not have the time—"

"And yet you have the time to roam the city?"

"I was taking care of certain business at Glaucus's request." Tessa remained at a distance.

Hermes' smile was again guarded, amused. "Yes, of course." He patted the seat again. "But tonight was not the first night you have had urgent business in the city when you should have been asleep. Was it?"

Tessa inhaled and straightened her shoulders.

"Hermes, if you have something to say to me, speak it now."

Hermes draped an arm along the back of the bench. "Tessa, we are simply talking. Do you not find it pleasant to pass the evening with me?"

*I have had enough.* She walked past him.

"Perhaps you would rather spend the evening with your new servant?"

She stopped. "He is not my servant. Glaucus acquired him."

"Of course."

She risked a glance at Hermes. His expression had hardened.

"Sit beside me, Tessa."

She returned to the bench and perched on the edge, her back straight. Her fingers traced the rough stone on the underside of the bench.

*Whatever he thinks, I can manipulate him to leave it alone. I can always make them do what I want.*

She eased back against the bench and smiled. "Hermes, you almost sound jealous. What would Glaucus say?"

He laughed. "Indeed," his eyes bore into hers, "what would Glaucus say?"

*He knows. By the gods, he knows.*

"What do you want, Hermes?"

He leaned against her. "I've come to see Glaucus, of course."

She shifted away from him.

"That old Jew insisted that I could not. And so I waited for the woman with the real power."

"You flatter me, Hermes. But I cannot convince Glaucus to see you either. He is a proud man, as you know."

"Hmmm." Hermes sipped his wine, then held out the cup to Tessa. She shook her head.

He slid closer, brought his arm around her shoulder, and held the cup to her lips. "Join me for a drink, Tessa. You have never had a cup with Hermes." He brought the cup to her mouth, forced it between her lips.

She shoved him away and stood.

"You take liberties, Hermes. Glaucus would not be pleased. Good night."

She whirled away and sped toward the back hall and the safety of Glaucus's room.

But Hermes caught her wrist in the hall and spun her to him. He pulled her close and whispered in her ear. She smelled the wine on his breath and, for a moment, thought she caught a whiff of the stench of the pit where she and Nikos had dumped Glaucus's body.

"Let us see what Glaucus thinks, shall we, Tessa? Let us see what he thinks about your midnight trips outside the city with his new servant. What he thinks about your flaunting decent behavior by moving into his home. How he feels about his servant and hetaera becoming heroes to the Jews."

"Hermes, I—"

His grip tightened on her wrist, and his voice was low like the purr of a cat. "No more games, Tessa. I will see Glaucus. And I will see him now."

## Ω

The oiled arm around Nikos's neck tightened to cut off his air. He dug his fingers into the slippery flesh and tried to take hold. The single sentence he spoke rasped from his throat.

"Persephone, get out of here!"

The girl took a step backward but did not run.

Nikos reached behind, flailing for his attacker's head.

*He is trained to fight.*

Nikos knew he had little chance of escape. But he must get Persephone to safety. He dug his heels into the street and thrust his weight backward. His attacker did not lose his balance but staggered back several paces. Away from Persephone. Nikos burrowed fingers into the arm again. The smell of the assailant's oil enveloped him.

He tried to send a message to the girl with his eyes. But then the darkness rolled over his vision. Red light sparked behind his eyes.

A moment later he was on his knees in the street, the grip on his neck released. He dragged in a desperate breath. Opened his eyes.

A man loomed above him, dressed in a simple tunic, but with a beard ornately braided. Nikos saw nothing more before the blunt toes of a sandaled foot drove into his ribs.

He gasped to regain breath, doubled over and clutched his stomach. A high-pitched shriek burrowed through the pain.

Another kick landed.

Then another shriek and a blur of gauzy white.

Nikos opened one eye, tried to breathe. Persephone had leaped onto his attacker's back and now pummeled his neck with her fists, still screaming.

Nikos dragged himself upright. Crawled the few feet to the fighter.

The wrestler clawed at Persephone's head. "Get off me, you wailing cat!" He tangled fingers into her hair and yanked her from his back. She hit the street with a *thwack*, next to Nikos.

Nikos clutched her hand. "Run, child," he whispered.

"He will kill you!"

The wrestler wrapped thick arms around Persephone's waist. He lifted her like a sack of grain and tossed her aside. Her shoulder hit the wall and she cried out, then slid to the ground. The man barked a laugh, then pointed at Persephone. "I will enjoy taking care of you next."

Nikos pushed to his knees, then to his feet.

The wrestler turned on him.

"What do you want?" Nikos managed. "I will give you what money I have."

The barking laugh echoed again through the empty street. "I have already been well paid."

His feet moved so quickly, Nikos had no time to react. Three steps and the man's fist connected with Nikos's jaw. The force flung him backward, off his feet again. Nikos felt the splash of gutter water beneath him, the taste of blood in his mouth.

Another kick. And another. Then lifted by his tunic and another fist landed on his face. Dropped back to the street, face down this time. The blood in his mouth mixed with the water running through the gutter.

The wrestler kneeled over him. "This is a message," he whispered into Nikos's ear. "Next time you will not live to hear it."

Nikos hung on to consciousness, needing to hear the words.

"Stay away from the Jews. Do not play the hero."

A palm smacked the back of his head. "Do you understand?"

Nikos spat blood from his mouth. "Crawl back to your gymnasium." He added a curse he hoped Persephone did not hear.

His attacker responded with another punch, this time to his lower back. Nikos lay still. The barking laugh sounded again, moving away from him.

Turned toward the wall where Persephone slumped.

"It's the little she-cat's turn."

Nikos breathed. Focused on the breathing.

*The girl needs you.*

The assailant moved away, his back to Nikos. "Persephone," he said. "Like the daughter of Zeus. Shall we see if you are as sweet as Hades found your namesake?"

Nikos struggled to his knees.

*One chance. I will have only one chance.*

He scanned the street for a weapon. The rutted, packed earth and narrow walk offered nothing.

He loosened the belt from his waist.

The wrestler had lifted Persephone from the street and pinned her against the wall. She slapped at him, her hands bouncing off his arms like tiny raindrops against marble.

Nikos held the belt in two hands, wrapping the ends around each palm once, twice. The leather cut into his palms and he snapped it taut.

His ribs, his back, everything hurt.

The wrestler pushed himself up against Persephone.

She screamed.

Nikos staggered forward, the leather cord stretched in front of him.

He lunged, looped the cord over the man's neck, then around. Yanked both ends with every bit of strength that remained.

The wrestler fell back against him, releasing Persephone.

This time, the girl ran.

His attacker tried to wriggle fingers between the leather and his neck, but Nikos held it tight. Nikos had never killed a man. He had no desire to kill his first. The two danced together there in street for a long moment. Nikos felt his strength draining.

And then the wrestler slumped. His weight pulled Nikos toward the ground. He let the man drop and retrieved his belt from the welted neck.

"Nikos, are you hurt?"

The girl was back.

Nikos gathered the loose belt with one hand, grabbed Persephone's hand with his other, and pulled.

"Come, child!"

They ran through the streets together. His attacker knew his identity, could probably find him again. His only hope was that the message had been delivered and there would be no need for another attack.

He brought Persephone to the back of the house, not wishing to wake anyone or concern them needlessly. The servant-boy of earlier was there again.

"Your father grows impatient!" he said.

Nikos had begun to wonder if the message had been a ploy. Apparently not. He dismissed the boy and turned back to Persephone. "Get to your bed!" he said, fuming at the delay.

"Nikos, wait!" Persephone clutched at his arm.

He wondered then, for the first time, what she had been doing there in the alley.

"Nikos, I wanted to speak with you!" Tears stained the girl's cheek.

"Were you following me?"

Her eyes dropped. "Nikos, I—I want to tell you—"

"What is it?"

Persephone raised pleading eyes to him. "Nikos, now that my father is dead, and my mother—my mother is not . . ." She clutched at him again. "I have been promised to a man I do not wish to marry."

Nikos sighed. "Persephone, I can't—"

"But now there is no one to make me marry him!" She smiled through her tears. "I want to leave here. Leave with Tessa. And I want you to come with me."

"Come with you?"

"I want to marry *you*, Nikos. Not that awful—"

Nikos peeled the girl's fingers from his arm. "Persephone." He tried to smile kindly. "I am a servant—"

"I do not care! Why should I care?"

"Persephone, I cannot."

"Why?" Her eyes filled again with tears. "What is wrong with me?"

He touched her face gently. "Get to your bed, Persephone. I have business to attend. We will talk again."

"Nikos—"

"Go, child."

Her eyes registered understanding at the use of the word. She drew back, dashed the tears from her face, and raised her chin. "Would that I *were* still a child, Nikos. But we both know that if my father lived I would have been married within the year."

"It simply cannot be, Persephone."

She whirled and strode toward the house. Nikos watched her go, knowing it was not class that separated them. There was a very different reason, one where class *would* prove a significant problem. But there was no time to think of that now.

His father awaited him in the bouleuterion.

Awaited information that Nikos did not have.

# TWENTY-FIVE

Tessa pushed against Hermes like a woman drowning will clutch at a twig that cannot save her. "Please, Hermes." The fear she had kept buried since Glaucus first fell in the courtyard flooded her, choking off her words. "Please."

Hermes shoved her aside. He retreated into the courtyard but was back a moment later, the torch in his hand. The flames flickered across his face, throwing angry shadows over his eyes. "Get out of my way, Tessa," he said.

A noise behind them startled them both. Someone stumbled into the back door of the house, moaning quietly. Persephone was as surprised to see them as they her. She pulled herself up, eyes wide, and clutched her dirty chitôn around her.

Tessa forgot the danger of the moment. "Persephone! What has happened?"

The girl sniffled and swiped the back of her hand across her cheeks. "Nothing. I needed to get some air. That is all." She tried to push past Tessa, looking at Hermes in confusion, then fear. "What is he doing here?"

Hermes grinned. "I have come to see your father, my dear."

Persephone took a step backward and looked to Tessa.

"Ah," Hermes said to Tessa, "I see you have allies in this house."

"Persephone, leave us," Tessa said. She tilted her head toward the courtyard and frowned at the girl. *Why is she coming in dirty and crying at this hour?* "Go, Persephone."

The girl's nostrils flared. "I am not a child! Do not treat me like a child!"

Hermes laughed, low and quiet. "Indeed. It appears the little girl has become a woman."

Persephone retreated at this. Her shoulders slumped and she studied the floor. "You are right, Tessa. I will go to bed. I am sorry to bother you."

Tessa studied her back as she slunk off, then looked at Hermes.

*What was that?*

Hermes watched Persephone's exit as well, then turned back to Tessa, smiling. "I have waited long for this day." Tessa frowned and Hermes laughed. "You do not know, do you, Tessa? Glaucus has not told you all his secrets, has he? Persephone has been betrothed to me for years. I have waited only for her to come to womanhood." He smiled again. "It seems my wait is over."

Tears sprung to Tessa's eyes, surprising even her. In Persephone, she had seen herself. And now the cycle would continue. Persephone would become a woman and be given over to this disgusting man, the freedom of her childhood gone.

Hermes stepped close and scowled. "Do you cry for the girl, Tessa? Am I such a monster?"

She blinked away the tears.

"It matters not what you think." He pointed to Glaucus's door with the torch and raised his eyebrows. "It matters only what Glaucus thinks, am I right? And now we shall ask him."

Hermes shoved her aside and pushed forward, swept away the curtain in the doorway and thrust the torch into the darkened room. Tessa followed, her heart dropping into the floor with each step.

Hermes waved the torch about the room. The light played on the furniture, the floor, the bed piled with blankets to resemble one large man. He glanced at Tessa, as though impressed with the extent of her deceit but took three quick steps to the bed and flung the top blanket from the pile.

*And so it ends.*

Hermes's laugh began slowly, then grew into a cackle that sickened her.

"How did you do it, Tessa? How did you kill him?"

She looked away, wishing herself anywhere but here. Now that it was over, she was surprised at how quickly her thoughts returned to the knife she had left at the feet of Helios. Perhaps those thoughts had never been far from her mind.

"Did he suffer?" Hermes replaced the blanket carefully, then moved across the room to her, still smiling. "Tell me how he suffered."

She turned back to him. "You make me sick."

He laughed. "At least I am not a murderer."

"I did not kill him."

"No, of course not. Let me guess. The new servant killed Glaucus, and you simply are helping him hide his crime out of kindness."

Tessa closed her eyes. *Just be done with me, Hermes.*

"Or perhaps it is not merely kindness," he said.

Even with her eyes closed, she could feel his leering smile and the heat of the torch as he brought it close to her face.

"You have learned my secret, Hermes. Why don't you leave now? There is nothing more I can do on my own behalf. We both know I will never escape this island."

"You give up so quickly? No begging, no bribery?"

She opened her eyes. "What do I have that you would want?"

He smiled. "What, indeed?"

She recoiled. "I would rather be executed."

He sneered. "Don't flatter yourself, woman. Not everyone on this island wants you. No, I need something more valuable than your body. I need information."

Tessa pushed the torch away. "What kind of information?"

"I think we both want the same thing. And perhaps we can help each other."

A chance. *Is there a chance?*

"Spiro," he said. "Neither of us wants to see him increase his political influence on this island."

Tessa inhaled. "I believe Spiro is behind the problems in the Jewish quarter and the violence that occurred in the southeast district," she said. "He works to discredit Glaucus. And yourself."

Hermes shifted the torch to his other hand and held it higher to better study her face. "What have you learned?"

"Not enough. But someone spread rumors in the Jewish district that the water would fail. The same person paid a man in the southeast district to say a Jew murdered the fountain house guard. And we found the splitting basin had been blocked to divert water away from the Jews, and a man murdered there as well."

"And how do you know Spiro is responsible?" Hermes asked, his eyes betraying his excitement.

Tessa shook her head. "That is what I have not yet learned. But I am certain—"

"And what purpose would he have?"

"I suppose simply to weaken Glaucus's position."

Hermes shook his head. "No, there must be more than that." He chewed his lip, staring above her, then looked back at her face. "And you can find out."

"How?"

"You will go to him secretly. The entire island knows that he is obsessed with you. You will tell him that you fear Glaucus is dying and you are worried about what will become of you. Tell him that you want to become *his* hetaera—"

"Never!" Tessa spit the word out, her stomach churning.

Hermes shrugged. "Then I am afraid the council and Assembly will soon hear that Glaucus's hetaera has murdered him and disposed of his body without a burial that will allow him to pass to the afterlife."

*Choices. Always a choice between death and more death. When will it end?*

"Why would I go to Spiro?"

"Because you are the only one who can get close enough to learn the extent of his plans. His obsession with you will overcome his wariness."

Tessa's knees felt weak. She moved to the bed and sank to it.

"I will go to him."

"Good." Hermes reached across and touched her face. She drew away.

"And you will get rid of the servant."

"What servant?"

Hermes chuckled. "Your pretense is foolish, Tessa. One only needs to see the two of you together to know the truth. And Spiro will never believe that you are loyal to him if he sees you with the young hero."

Tessa stood and stared into his eyes. "You are mad, Hermes. He is a servant and has been helping me. Nothing more."

"Perhaps someone should tell him that."

Tessa crossed her arms in front of her. "I will play your game with Spiro, but do not misunderstand. No man will ever own me again. Not you. Not Spiro. And not a servant." She dropped her arms and drew up close to him, her height almost matching his own. "No man."

Hermes smiled. "As you say, Tessa. We each have our role in this little play." He dipped his head. "And I will leave you to yours."

He moved to the doorway but stopped and looked back. "One more matter. I want Persephone. Convince the mother to accomplish the wedding before Glaucus is to leave for Crete."

"The wedding would have to begin in two days!"

"Exactly. I have waited long enough."

Tessa thought of Hermes's young boys. Of the hetaera, Berenice. She loathed this man. "Don't do this, Hermes."

He smiled. "Do not be long about your tasks, Tessa. Give me Persephone. Get rid of the servant. And learn Spiro's plan. I will return soon."

And then he was gone.

## Ω

The empty agora yawned before him, its marketplace awaiting the merchants who would return in the morning. To the right, the bouleuterion appeared empty as well, but as Nikos walked past the fountain at the center of the agora, he could see that a small light filtered out through the entryway.

He climbed the five steps to the columned porch.

A man stepped into the doorway, blocking Nikos's entrance.

Nikos drew himself up on the top step in surprise. The man in the doorway was unfamiliar to him. His eyes narrowed as he took in Nikos from head to foot.

"Who are you?" the stranger asked.

"I have business in the bouleuterion."

"Business with whom?"

Nikos crossed the porch. "Let me pass."

The man placed a hand on Nikos's chest. There was no pressure, but the threat was clear.

"I have come to see my father."

From inside the bouleuterion, a voice called out, "Nikos, is that you?"

Nikos raised an eyebrow at the slave in the doorway. The other man stepped aside, if reluctantly.

Nikos crossed into the large council room, led by the oil lamp that perched on the marble ledge on the open gallery's left side. Beyond the light his father, Andreas, sat in one of the council seats, four rows up from the gallery floor.

Nikos bowed his head. "Are you well, Father?"

"I had nearly given up on you." The words were spoken with a quiet disapproval.

"I had some difficulty in getting away."

Andreas stood. He descended the tiers, pausing on each step as though he attended a coronation. Nikos took note of the ever-present deep crease between his eyes, the full lips and closely cropped hair. The man's body belied his age. He had always disciplined himself, abstaining from rich foods, and the leanness of his body made him look years younger. At the moment, his father's handsome features were distorted in disgust.

"When I suggested you play the part of a servant," his father said, "I did not intend that you roll in the gutter."

Nikos was aware that the scuffle in the street had left his clothes dirty, torn, and foul-smelling. No doubt his face betrayed the beating he had taken.

"As I said, I had some trouble."

"Were you followed? I do not wish my presence here—"

"I came alone."

Nikos's father lowered himself onto a seat at the edge of the gallery floor. His position left Nikos with the choice to stand or to sit in a seat where speaking together would be awkward. He stood before his father, his hands clasped behind his back. On the floor beside him lay a mound of tiles and a tradesman's tools, including a pot of water. A section of the floor had been ripped up but not yet repaired.

"Well?" Andreas asked. "How do the strategoi stand in the matter of the League?"

*I am well, Father, thank you. I have missed you, too.* Nikos fought back the thoughts. His father had done more for him than any other person. Perhaps he should not demand affection as well. But he did wish for approval, that he knew.

"I am not certain yet how each of them would vote. I have secured a position in Glaucus's home—"

"And how will Glaucus vote?"

Nikos swallowed. *Tessa, how can I keep your secret from my father?*

"Glaucus has always been a strong supporter of democracy," he answered.

"Bah," Andreas spit. "Do these fools not know that such a flawed system cannot last?"

"I also suspect that Spiro—"

His father's eyes shot back to him. "Yes? What of Spiro?"

"He seems to be involved in some sort of plot to discredit Glaucus and those who support the Jews."

"The Jews? Of what consequence are the Jews?"

Nikos shook his head. "I have not yet discovered—"

"What *have* you learned, Nikos?"

Nikos bent to the floor and absently sorted the mound of colored tiles into differing sizes. "Glaucus is ill," he began, placing a jagged blue tile to the right. "His hetaera is well-respected on the island and speaks for him presently. She requested that I accompany her to the Jewish district, where we found—"

"You were seen in public with another man's hetaera?" The amusement in his father's voice carried across the dimly lit bouleuterion.

"We learned that someone has been inciting violence among the Jews. We are certain that Spiro is responsible, though we have not yet proven it."

"It sounds as though you did more than simply *accompany* the hetaera."

Nikos nudged a yellow tile into the pile. "Tessa needed protection."

Andreas laughed. "You have not been in my household long, Nikos. But long enough that I know your propensity for rescuing those in distress."

Nikos scooped a handful of mortar dust from the tradesman's pot and poured water over it.

"What of the other eight strategoi?" his father asked.

"Xenophon has been murdered."

"Eh?"

"Yes. It is not known by whom, but he stood in opposition to the League, I believe." Nikos used a trowel to mix the mortar to a paste. The mortar's sharp smell blended with the stench of his clothes. He smoothed it over a section of the missing floor.

"And the others?"

He set the first tile into the mortar and applied a steady pressure to release the air bubbles. "I do not know yet." He increased the pressure.

Andreas sighed. "I sent you here to learn whether the island was ready to join the League, and instead you have spent your time helping a whore—"

The tile cracked under Nikos's hand. He lifted his head and stared at his father. "Do not speak of her in that way again."

The amusement on his father's face faded. Andreas stood and towered over Nikos. "You are not a peasant any longer, Nikos. You are my son. This woman—"

Nikos stood. "Let us not speak of her at all, Father."

His father scowled. "I *will* speak of her, and you will listen. No son of mine will degrade himself by consorting with another man's hetaera." His face softened. "If this Tessa is that important to you, perhaps you can secure her services—"

"Stop!"

The scowl returned. "Enough of this, Nikos. You must complete the task I sent you to perform. Learn the opinions of the strategoi. But above all, learn not only what Spiro says, but what he plans. I do not trust his apparent support of the League. He has always been more ambitious than that."

"You think he wants to rule the island himself?"

Andreas turned and dropped to his seat again. He crossed his arms over his lean chest. "Of course he does. He craves power like some men crave undiluted wine."

Nikos used his foot to nudge the stones he had placed into a more pleasing position, then moved away from his work and stood before his father.

"I will learn what he plans, Father. I will not disappoint you."

His father nodded. "You have much to learn, Nikos, about leaving your heart out of politics. But you have the strength of character necessary to lead." He rose and placed a hand on the young man's shoulder. "I do not believe your brother has the same strength. And that is why one day *you* will lead Kalymnos."

Andreas squeezed his shoulder.

"And why your brother Spiro will never have what he most desires."

# TWENTY-SIX

### ✦ *Two Days before the Great Quake* ✦

The heat of the day had not yet built. Spiro climbed the hillside early, not wishing to mingle with the more than five hundred jurors who had been chosen to hear the case against Ademia for the murder of her husband, Xenophon. The remaining strategoi would also be present, out of respect for their former colleague.

The path led up the hill in a slow, winding fashion, but Spiro did not mind the walk this morning. The grass seemed especially green in the morning sun, and the pines at the top of the hill led him upward with the spicy scent of resin.

*All is well. In spite of Tessa and her peasant hero, all is well.*

His plans would not fail. The Jews were still under a cloud of suspicion, and tomorrow the final piece would fall into place. By now Glaucus's new servant had been warned to forego heroism and focus on his own survival. Spiro had never laid eyes on the servant, but he wished to see him this morning, a morbid curiosity to see the damage that Calisto had inflicted in the night.

Behind him Spiro could hear the crowds beginning to ascend the hillside. In addition to the five hundred jurors chosen from the annual panel, many would be there simply to enjoy a day's entertainment. Spiro stopped to pull a skin filled with water from under his himation. The climb had already parched his throat, and the water was still cool, sliding down his throat like a fine wine.

*Only one more day.*

By nightfall tomorrow, only four strategoi, including himself, would remain alive. The other three, though weak-kneed in their ability to lead, remained firm in their support of Spiro. The chaos resulting from the deaths of the other six would ensure the island's entry into the Achaean League. A temporary measure, to be sure, but a necessary step in his plan to rule.

*You will see, Father. You will see.*

He pushed away thoughts of Andreas. The man's unconditional disapproval rankled him beyond what he would admit. He had never been able to please the man. And in his failure, his father had apparently found someone else to please him, the bastard son who had appeared out of the gutter.

*He is nothing. And my father will soon see that.*

Ten large boulders were set at the hilltop, one of the privileges of leadership on the island. The strategoi would not be required to sit on the grass with the rest of the jury and spectators. Xenophon's, of course, would be empty. And what of Glaucus? Would he be well enough to appear? Or would he send Tessa to perch on a rock in the sun? Spiro smiled at the thought.

He chose a rock for himself and watched the crowd gather. Those who had been chosen from the panel of potential jurors to serve in this trial each wore a bronze *pinakion* with their name inscribed on it, to indicate their official position. Each of these came to the top of the hill to receive their bronze markers—one to vote guilty and one for a not-guilty vote. They would be collected after the prosecutor and the defendant had each presented his and her case. It promised to be an entertaining morning.

The crowd swelled, and the noise grew until it drowned out the sounds of the birds and the sea. One by one, the other strategoi arrived. Spiro nodded to each, offering a particular smile to those who would soon be dead.

And then Tessa appeared. She walked alone, with deliberate steps and head held high. Her dark hair hung in loose ringlets below her shoulders, mute testimony to her rebellious heart. She took Spiro's breath away.

*Soon. So very soon.*

Tessa raised her eyes and met his own.

*Hmm. She looks at me differently.*

Spiro never had illusions about Tessa's feelings for him. But the usual contempt he encountered in her eyes was absent today. She lowered her eyes with a slight smile that almost bespoke shyness.

A sudden dryness in his mouth prompted him to pull out the water skin again, but he barely noticed the liquid this time. Tessa came to sit on the stone beside him. "You grow more beautiful every day, my dear," he said. "Pity Glaucus is too ill to appreciate it."

The trial began with a brief statement by Lysander, the prosecutor. The water clock was filled. Each party would have four amphorae to make their case, with the water pouring from a drilled hole at the base of one clay bowl, into the bowl placed below it. When the water ran out, time was up.

Ademia spoke first. She stood tall before the jury, elegant and austere, describing the abuse she had suffered at the hands of Xenophon as though she were instructing her servants on their tasks for the day. Her words fell mainly on the ears of men who no doubt treated their own wives in similar fashion. Spiro watched the spectators, knowing that the only sympathy Ademia received would come from the women, many of whom murmured and shook their heads. True, they would have some influence with their husbands, but everyone knew before the trial began how it would end. Ademia seemed to sense the jury's mood, and her speech turned into a plea, gaining in desperation. Spiro fought the impropriety of laughing at her humiliation.

The water clock ran dry. Ademia cried out and turned back to the jurors. "Have mercy," she screamed. "Have mercy! He was——"

A council member appeared behind her and grabbed her by the arms. She cried out again. He yanked her backward and down to the grass. She fell and curled up on her side, her knees pulled to her chest. The crowd's murmur crescendoed into a roar.

The prosecutor, Lysander, raised his arms to quiet the crowd. A frail man, well-advanced in years, his voice nonetheless carried to the far reaches of the assembly. "Xenophon led this city well. And now he is dead." He pointed to Ademia. "She would have us believe that his life held no value simply because *she* was not happy!

"By her own admission, she poisoned his figs. She wished him dead, and she succeeded. He died in agony, like an animal that must be destroyed because of disease."

The crowd responded as Lysander no doubt hoped, with disapproving frowns and bitter comments to one another.

Lysander's voice rose. "He did not deserve to die in such a manner! And she is responsible!" His long arm raised a finger of accusation at Ademia. He turned to the water clock, still gushing, and in a favorite trick of confident prosecutors, he waved an arm at the clock. "Throw out the water!" he shouted and dropped to the grass, his statement concluded.

The crowd roared its approval. The epistates in charge brought Ademia before them, where she was forced to stand while the ballots were collected.

Spiro glanced sideways at Tessa. She had observed the trial in silence, and now her chin rested on her chest. He squinted. Did she weep for Ademia?

The ballot collectors brought their pots to the top of the hill. Each emptied the contents at the epistates's feet. There was no need for a count, though it would be performed as a formality.

*Guilty.*

The word swept through the crowd, and the response was jubilant. Ademia fell to the grass, weeping. Two council members dragged her away from the crowd. She would be dead before night-fall, and her body would be displayed for all who wished to honor Xenophon by spitting upon it.

The crowd dispersed, some socializing on the hillside, some wandering home to the day's tasks.

Spiro tried to speak with Tessa, but she shook her head and fled through the crowd. He watched her run.

A stranger appeared beside him, too close to be simply pushing through the crowd. Spiro turned to the man, younger than he and well-built. He was clearly a servant, and had perhaps recently been in a fight. A purple shadow about his left eye looked as though it had disagreed with someone's fist.

"You enjoyed the trial?" the servant asked.

Spiro raised his eyebrows at the presumption. "Your master must be quite lenient to allow his servants the leisure to attend to trials rather than their tasks."

The younger man shrugged and surveyed the hillside. "It is fascinating to watch the display of power, whether in the hands of many or in the hands of a few." He turned to Spiro. "I am certain you find it more interesting in the hands of the few, do you not?"

*I know who you are.* This was Glaucus's insolent servant who had been helping Tessa. He smiled. "You are Nikos."

The servant looked away. "To be known by a man such as you is a kind of power in itself, do you not agree?"

"And power in the hands of inferiors makes them look as foolish as dogs dressed as kings."

Spiro turned his back to Nikos and hurried down the hill, disgusted that the peasant had even spoken to him. It did not appear as though his message had been conveyed as clearly as Spiro had intended. But it was another message, whispered to Spiro moments later by a servant who rushed up the hillside to meet him, that soon occupied his thoughts.

A ship had arrived in the harbor last night with a surprising passenger—one who wished his presence on Rhodes to remain unknown. But there were many on the docks who knew information was often well-rewarded, and one of them had slipped off to Spiro's home this morning with a message.

*Your father has come to Rhodes.*

## Ω

Nikos skirted the crowd and ran downhill, past Spiro, who had stopped to speak with a servant. Toward Tessa, who had not looked at him at all during the trial.

He caught up to her on the gravel road to the city. She had slowed and walked alone. Her hair hung down her back, and she had woven colorful strips of cloth into it today. He drew close and whispered her name.

She inhaled sharply and looked about, as though to see if they were watched.

"What is your plan?" he asked.

She spoke quietly, without looking at him. "I have no plan."

"We must be able to prove that Spiro is planning something more than random violence."

"It is not your concern, Nikos. I will deal with my own—"

"Tessa." Nikos wrapped his fingers around her arm.

She shook him off and scanned the crowd around them again. The look she turned on him was not favorable.

To the right of the road, the pines grew tall. Beyond them, the foliage thickened and smaller trees grew up under their taller counterparts. Nikos pointed there. "Let's get off the road where we can speak without being seen."

Tessa hesitated, then nodded. Nikos turned into the trees, leaving her to follow in a moment. He kept his head down, hoping they would not be noticed.

The sunlight barely pierced the treetops here, and light filtered down as though from pinholes in a green canopy. Nikos made his way between the smaller trees, the pine needles softening his footfalls.

Tessa whispered his name from behind, and he stopped and closed his eyes. The sound of the crowd had already faded, and even the sea roar grew faint here. His father's face appeared in his mind's eye.

*You can do this.*

After meeting with his father, Nikos had lain awake until the sun crested the sea, until he had convinced himself that the best way to get the information he sought was through Tessa, though it would mean deceiving her.

He turned and looked at her face. She had been crying.

"The trial was difficult," he said. "To see her disgraced. I could not help but think—"

"It will not come to that," Tessa said. She hugged her waist. "I will throw myself into the sea first."

He reached for her, touched her arms. "We will stop Spiro. We will learn what he plans and stop him. I will not let him hurt you."

*And so the ruse begins.*

Tessa ran her hand over a pine bough, stripping its needles into her palm. "I do not need your protection, Nikos. Not any longer. I will stop Spiro myself." She let the needles flutter to the ground. "I have been unwise involving you."

He pulled her closer to him and waited until her eyes found his. "Unwise?"

Her eyes grew misty. "I have the means to make Spiro trust me. To tell me what he plans. But I must go alone."

"I will be nearby. I will wait for you to meet me."

Tessa closed her eyes. "Why?"

"So I can be certain you are safe."

Nikos hated himself. Hated the lie and the way it made him feel. To use Tessa for the information she could give him made him feel no better a man than the brother he was beginning to know and despise.

She raised her face to his. "Do you care so much that I am safe?"

The pressure in his chest made it impossible to speak. He cursed Spiro, cursed Glaucus, even cursed his father and what they all had forced him to. Tessa waited, her eyes on his.

He breathed out his frustration, tried to formulate his deception. But when the words rose to his lips and poured out, they felt more true than any words he had ever spoken.

"Yes, Tessa." He pulled her closer and felt her heartbeat, knew that she held her breath. "Yes, I want you to be safe." He reached for her face with both hands. Ran his fingertips along her jaw line, down to her lips. Traced her lips with his fingers. "All I want is for you to be safe."

A single bird sang above them. Thoughts of politics, and of pleasing his father, floated away with the bird's song. The play of light through the trees sparkled through Tessa's hair and lit her eyes.

"Tessa," he whispered, his voice ragged.

She seemed as still as marble beneath his fingers, but he knew better. He bent his head to her, touched his lips to hers. She tasted of honey and flowers. And nothing else mattered.

"Tessa," he said again.

*I am lost.*

## Ω

The pines, the birds, the world faded to nothing for Tessa. She knew only the touch of Nikos's fingers on her skin, his lips on hers.

*This is what it feels like to be loved.*

The thought floated through her, like the puff of a feathery cloud across a jewel-blue sky.

Nikos's hands slipped to the back of her head, pulled her further into his kiss. She felt again the shifting inside her, the shattering of pieces she had thought were stone. Her hands found their way to his chest and she could feel the pounding of his heart beneath her touch. He kissed her eyelids, her forehead, then returned to her lips.

*Is this part of the joy I have denied?*

But then, as though something dark, something ominous had blacked out the sunlit sky, Tessa felt the fear that had long been her companion descend and wrap cold fingers around her heart. The fear burrowed through her chest, into her arms, and forced itself out through her fingers. She shoved Nikos backward and stepped away.

"No!" she said.

His eyes seemed to reach for her. "Tessa—"

*He is a man. He is a man like all the rest.*

She put her fingers to her lips and took two more steps backward.

*You cannot trust him. He will use you, like all the rest.*

She remembered Hermes, his accusations of impropriety that were truer than she had acknowledged. And she remembered his threats.

*Get rid of the servant.*

"Tessa, don't pull away from me now."

She shook her head. Hermes or no Hermes, she would never again allow a man to get close enough to use her. Crete was still within her grasp.

"You go too far, Nikos!" she said, the anger of ten years flowing through her words. "You are a servant. I do not belong to you. And you have no right."

Nikos reached for her face again. She smacked his hand away. "Do not touch me!"

"You cannot convince me that you feel nothing."

She tried to smile. "You think you know me. But you know nothing. I have played you for a fool from the day we met."

Nikos dropped his arm. His lips parted.

She tossed her hair behind her shoulders. "You pushed your way into Glaucus's home and learned the truth about his death almost immediately. You had enough information to ruin me." She raised her chin. "What was I to do? I did what I do best, of course. I manipulated you into believing I cared for you. Just as I have done with Glaucus for years. Just as I was trained to do. And you are as much a fool as he ever was."

The hurt in Nikos's eyes went deep, and she knew it. Her years of acting were serving her well. But she was not finished yet.

"I have kept you quiet since that first day, have I not?"

Nikos closed his lips and she saw him swallow with effort. He looked at the floor of their private grove.

"But I overplayed my role. In spite of my complete distaste for you, I somehow made you so confident in my affection that you took liberties I did not intend." Tessa removed the burgundy strip of linen she had woven into her hair that morning and used it to tie her hair atop her head.

"But it is over now, Nikos," she said. "You will remain quiet, for you are as guilty as I in disposing of Glaucus's body, and no one will believe we did not plan it together." She smiled. "I will make sure they do not believe you are innocent."

*Yes, this is better. This is how it should be.*

She backed away, her eyes not leaving Nikos.

*Much better not to trust. The marble Athena—she is always safe.*

She turned, finally, and ran back toward the road. The song of birds ceased as she ran, and the grove seemed as silent as the grave.

# TWENTY-SEVEN

Tessa chose to walk across the city to Spiro's home, her mind set to her task. She had never handled the ox cart herself, and she would not call Nikos.

She had bathed before leaving Glaucus's house, dressed with care and perfumed herself, preparation for the part she was about to play.

Daphne had seen Tessa before she left. Seen her dressed elegantly and with painted face. She had said nothing to Tessa, only stomped forward and slapped her, hard across her cheek, then walked away. Tessa touched her face now as she walked, remembering how the slap seemed painless, because it was so well deserved.

Through the streets, she did not attend to the children who played, the women fetching water, the servants dragging goods home from the market.

She hoped to find Spiro at home. Hoped to find him as foolish and presumptuous as usual. Needed him to be.

Spiro's home wedged into a hill, with a series of smaller homes on either side. Its whitewashed walls gleamed brighter than those beside it. One gnarled palm grew at the corner, its trunk bent and twisted.

The walk up the hill left Tessa breathless. She paused in the street below Spiro's house and composed her thoughts. To approach her enemy as though he were a friend would cause nothing but suspicion. Tessa's plan called for more subtlety.

She approached the steps to the house, and a servant appeared from behind her, pushed past her as though she were not there. A crate rattled in his arms, and sweat beaded on his forehead.

She followed him up the steps and paused at the door.

A shout from inside the house greeted the servant. "That had best be the pomegranates!"

Tessa recognized Spiro's voice. She glanced at the servant, who noticed her at last. "There is still much to do," the servant said with a shrug. To the empty hallway, he called, "I have brought the pomegranates, yes."

Tessa waited inside the door, taking in the expensive statuary and hanging tapestry in the entry to the home. She had been here once, for a symposium with Glaucus, but they had spent the evening in the andrôn, and she had never seen anything beyond this entrance and the room where the men had gotten drunk and argued about city government.

Sandaled feet slapped along the hall and Spiro shot into the entry. "Well, take them to the kitchen!" he said to the slave.

"Tessa!" Spiro's hand went to his hair and smoothed it back.

Tessa thrust her chin forward and let her voice carry. "I came to speak with you, Spiro."

His eyes narrowed for only a moment. "Of course. Come in."

He led the way through the hall. Tessa peered into the andrôn as they passed. Inside, three female servants placed cushions on the couches and punched them into a pleasing arrangement.

"Guests tonight, Spiro?" she asked.

A male slave slowed in the hall, and Spiro stopped to whisper something to him. They carried on, and he tossed his comments over his shoulder to Tessa. "Yes, a symposium. Of course all the city leaders will be there." He led her into his central courtyard. "Will Glaucus be in attendance?"

Tessa sniffed. "Do not pretend to care for Glaucus's company, Spiro. I know the truth."

Spiro turned in the center of the courtyard. The space was similar to Glaucus's home, but the extravagant plantings and fountain showcased Spiro's lavish spending.

"Why, Tessa," Spiro said, "you wound me. How could I wish Glaucus anything but good health at this delicate time?"

"You have done all you can to weaken his position, Spiro. I am well aware of that. I also know you have failed."

The sun beat down through the center of the house, warming the stones beneath Tessa's feet. She waited for Spiro's reaction. Much depended on it.

"You are confused, Tessa," he said, running his fingers down her arm. "Glaucus and I may not agree about everything, but I would never wish him harm."

Two servants entered the courtyard, each with a dead pheasant in his hands. One held his bird up. "The larger?" he asked. "Do we have a count of guests?"

Spiro lifted the tail feathers of the pheasant and examined all sides of it, then did the same with the other. "Yes, the larger," he said. "I expect that all invited will join us." He turned to Tessa and bowed slightly. "Including Glaucus."

The servants disappear toward the hearth room. With her head turned away from Spiro still, Tessa spoke, in a low and threatening tone. "I know of your manipulation of the Jews," she said. "But your plans were disrupted."

"Ah, yes, the servant Nikos, whom I have heard so much about. Hero to the Jews."

Yet another servant came to Spiro, this one with a platter of fruit for his inspection. When the fruit passed her, Tessa snatched a cluster of grapes from the platter. The servant's eyebrows shot up, but he continued. Tessa pulled a grape from its stem and slowly placed it in her mouth, her eyes on Spiro.

"You must admit, he was smarter than you."

He laughed. "I have no idea what you speak of, Tessa. You suspect a conspiracy where there is none. The Jews caused a riot when their water failed. One of them killed a Greek. That is all that I know."

*Now, Tessa. Now you must play your part well.*

She picked another grape from its stem, and this time held it to her lips with her fingertips for a moment. Pulling it away, she looked over at Spiro, letting a slight concern cross her face.

"I know you seek power, Spiro. That is why you act against the Jews." She twirled the grape cluster in her fingers, and lowered her eyes to it as she spoke. "But a hunger for power is something we have in common. Something I understand."

Spiro took a step toward her.

*Yes.*

"Tessa, I have been telling you for years that we are more alike than you wish to admit."

She shrugged and placed the grape in her mouth. "I can admit it. But I have no power. Not really. I live at the whim of Glaucus."

"Glaucus is a very ill man."

Tessa kept her head down, but not so far that Spiro could not see her slight smile. "Yes. Yes, he is."

Spiro was now close enough to touch.

More servants paraded through the courtyard, carrying armfuls of cushions, small tables, and oil lamps. They glanced at Spiro and her but continued at their tasks. From somewhere, the smell of the hearth drifted in. The pheasant must have been placed on the spit. Tessa's mouth watered. Aside from the grapes, she had not eaten yet today.

Spiro spoke softly. "Perhaps you will soon be free of Glaucus."

She looked into the distance. "Never free to pursue one who understands me, however."

*Careful, Tessa. So careful.*

Spiro leaned in, his eyes warm on her. "You know you belong with someone else."

She inhaled deeply and looked back at him. "I have learned one thing well in all these years: It is best not to speak of things that can never be."

Spiro lifted a hand toward her face, but she pulled back and pushed lightly against his chest with her hand. She let it linger there for a moment longer than necessary, then smoothed the fabric before she dropped the hand to her side, masking well her utter revulsion.

Spiro's breathing had grown shallow, she sensed.

"Tessa, I must tell you—"

A shout from the entryway pushed them apart, as though they had been caught in an illicit embrace.

A man's voice called, "Let me pass, filthy peasant!"

Tessa watched Spiro's face drain of color.

"What is it?" she asked.

He cursed. "My father."

"Here? On Rhodes?"

A man a full hand taller than Spiro strode into the courtyard. Tessa watched Spiro, certain he would say he was mistaken. This man could not be his father. His body and carriage were that of a man only a few years older than the man next to her.

"Father!" Spiro said, feigning welcome. "The symposium is not until this evening. I did not expect you so soon."

Andreas waved an impatient hand at his son. "My schedule is my own, Spiro. I wanted to speak to you before the rest of the sycophants arrive."

Andreas's eyes traveled to Tessa. With only a moment's hesitation, she slid closer to Spiro's side, her attention on Andreas.

"You have added someone to your household?"

Tessa tossed her hair back. "I have heard much of you, Andreas of Kalymnos. You are even more commanding a presence than people say."

Andreas gave her a half-smile and a raised eyebrow in response. His gaze returned to Spiro, a new respect gleaming in his eye. "I have heard the hetaerae on this island are a spirited breed," he said. "I see the rumor is true."

*He knew what I am without anyone telling him.*

Somehow, even in the midst of this game she played, that truth went deep, to a painful place.

"Master," a servant called from the hall. "Forgive me. The wine merchant has arrived and is in the street awaiting your selection."

Spiro looked from his father to Tessa, as though they would snatch the island from him if he left them alone for even a moment.

Andreas inclined his head toward the hall. "Choose wisely, son. I have traveled far for this evening."

Spiro dipped his head and moved to the front of the house. Tessa marveled that even the way he walked had changed. He had gone from master politician to wayward child in only a moment's time.

Andreas turned back to Tessa.

"My son rarely does anything to make me proud, but it seems he has surprised me today."

She smiled. "The symposium will certainly be lavish for you."

He laughed. "Your modesty is noted. We both know I spoke of his surprising success in acquiring a hetaera who is both beautiful and intelligent."

Tessa weighed her options, made a quick decision.

"I am not his hetaera," she said.

Andreas scowled. "Do not tell me he has been so foolish as to take you for a wife!"

Tessa exhaled, the air struck from her chest.

*Nothing so terrible as that, no.*

"I am another man's hetaera," she said. "Spiro is . . . an acquaintance."

"Another man's?"

She shrugged. "One does not have a choice in such matters."

"And what Rhodian has been fortunate enough to secure you?"

"One of the other strategoi. Glaucus."

Andreas recoiled as though slapped. "Glaucus!"

Tessa watched him carefully, trying to gauge his reaction. Surprise, yes. Disgust? Curiosity? He was difficult to read.

"You are Tessa."

She did not expect recognition. What else did he know?

She raised her chin. "I am."

His smile was slow and its meaning still hard to discern.

"Yes," he said. "I am beginning to understand."

Spiro returned to the courtyard, his wary eyes dodging between both of them.

"We have cleared up the misunderstanding, Spiro," Andreas said. He turned to Tessa. "We will see you and Glaucus tonight at the symposium?"

Spiro stepped between them. "Glaucus is ill, I am afraid."

"Ah, yes. I had heard that." Andreas reached for Tessa and ran a finger through her loose hair. "But may I insist that Tessa be present nonetheless?"

Spiro's eyes shifted to hers.

She hesitated only a moment, then bowed slightly, turned and retreated to the hall. Over her shoulder, she called back to them with a calculated smile.

"I will be honored to spend the evening with two such powerful men."

Ω

Tessa's departure sucked the life from the room. Both men watched her disappear into the hall, then watched the empty doorway a moment longer.

Spiro finally faced his father. "My apologies. I received word that you were on the island but expected that you would be visiting with friends until this evening's festivities."

"I did not expect you to welcome me in any other fashion."

Spiro bit back his first reply. "Was your voyage smooth?"

"Must we stand about in the heat of the yard, Spiro?" Andreas lifted a corner of his himation and dabbed at his forehead.

Spiro sighed. "Let me show you to your room, Father."

"And some food and water if you can spare time from your preparations."

Spiro led the way to the guest room, cursing himself for not having the bed readied earlier. The unprepared room did not go unnoticed, as Andreas sighed heavily and shook his head.

"I will send servants with bedding." Spiro ducked out of the room.

"And food!" his father called after him.

Spiro returned soon with four servants in his wake, their arms loaded with clean bedding, a pitcher of fresh water for bathing, a platter of fruits and cheeses, and an amphora of wine.

Andreas paced at the center of the room, arms crossed. "So," he said, "where lies the allegiance of the council, and hence the Assembly?"

Spiro eyed one young servant, wishing he had assigned one with more experience to make up the bed. *Straighten that covering.*

"The situation is volatile," he answered. "You have heard, I am certain, that Xenophon was murdered by his wife."

"His wife?"

Spiro shrugged. "Once again they prove they are best kept locked away."

"And Xenophon was still a proponent of democracy?"

Spiro motioned to a nearby set of chairs. They sat, and the flurry of servant activity continued around them.

"With Xenophon dead and Glaucus's future unknown, there are only three who still hold firmly to democracy. Two others support me in the belief that Rhodes should join the Achaean League. Two hold weakly to our position."

"The right man must be elected to Xenophon's place, in order to see the League come to Rhodes."

Spiro set his jaw. "Or we must see that those opposed can no longer exert their influence."

"And how will you accomplish this?"

"I have the situation in hand."

Andreas motioned to a servant, who brought a small table and placed the platter of food on it.

"And once Rhodes abolishes its hold on democracy, it will— *you* will—gladly embrace the League?"

Spiro reached for a square of goat cheese. *Trade true power for peace as you would, Father?* Spiro longed to share his entire plan with his father, to watch respect return to his eyes, but he could not take the chance. Perhaps Andreas carried more loyalty to the

League than Spiro imagined and would be displeased with his plan to use the League as a stepping stone to tyranny. Even worse, Andreas might scoff at the very idea of Spiro's ruling the island.

"Of course, Father," he answered. "The League will bring even greater peace and prosperity to Rhodes."

"Hmmm." His father chewed a fig and studied him. Spiro looked away. "So you say you have a plan to strip those who favor democracy of their influence?"

Spiro replaced the cheese on the platter. "The position of Glaucus and the others is not as secure as they would think."

"One should never underestimate a politician," Andreas said. "Or his hetaera, it would seem."

Spiro smiled. "I do not believe one could *overestimate* Tessa of Delos."

"Be careful, Spiro. Men have found a knife in their backs for less."

Spiro leaned back in the chair. The servants finished their tasks and left the room. "She is not as loyal to Glaucus as many believe."

"Yes, I am growing quite certain of that." His father rose and strode to the water pitcher and basin on a side table. He poured the water over his hands and dipped a white cloth into the small pool in the basin. "Still, Spiro. She is not yours. You must be careful."

"I am always careful, Father."

Andreas squeezed water from the cloth and ran it over his face. "Perhaps Glaucus will not live long anyway," he said.

Spiro smiled and looked away.

*There is no 'perhaps,' Father. Glaucus will not live another day.*

# TWENTY-EIGHT

Tessa arrived on Spiro's steps well past sundown, hoping to have missed the evening meal. Simeon had clucked and fussed at her decision to come. She could not make him understand that it was necessary. Hermes would keep her secret only if she helped him bring down Spiro. And she was about to use the only weapon she possessed. She paused on the steps, straightened her chitôn, pinched more color into her cheeks, and assured herself that the flowers woven into her hair remained intact.

From the sounds of the house, the party was well underway. The thin notes of a flute drifted to her, and memory jolted her back to the night of Glaucus's symposium, the night that started it all. She clutched her stomach at the reminder.

*Think only of tonight, Tessa.*

She entered the home without waiting to be announced and glided to the andrôn. One deep breath outside the door. She rounded the doorway and waited, framed there.

Slaves moved through the room, laying out the evening meal on long tables set before the couches. The height of Rhodian power reclined around the room, nearly all the strategoi by her quick count.

The girl with the flute saw her first. Their eyes connected, and Tessa realized why the music had so reminded her of Glaucus. It was the same girl who had played that night.

Tessa looked at Spiro, engaged in conversation with his father beside him.

*Still trying to prove you're as great as Glaucus, Spiro?*

As if in answer, Spiro's head lifted. He focused on her, outlined there in the doorway. A warm smile crept across his lips. Andreas followed his son's gaze, and Tessa met his look with a smile of her own.

Aside from the flute player, Tessa was the only woman in the room. Spiro had made certain of it, she knew.

"Tessa," Spiro pulled himself up from his couch. "Come in." His gaze swept the room, taking time to catch every eye. "Tessa honors us by taking time away from Glaucus to meet with us tonight." He motioned Tessa toward him. "And Glaucus, he is improving, I hope?"

Tessa stepped past a table piled with roast pheasant and cooked apples. She slid to the space on the couch that Spiro had indicated, opposite of his father.

"Yes," she said. "Much improved."

"Wonderful. We look forward to hearing him tomorrow at the Assembly meeting."

Spiro waved a hand to his guests. "Eat everyone, eat. Tessa is here."

The guests plunged in, giving Tessa a moment to survey the group again. Seven of the nine remaining strategoi were here, with only Glaucus and Hermes missing. Several other men of influence or money had joined them.

Her task tonight would be no less delicate than earlier in the day. She had to win Spiro's trust and pry his secrets from him, but she must be careful. If she went too far, he might accuse her of disloyalty to Glaucus and create more of a problem for her.

Spiro reached for a hunk of pheasant on the table, shifting so that his shoulder grazed against her. A subtle message, but clear nonetheless.

*Nikos, where are you?*

Spiro offered her a bite of pheasant from his fingers, but she shook her head, smiling. He shrugged, shoved the piece into his mouth, and licked his fingers, looking at her.

At his right Andreas leaned forward. "Spiro, do you plan to keep the most interesting guest here all to yourself?"

Spiro's smile faded and he turned to his father. "Perhaps Tessa does not want to be the center of attention."

"Nonsense! What woman doesn't?" Andreas slid to his right, opening a narrow space between himself and his son. "Sit here, Tessa, so I can get to know you."

Spiro scowled but bent his head and shifted to his left to allow more room between them.

Feeling like a meaty bone between two dogs, Tessa squeezed into the space, then repositioned herself to recline with her head toward the table. The position was awkward, as she would have had to place her back to one or the other of them, and it seemed that neither was willing to give up her company.

"There," Andreas whispered in her ear. "Now you will not be at the mercy of my son."

Tessa leaned her head away from Andreas to look into his eyes.

*You are very different than he.*

Spiro nudged her again. "Eat, Tessa. The food will grow cold."

Her stomach rebelled at the thought. "I am not hungry tonight, Spiro." She saw his disappointment. "I am sorry. Some of your fine wine, perhaps?"

He smiled. "Brought in this morning, from Lesbos." He reached for a cup and ladled it full from the bowl before them.

The girl in the corner began another sorrowful song on her flute, but Spiro called to her. "Something lively, girl! This is an evening to enjoy!" The music picked up, and Spiro turned to Tessa. "There will be more entertainment later. I have something special arranged for you."

*Wonderful.*

She smiled. "You are an impressive host, Spiro. I had forgotten how lavishly you entertain."

"That is high praise from you, accustomed as you are to Glaucus's symposia."

Ah, here it was. The dance would begin.

"Hmmm," she sighed. "Glaucus does like to spend his money." She leaned closer to Spiro, revulsion coiling through her. "But he lacks a certain . . . sophistication, one might say."

Spiro turned his face away slightly, his smile revealing that she'd hit the mark.

"You know, Spiro, Glaucus has never spoken well of you."

The smile disappeared and Spiro glared at his cup.

She shrugged. "But I have never understood his opinion. And being here tonight," she waved her fingertips at the room, "shows that you have the respect of those who matter."

His chest puffed out again, and Tessa was amazed at her ability to pull the strings that would make him dance.

"This illness of Glaucus's has given you the freedom to form opinions apart from his," Spiro said. He sipped his wine, and Tessa lifted her own cup to her lips. "For that, I am almost glad that Glaucus has been stricken."

Tessa lowered her cup and looked up at Spiro through her lashes. "Of course, I could never say such a thing." She paused. "Even if I agreed with you."

He smiled and reached for a large mushroom.

Tessa leaned away from Andreas, hoping his attention was elsewhere.

"Spiro, do you ever feel that perhaps you were meant to be more than simply a strategos?" She tilted her head at his father. "You come from power. Don't you . . . ever want more of it?"

He inhaled deeply. "Joining Rhodes to the Achaean League will—"

Tessa lowered her voice to a whisper. "I'm not talking about the League."

"Radical change will need to take place before true leadership can emerge."

"You don't seem to be a man intimidated by radical change."

Spiro looked down into her eyes, a question there.

Laughter erupted from the other side of the room. A skinny man, wearing only a cloth at his waist, cartwheeled into the room and leaped up at its center.

Spiro clapped. "Ah, my surprise has arrived. Men, I give you Jason, the finest juggler in the Aegean!"

The audience clapped its appreciation, and Jason pulled three oysters from the tables of food and tossed them into the air. The flutist piped a lilting tune that soon had the guests clapping in time.

Spiro's attention was now on his guests and entertainment. Tessa sipped her wine. She would wait for her next opportunity; it could not be rushed.

"What are you doing?" Andreas's voice was low in her ear.

She turned to him. "The juggler is quite good—"

"And I am not a fool."

Tessa kept her eyes on the entertainment. "I do not know—"

"Spiro's lust blinds him. But I hear what lies below your words." He touched her arm. "Even from here I can feel the tension in your body when you speak to him."

Tessa sipped at her wine with a furtive glance at Spiro, but he laughed and clapped along with the rest.

Andreas' voice was still a mere whisper in her ear. "I think you mistrust my son almost as much as I do."

Tessa's heart slowed a bit.

"Do you think my son would make a capable ruler?"

The question seemed sincere. She looked to Andreas, saw the frankness in his eyes. She gave a subtle shake of the head.

"And why not?"

Tessa shifted her body to face Andreas, placing more of her back toward Spiro. She lowered her head to his. "There is a certain strength of character needed. An integrity. A love for people and a concern for their welfare." She placed her lips near Andreas's ear. "I believe Spiro has none of this. His only concerns are his own pleasure and power." She pulled away, hoping she had not been too honest.

But Andreas studied his cup and simply nodded. Then he smiled at her. "I have another son, you know?" Though his voice was still low, his attention was fully on her.

"No. I did not know. Does he serve with you on Kalymnos?"

"One day he will."

She smiled. "Then I am glad you have fathered a man like yourself."

Andreas regarded her in silence, until she grew uncomfortable and dropped her eyes. Her cheeks felt hot. *Too much wine.*

The juggler had moved on from oysters to apples while she and Andreas talked, and now, to the delight of the crowd, he had picked up three small terra-cotta amphorae and spun them in circles around his head. The flute played faster, the crowd clapped in time, and the juggler's hands blurred through the air.

It could not last forever, though. One hand came up too slowly, and the lip of one amphora caught his thumb. It tumbled from its orbit and hit the floor with a crack. Pieces of pottery shot in all directions. The flutist screamed.

Jason caught the other two amphorae. He stepped away from the shattered pottery.

Spiro jumped to his feet and called for a slave to clean up the mess. He laughed brightly. "Such fun, eh, men? Shall we smash a few more?" He lifted a jug above his head, and the crowd laughed.

Tessa noticed the girl in the corner, still whimpering and covering her face with her hand. Had the accident scared her that badly?

Then Tessa saw the blood.

She pulled herself from the couch and tumbled across the room to the girl.

Blood ran from her palm-covered cheek, down through her fingers, soaking the flimsy fabric at her shoulder.

"Come," Tessa said. "Lie down over here." She pulled the girl to the nearest couch and glared at the man lying there until he lifted himself out of her way. The girl fell to the couch, and Tessa bent to her and touched her face.

"What is your name, child?"

"Amara."

"You will be fine, Amara. Let's look at it." She peeled the bloody fingers away from the girl's cheek. The cut bled profusely but did not appear life-threatening.

"Get some clean cloths," she called. "And some fresh water."

Spiro summoned a slave in the doorway.

Andreas stood beside Tessa. "Shall we call a physician?"

Tessa looked up at him from where she knelt at the girl's side. That he would call a physician for a slave girl's injury told her more about the man's character than anything he might have said.

"I do not think that is necessary," Tessa said with a smile. She turned back to the girl. Her gauzy chitôn had fallen away, and Tessa carefully covered her. A slave returned with cloths and water.

"You remind me of my son," Andreas said. "Always trying to fix things."

Tessa saw the look that passed between Andreas and Spiro and knew that Andreas did not speak of the son who was present. She applied pressure to the girl's cheek to staunch the flow. "Have you family?" she asked.

The girl gazed up at her, then shook her head. "I am alone," she whispered.

Tessa studied her eyes, saw that the simple words held more than statement of fact but opened a window to her very heart—to a place that Tessa understood, a truth she feared more than slavery, more than anything. She brushed away a strand of hair that had fallen across Amara's eyes, then leaned in to speak in the girl's ear, words that no one else could hear.

"You are not alone."

It took Tessa only a few minutes to clean the cut and apply the poultice brought by a slave boy and send Amara home.

In the meantime, Spiro had worked to restore the gaiety of the party. Another musician had already been found, the shattered pottery swept away, and Spiro laughingly gave the juggler three small sacks of wheat to begin again. The crowd settled back into their couches, and Spiro disappeared to arrange for the next course. Tessa reclined again beside Andreas, glad for the temporary respite from Spiro.

One of the strategoi, Vasilios, called above the music of the lyre, "Fortunate for the girl that a woman was in attendance this evening."

Tessa raised her cup in acknowledgment. "Women are useful in so many ways, are we not?" The room laughed.

Andreas resumed his attention on her. "Why do you do that?" he asked.

"Speak when I am spoken to? Would you rather I be silent?"

*Definitely too much wine.*

"That is not what I meant. Why do you answer them as if you are nothing more than a plaything for men?"

Tessa swirled the wine in her cup. *I am supposed to ask the questions tonight, Andreas.* He was nothing like what she might have expected from the father of Spiro. Something about him begged her trust, against all her innate tendencies.

Like Nikos.

Vasilios spoke to her again from across the room. "Tessa, it would seem that Rhodes barely misses the presence of Glaucus when you take his place."

She smiled and wished the attention of the room would shift elsewhere.

Demetrius responded, "Perhaps Tessa should be a strategos. Leave Glaucus to his other pursuits." Everyone laughed, but the humor had taken on a serious undercurrent.

"As Tessa says," Vasilios answered, "women are good for many things. Politics, however, is not one of them."

More wary laughter. Tessa studied the floor.

"Still, Glaucus has not proven much better than a woman of late. Perhaps the stress of leadership is simply too much for him."

The mood of the group was growing more negative. Tessa groped for a response that would not sound desperate.

"Perhaps," Demetrius said, "the representation of our island at the naval talks on Crete would be better served by someone other than Glaucus."

Tessa raised her head. "Glaucus has served well for many years. Do not begin to doubt his leadership after such a brief illness!"

There was a pause, then Vasilios spoke loudly. "I think Spiro should be sent to Crete." All eyes turned to him. "Allow Glaucus more time to recover. Then we can be certain we are well represented." He shrugged. "If Glaucus were to have a relapse or—may the gods forbid—cross to the afterlife while in Crete, our island's welfare would not be championed at the talks."

Tessa swallowed. "Glaucus is fully able to speak for Rhodes in Crete!"

"But Spiro—"

She slammed her cup to the table in front of her. "Not even Spiro's father trusts Spiro! Why should we?"

Her accusation rang through the room, stopped the fingers of the lyre player, and seemed to bounce from the walls and repeat.

All the way to the door, where Spiro stood holding another large jug of wine.

# TWENTY-NINE

The day had been long and tedious. Nikos had been given countless menial tasks around the household. Tessa refused to see him. And he had gained nothing of the information his father sought. Tonight Nikos slunk along a back alley, hoping to have something for his father before the day ended.

He watched his feet, skirted garbage that had been mauled by dogs, and stepped over the gutter channel that ran waste water through the city. Even in the finest sections of town.

He had to stop twice to ask for help finding Spiro's home. He hoped the boy and the servant girl would not remember his face. Now standing in the street below, it seemed to Nikos that Spiro's home glowed. The andrôn must be filled with oil lamps. He could hear laughter and music.

Tessa. Spiro. Andreas. All of them reclined in that room while he stood in the street. Longing filled him. Was it wrong, this desire to be loved by his father? To love her?

Spiro's home was built into a hillside and had no alley running behind it from which he could approach. There were, however, darkened areas on either side of the house where one could possibly slip in unnoticed. He avoided the steps and climbed the hill to the left.

He had no plan, really. Only to get inside the house and learn whatever he could. The bare dirt beside the house had been well-traveled by slaves, he could see. Garbage reeked where it was piled against the house. Each stinking pile crawled with rats that poked their long noses in search of treasure.

A shadow moved near a doorway. Nikos pulled back against the house. A man emerged, stuffing something into a large sack. He tied the sack shut as he walked. He walked past Nikos without looking up.

The man was huge. And bald.

Nikos followed.

Remaining unseen required several dodges into alleys. Once the bald man turned, and Nikos stopped to talk with a servant in the street. They continued their game, until Nikos saw the torches that blazed around the feet of the harbor statue. The bald giant was headed for the docks.

Almost to the water, the bald man approached a cluster of others, maybe three or four, Nikos could not tell. He slowed and drifted toward the barges, glancing in the direction of the men.

*He will not know me. Get closer.*

Nikos shuffled, head down, as though he were dragging himself to work for another tedious night. Slowly he made his way past the small group.

"All of you will be there tomorrow?" the bald man was saying.

There was murmured agreement.

"Here." The sack was exchanged. "Here are the clothes. You know what to do with them after?"

"Adelphos pointed out the house to us. We'll drop them there."

Nikos circled around the group and headed back on the other side.

"They all have to die, you understand?" the bald man said. "Your knives must find their marks, no mistakes. You will not be paid for mistakes."

"We understand. Everyone on the stage. Dead."

He nodded. "And then dispose of the clothes. And then you get paid."

The bald man glanced up at Nikos, then back to the group. "You remember what you must yell as you do it?"

"You've told us, Ajax! Enough! We are ready."

"Good."

Nikos continued past the group. The bald man, however, moved quickly for his size. He was on Nikos in only a few steps and grabbed him by the hair.

"Who are you?" Ajax asked.

Nikos smacked the arm away. "Going to the docks. To work. Let me pass."

"You were listening to us."

"A bunch of men arguing over a sack, that's all I saw."

Ajax turned to the others. "You see?" he said. "Your task is so important, there are spies everywhere."

His arm shot out without warning. The punch landed in Nikos's stomach, doubling him over.

*Not again.*

Nikos fought hard, but Ajax was larger, and his friends landed the occasional kick for good measure.

After a few minutes Nikos lay still, hoping they would leave him for dead.

"Grab his ankles," Ajax ordered. Another pair of hands reached under his arms. Nikos felt himself lifted from the ground.

"Throw him in the water," a voice said.

"No, he'll wash up on shore by morning."

They carried him in jerking steps. Every muscle hurt. A welcome and heavy blackness started to descend.

They tossed him somewhere, Nikos cared not where. He hit the ground with a stabbing pain to his shoulder. From somewhere far off, he thought perhaps the ground swayed beneath him. But then the darkness came.

*I am sorry, Father.*

## Ω

The andrôn remained silent. Tessa watched Spiro's face at the door, waited for his anger to erupt.

*Stupid, Tessa. Such a fool.*

Instead, he inhaled and lifted the jug of wine with a smile. "Refill your cups, men. The supply holds well."

He handed the jug to a slave and crossed the room to resume his seat beside Tessa. The young lyre player plucked a few strings on his instrument, a shaky melody that took several moments to be recognizable.

"Spiro," Tessa began.

He held up a hand. "Your opinion is noted, Tessa. There is no need to speak more of it."

"I have had too much to drink, Spiro. I spoke without thinking."

He swallowed and turned to her. His eyes held the anger she expected, but something else as well. When he spoke, his voice was low. "You wound me, Tessa," he said. "I am accustomed to his disapproval." He jutted his chin toward Andreas. "And soon he will see the error in his judgment. But," he looked away, "I had come to believe . . ."

"Spiro, my first loyalty must be to Glaucus." Tessa lowered her voice. "They try to undermine his authority. I cannot allow those statements to go unchallenged. What if Glaucus were to hear that I sat quietly as he was openly criticized? He allows me to be here to speak on his behalf, and that is what I must do."

*I sound like a senseless, rambling child.*

"Please, Spiro," she touched his arm with her fingertips, "do not be offended by my words."

Spiro called something to another man across the room, clearly unwilling to continue with her.

She allowed the conversation to flow around her. Both men beside her engaged themselves with others, and at times the talk included the entire room. They spoke of city politics at first, then of financial matters of concern to the island, of trade and local sales. Tempers rose and fell along with the wine cups, and before long most of them were too drunk to speak intelligently.

Tessa searched for a way to return to her intimate exchange with Spiro. Thus far he had revealed nothing about his plans. If she did not learn more, Hermes would be unwilling to keep her secret. Not that she was certain he would keep it anyway, but she had no other choice.

As though he had been reading her thoughts, Hermes suddenly appeared in the doorway.

"Ah, Hermes," Spiro called. "I wondered if you would make it."

Hermes bowed. "I apologize for my late arrival. I had important business to attend."

Tessa nearly laughed. The incessant efforts of every one of them to appear more important than the others were humorous, if not tiresome. She was grateful, at least, that the suggestion that Spiro replace Glaucus on their trip to Crete had been abandoned. Someone had mentioned that they would all feel reassured when Glaucus spoke at the Assembly tomorrow, and the topic had been dropped.

*I will worry about that tomorrow. First, I must find a way to keep Hermes quiet.*

An oil lamp sputtered in the wall niche beside her. Tessa used the excuse to speak to Spiro. She forced herself to touch his forearm on the cushion beside her. "A lamp needs attending," she whispered and nodded her head toward it. A pathetic attempt to reestablish their connection, but she was growing desperate.

Spiro turned to her, searched her face. "You are a mystery to me, Tessa of Delos."

She smiled and let her lashes flutter. "I hope that is a good thing."

He said nothing, only looked at her hand, still on his arm.

On her right, Andreas leaned in. "You are a mystery to me, as well."

Tessa's smile for Andreas was genuine. "I am not so complicated, Andreas."

The evening was growing long, and the wine truly was beginning to take effect. She clearly was losing her ability to speak carefully. She shifted her position on the couch.

From across the room, Hermes frowned at her, as though he knew she had been unsuccessful thus far.

"Spiro, you spoke earlier of radical change," she tried. "Tell me your hopes and dreams for Rhodes."

Spiro had no chance to respond before Hermes called across the room. "How is Glaucus, Tessa? Still unwell?"

She glared at him. "Improving, Hermes. Thank you for inquiring. He sends his regrets that he could not be with you for this fine evening of entertainment."

"Tell him he was sorely missed."

The antagonism in his voice did not go unnoticed by those in the room. Others exchanged looks, no doubt wondering why one of Glaucus's usual allies spoke with such sarcasm.

Vasilios addressed Hermes. "Tomorrow's Assembly meeting will present an opportunity to hear all four of you speak your position about democracy in Rhodes." He nodded to the other two strategoi allied with Hermes.

"We have long tried to explain our position, Vasilios—"

"I think," Spiro said, "perhaps the hour has grown too late, and the wine too scarce, for us to talk further of politics. Besides, Hermes, you have us at a disadvantage, having missed much of the wine."

Hermes laughed. "Yes, it would appear that some of you have grown quite friendly through the long evening," he said, looking at Tessa.

"I think it is time for me to return to Glaucus," she said quietly, rising.

Spiro reached for her wrist and wrapped tight fingers around it. "Hermes is not pleased with you."

"No. Hermes holds little affection for me, I am afraid."

Spiro pulled her downward, into himself. "Glaucus and Hermes, they have you trapped," he said. "You do not belong with any of them."

"My life has never been of my own making, Spiro."

He bent his head to hers, until she felt his breath on her ear. "Do not fear, Tessa. Soon everything will be changed. I will free you from him."

She tensed, held still. "I would not want you to harm Glaucus. And it would not matter anyway," she said. "If you should free me from Glaucus, I would only be given to the next in line to have paid for me."

His silence drew her eyes to his, their faces almost touching. What she saw there filled her with a deeper dread than anything she had ever known.

Triumph.

*It cannot be.*

"Spiro?" His name scratched out from her throat and tumbled past her lips.

"My Tessa," he whispered with a smile. "Servia's price was high, and my wait was long, but soon . . . soon it will be worth all I have paid." He released her wrist, slid his hand into hers, and kissed her fingers. "Soon, Tessa, you will be mine."

Ω

A slow awareness of the sun's warmth on his neck caused Nikos to stir. He lifted his head, groaned, and dropped his head once again to allow himself a moment to orient.

He lay face down on some kind of wood, and something heavy covered most of his body, up to his shoulders. He shifted and several woven sacks slid from his back. Near his head lay a coil of thick rope, stained black from use. The ground bucked beneath his body, and he recognized the sway at once.

A boat.

Head throbbing, Nikos pushed to his hands and knees. Above him, three sea-crows swooped, their angry calls indicating a disagreement over food. He followed their flight and saw over the edge of the boat that he was in port.

*Thank the gods it did not sail with me aboard.*

The boat was a fishing vessel, not very large. A fisherman trudged up the plank onto the boat, nets in hand, and drew up in surprise when he saw Nikos.

"Where did you come from?"

Nikos shook his head and staggered to his feet. "I am not certain. I was attacked—"

"Did you just come aboard?"

"No. Sometime in the night."

The fisherman tossed the roped nets at Nikos's feet. "Last night we put in at Rhodes."

"Yes, Rhodes."

*No. It can't be.*

Nikos looked away from the fisherman, out to the harbor. *No!* Houses lined the harbor, pushed into a rocky hillside. Houses he had never seen before.

"This is not Rhodes."

He looked back to the fisherman, whose amused grin did little to comfort him.

"Halki, friend."

Nikos pushed up to the fisherman and grabbed his tunic. "I must get back to Rhodes!"

The man pulled Nikos's hand from his clothing, his amusement turning to annoyance. "You should be more careful about the boats you board, then."

"I told you, I was attacked—" Nikos broke off in frustration. There was no reason to argue with the man. "Are you going back to Rhodes?"

"Fishing is better here. We go to Rhodes to unload. Won't be going back until we have a full cargo."

Nikos growled and pushed the man aside. He ran down the narrow plank and out onto the dock. Sailors, merchants, and fishermen crowded the port. The early morning sun warmed the stones already and glistened on the white-washed houses. A holiday spirit seemed to pervade the harbor, and Nikos grew more frantic with every moment.

The murderous plans he had heard last night had to have been about the Assembly meeting today. Spiro had used the bald giant to contract the murder of everyone on the amphitheater's stage during the meeting.

*Tessa?*

He was unsure how early the meeting would begin, but there was no doubt that he needed to start back now. It would take at least a few hours to return to Rhodes.

Nikos cursed his stupidity, the weakness that stranded him hours from Tessa when she needed him most.

And his father. Andreas would be at the Assembly meeting as well, perhaps on the stage, if he were considered an honored guest on the island.

Nikos ran to the nearest boat and up the plank.

"Hold!" A sailor, perhaps the captain, held up a hand, his face stern. "Who are you?"

"I am looking for passage to Rhodes." He felt for the pouch he kept strapped under his tunic. "I can pay."

The sailor frowned. "You look like an escaped slave to me."

Nikos waved an impatient hand. "I assure you, I am not. Are you going to Rhodes?"

"To Kos."

Nikos groaned and ran back down to the dock. He inquired at the next boat and found it would leave for Rhodes that evening. Too late.

His options were fast dwindling, and he had not found anyone leaving for Rhodes within the hour. There were trading vessels, larger ships waiting at sea while barges carried their wares out to them, but any of these still being loaded would be hours before shoving off.

"You there!" someone called from the deck of a fishing boat. "You looking for work? We are in need of extra hands."

Nikos shook his head. "I am looking for passage to Rhodes."

"Rhodes, you say?"

Nikos nodded and shielded his eyes from the sun.

The sailor stood on the edge of the deck, a silhouette. "We leave for Rhodes as soon as we get this leak repaired. Trade your hands for passage?"

Nikos jogged up the loading plank and leaped over the edge. "Show me what to do," he said.

The sailor laughed. "In a hurry, are we?" He eyed Nikos's clothing. "Who are you trying to get away from?"

"Back to. Trying to get back to someone."

"Ah," the sailor laughed again, "a woman."

*Yes.*

Nikos accepted a fistful of iron nails from the sailor's rough hand. He glanced at the sun, only just risen above the horizon, and wondered how long it would take to sail back to Rhodes. To sail back to the Assembly meeting.

Yes, to sail back to a woman.

## Ω

Tessa stood in the hall outside the women's quarters of Glaucus's home and listened. She had put off this task, wrestling with her growing attachment to Persephone and the demands Hermes had made of her.

The spinning of the loom, accompanied by Daphne's off-key tune, formed a continuous hum from behind the curtain hung in the doorway. Tessa took a deep breath and pushed the curtain aside.

Daphne's fingers paused in mid-air, though the loom continued to spin, abandoned, for several moments.

"My rooms," Daphne said, standing. "My rooms!"

"I am sorry to intrude," Tessa said.

Daphne's nostrils flared with each labored breath, as though Tessa's presence had somehow cut off the room's air.

"I need to speak with you." Tessa bit her lip. "A message from Glaucus."

Daphne plopped back onto her seat and ran fluttery fingers over the flax stretched tight across her loom. "My husband now sends you to speak even to his wife."

It was not a question, but Tessa wished to give the woman an answer that would comfort. "He is concerned for your health," she said. "He does not wish to expose you to his illness."

Daphne raised her face to Tessa, but her eyelids seemed weighted with distrust. "Yet he is so willing to sacrifice his prize?"

Tessa waved away the question. "I am of no consequence. In fact, Glaucus's message concerns your family, always his chief interest."

Daphne snorted. "And what does Glaucus wish you to tell me?"

Now that the moment had come, Tessa's heart dropped to her feet. *I am sorry, Persephone.* "Glaucus tells me that Persephone has been betrothed to Hermes these many years."

Daphne smiled into her flax. "Ah, so you do not know everything. But no, you were not there when I bore Glaucus a child, were you? Nor when she was betrothed."

Tessa closed her eyes. "No," she said. "No, I have only just learned, from Glaucus, about the betrothal. And Glaucus has decided that Persephone is past the age of marrying and should be given to Hermes immediately."

Daphne's glance shot upward. "No!"

Tessa swallowed. "Glaucus insists that the ceremony begin tomorrow, so that the two days of *proaulia* and *gamos* can take place before he sails for Crete."

"Before you both sail for Crete."

Tessa nodded, a short jerk of her head that she wished were not necessary. "Yes. The proaulia must begin tomorrow."

Daphne stood again and walked to the small window over-looking the street and, beyond, the sea.

"I had no son."

Tessa waited, but there was nothing more. "I am sorry," she finally said.

"Only a daughter. One daughter. He has never forgiven me."

"Men forget that these things are beyond our control," Tessa said to Daphne's back.

The woman's shoulders slumped. "We are trusted for nothing but bearing children. But if we do not produce them adequately, we are blamed as if we controlled the world's destiny."

"It is unfair."

Daphne laughed without turning. "I hate you. Do you know that?"

Tessa tried to still the quiver in her chest. "Yes. I know."

"You have taken my husband from me. And now you come to take away the only thing that remains—my daughter."

It was unbearable, what Hermes had forced her to do. And yet the words poured from her as though she spoke them gladly. "It is a good match. Hermes is a rich man and a powerful one."

"Hermes is a monster."

*Yes, he is. May the gods forgive me.*

"She will be well-provided for. It is a favorable marriage."

Daphne turned then, turned on Tessa with all the hatred of the years in her eyes. "There is no such thing as a favorable marriage. Not for a woman. But why should Persephone expect anything better than her mother or the mothers that came before?"

Tessa's breath came in short gasps now, and she wished nothing more than to be finished with this awful task. "So you will make the arrangements for the proaulia to begin tomorrow? I will tell Simeon to prepare for the feast and to send word through the city."

Daphne turned back to the window, wordless.

"Be on your way, Tessa. You have Glaucus. And now I have nothing at all."

Tessa backed from the room, until her shoulders brushed the doorway curtain. She turned, swept it aside . . .

And faced Persephone.

The girl had been in the hall, listening.

Tessa could not move, could not even speak the girl's name.

Persephone's cheeks were wet with tears, but her eyes had already grown cold and dry. She breathed heavily, her chest rising and falling in rhythm.

"Tessa," she said. "Tessa."

Only that one word, yet filled with betrayal.

*I have only one daughter.* Daphne's voice in her head.

*Mother, don't leave me. Don't leave.* Her own voice, years and years ago.

She reached for the girl, but Persephone shoved her away. Her voice was low, and her eyes like cold blue stones. "You have freed me from one man," she said, "only to deliver me to another." Her eyes moved to the curtain that kept Daphne from the world. "You destroy everything you touch, Tessa of Delos."

Tessa covered her mouth, stifling the cry that can only come from a breaking heart, and ran for the stairs.

# Part III

*An earthquake achieves what the law promises
but does not in practice maintain—
the equality of all men.*

Ignazio Silon

# THIRTY

### ✦ *One Day before the Great Quake* ✦

Nothing brought out the people of Rhodes like an Assembly meeting. Families flooded into the amphitheater, carrying food for their midday meal. Spiro watched from the hillside above the theater, anticipating the show he had arranged for them.

It would take some time yet for the entire Assembly to be present and for those scheduled to speak first to be seated on the stage. Spiro crossed his arms and dug his heels deeper into the soft dirt of the hillside. He studied the sky and sniffed the air. Rain threatened.

Hermes had arrived and stood at the back of the theater, slapping shoulders and smiling at the men who filed in. Demetrius and Vasilios were there; these two supported Spiro, though they had no idea what he had planned for today.

Glaucus had not yet arrived, though he would not dare to miss it, Spiro thought. Last night's symposium had made it clear that if Glaucus hoped to retain his position, he needed to make a showing here today. Tessa would have conveyed this necessity to him, Spiro was certain.

Tessa. Would she come on Glaucus's arm—for the last time?

This day had been inevitable, evolving and taking shape since the night Xenophon had been conveniently murdered. Spiro had quickly recognized the opportunity to swing the council in support of the League, if certain opponents were eliminated. It had been a simple thing to create the impression that the Jews were unhappy with the island's leadership, and despite unexpected interference, there remained a general malaise toward the Jews. Now in a matter of minutes a group of Jews would storm the amphitheater's stage and, screaming their defiance, murder the last four roadblocks to his eventual monarchy.

The hillside theater provided seating for nearly ten thousand people, and from the crowd already formed, Spiro suspected that all the seats would be needed. Xenophon's murder and the Jewish riot had left people concerned for their safety and the peace of Rhodes.

The row of seats nearest the stage would be reserved for priests and other officials. The performance space was a simple half-circular space, the orchestra, where stone benches had been placed. Here Hermes, Glaucus, and the other two holdouts for democracy would sit, and here they would meet their fate.

*It will all be over soon.*

A voice at his shoulder startled Spiro.

"Shouldn't you be taking your seat?"

Spiro turned to face his father. "I did not expect you so early."

"I did not want to miss any of the speeches."

"Those who oppose our joining the League will speak first."

"And are you prepared to speak eloquently in the League's favor?"

*This meeting will end before that becomes necessary.*

"Of course, Father."

Andreas grunted his doubt. "I do not see Glaucus."

"He has not arrived."

Andreas raised his eyebrows. "I think I will wander down there and make certain that our position is well received."

Spiro extended a hand toward the stage in invitation. He watched Andreas descend and felt a sudden desire that his father would join those about to die.

"All is arranged," Ajax said from behind.

Spiro turned and led him farther up the hill, away from the theater and prying eyes. "I thought I told you we were not to be seen together in public. You are certain those you hired understand their role?"

"There will be no mistakes. Oh, and I took care of a curious servant who may have heard too much."

Spiro hissed, "What servant?"

Ajax shrugged. "Only a young Greek, hanging about the docks and listening where he didn't belong. But he won't be talking to anyone."

"Describe him."

Spiro frowned as Ajax described the build and appearance of the man he was certain was the problematic Nikos, servant to Glaucus.

"What did you do with him?"

Ajax sneered. "Beat him well and threw him unconscious on a fishing boat about to sail."

Spiro sighed and patted Ajax's arm. He would have preferred to see Nikos dead. But after the Jews had turned him into a hero, Spiro knew it would not be wise to make a martyr of him. Only now the servant had become a bothersome insect, buzzing around Spiro's head. But Ajax could not have known whom he dealt with.

"Perhaps an angry Poseidon will toss his boat into the sea."
He slapped Ajax's shoulder. "Stay back here, should I need you for
anything. It is time I take my place."

He left the slave under a tree high above the hillside theater and
descended to the horizontal *diazoma* that cut across the topmost
tier of seats. Pausing there, he squinted at where the strategoi were
to be seated.

*I still do not see Glaucus.*

He took the steps quickly, passing the upturned faces of Assembly
members and other spectators without meeting their eyes. He found
a seat in the first row and nodded to Demetrius and Vasilios.

The epistates of the council crossed the circle and approached
the three of them. "Glaucus has not yet arrived," he said, "but I do
not wish to wait any longer. Therefore I have decided to make a
change. We will hear from you first as to why Rhodes should join
the Achaean League, while we wait for Glaucus to arrive. When the
three of you are finished, Glaucus and the others will speak."

Spiro felt his jaw go slack and scrambled for a reply.

*We cannot speak first. Those first on the platform will be
assassinated.*

He rose to his feet, calling up all the indignation he could muster. "For days we have been assured that Glaucus is fully capable
of maintaining his leadership of Rhodes," he said. "We have seen
no proof of this, but still the council supports his leadership, insists
that he represent our island in Crete. And now he insults the entire
Assembly with this delay, and *you* accommodate him!"

Spiro eyed Demetrius and Vasilios beside him, and they
jumped to their feet. The epistates exhaled, not wanting to deal
with conflict on either side.

A figure in white glided toward them from the far side of the
orchestra where the *skene* provided storage and changing areas for
performers.

Tessa.

The epistates turned on her without the courtesy of a greeting. "Where is he? It is time to begin."

Tessa's white chitôn gleamed like a summer cloud on a gray day. She smiled and dipped her head toward Spiro and the others. "Glaucus is much improved but felt that he should save his strength and prepare for the coming journey to Crete. He is confident that Hermes and the others can speak adequately to the question of the League."

Spiro spoke loud enough for the entire Assembly to hear. "The council will no longer tolerate Glaucus's presumptuousness."

The epistates agreed. "The people cannot abide his continued absence. They wish to hear his thoughts."

Vasilios spoke beside Spiro. "Have Tessa speak for him."

"No!" Spiro gripped Vasilios's arm to silence him. "Tessa cannot be allowed to speak in the Assembly."

*Not on stage. Not first.*

The epistates shrugged. "She has already spoken to the council. Why not the Assembly?"

Tessa moved closer to the epistates. "There is no need—"

He shook his head. "You will speak for Glaucus. Or should the people assume that Glaucus cares more for his own comfort than for the welfare of Rhodes?"

"No. I will speak." She bowed.

Spiro growled, "I have a moment's business to attend. I will return." He stared down the epistates. "Wait for me."

He turned and sprinted up the steps, then up the hill, to the olive tree where Ajax waited, reclining on the grass.

"Ajax!"

The slave bolted upright, then stood. "What is it?"

"Tessa will be on the stage. You must get word to those you hired. She must not be harmed."

Ajax scanned the crowded amphitheater. He shook his head, then stared at Spiro. "I cannot! They have hidden themselves among the crowd and will not emerge until the first speaker begins. I do not know where they are, nor would I even recognize them dressed as Jews."

Spiro huffed his frustration and pressed a hand to his forehead.

"Perhaps," Ajax said, "Glaucus will protect her—"

"Glaucus is not here! He prepares for Crete . . ." Spiro pounded a fist into his palm; he could not allow Tessa and Glaucus to sail. He turned to Ajax. "Go!" he said. "Go to Glaucus's house. He must die this morning with the others. Kill him in his bed, then get out."

"How will I—"

"I do not care! Just do it!"

Ajax nodded. "I will return when it is done."

Spiro watched the slave flee toward the city for a moment, then began his own quick descent.

*So it comes to me to save Tessa's life.* It was fitting somehow. He wondered briefly what form her gratitude might take.

Ω

Tessa took her seat in the front row, listening numbly to the epistates rant about Spiro's arrogance. To her far left Hermes, Philo, and Bemus waited as well. She had been told that the four of them would present their position first. She did not know in what order they would speak. If one of the others were to go first, perhaps she could sound knowledgeable by repeating their words using different rhetoric and convincing passion. If she were called upon first, however, she had no idea what she would say, and her mind seemed unable to recall any details from past symposia or conversations.

*What is happening to me?*

Since Spiro's announcement last night that he waited next in line for her services, she had been unable to think clearly. She had stumbled back to Glaucus's home, the abundance of wine she had drunk slowing her steps and Spiro's terrifying smile haunting her thoughts.

Only a few hours remained of this drama, and yet they stretched before her like a vast desert, and she feared she would not survive the crossing of it.

Hermes moved from his seat and came to sit beside her.

"I did not expect to arrive at this meeting with no information with which to bury Spiro," he whispered, his tone threatening.

She recalled Spiro's promises of the night before. "He is planning something," she said, her eyes forward. "Something to get rid of Glaucus and the rest of you. But I have not yet learned what it is." She turned to Hermes, pleading. "Give me more time."

"Hah! More time! Until you and Glaucus supposedly sail for Crete?" He frowned. "And how do you plan—"

She swallowed. "I will find a way to make people believe he is on the ship. And I will leave with him."

"And never return to Rhodes, I assume."

She nodded, knowing she sealed her fate.

"So you will be across the sea, where I have no use for you."

"Please, Hermes," she clutched his hand, "do not reveal my secret."

He snorted. "My allegiance is foremost to Rhodes," he said. "And this continued deception does not serve her well."

The sky deepened its shade of gray, and the clouds over the theater looked low enough to touch. Tessa prayed that the heavy clouds would release and send them all home. She feared it was her only chance.

Hermes pulled his hand from her grip. "I will say nothing as yet, for I do not want to damage our position here this morning."

Tessa nodded her gratitude. "But you will not sail to Crete, Tessa. I will make certain of that."

Spiro strolled back down the steps, then nodded to the epistates as if the entire proceeding were under his authority. The epistates scowled, then signaled the four of them to take their places. Spiro did not resume his seat. He crossed to the row behind her, slipped down through the seats until he was at her back. She stood to move to the orchestra, but he grabbed her wrist from behind and held her back.

"Do not go up there," he whispered in her ear.

She half-turned, but he used his other hand to turn her face to the front. "Say nothing, but remain in your seat here."

"What is happening?"

"You were not supposed to be up there."

"The epistates insisted—"

"It was not the plan!"

Tessa tried again to turn to him, but he leaned forward, bracing her shoulders with his own. Tessa felt her face flush with embarrassment at the closeness of his body. Certainly, all on either side of them were observing the scene with curiosity.

"Step to the *parados* with me, Spiro. We can speak there."

On either side of the orchestra, a passage provided access for the performers, blocked from the spectators' view. He released her and together they moved to the passage on the right. Hermes, Philo, and Bemus took their places in the orchestra.

*At least I will not be called upon first.*

What little light came from the overcast sky barely seeped into the parados. Tessa turned in the semi-darkness and found Spiro close enough to touch.

"What is happening, Spiro?" She fought to keep anger from her voice, knowing this man was better managed with a softer attitude.

Spiro reached for both her hands. "It will not be much longer, Tessa. But I cannot let you join them. Wait a few moments, and all will be clear."

*He is going to kill them.*

"What have you done?"

He shook his head, then laid a gentle finger on her lips. "We will soon rule this island together, Tessa. You will be the most powerful woman—"

"*All* of them?" Tessa said, her voice rasping in the stone corridor. "You are going to kill all of them?"

He nodded. "And do not concern yourself with Glaucus. I have taken care of him."

In the amphitheater, the crowd hushed as the epistates stood in the center of the orchestra to make his opening remarks.

"Glaucus?"

"I have sent someone to take care of him this morning. It will all be blamed on the Jews, vengeance for the water disruption." He smiled. "That troublesome Jew in Glaucus's house instigated the plot, did you hear? The evidence was found in his family's home in the Jewish district."

Tessa closed her eyes. Finally, the reason behind the Jewish riot. The plan Spiro had been executing for days. All the information she needed to pass to Hermes to keep him quiet.

She opened her eyes and looked out at Hermes, waiting on the bench for his chance to speak. In a short time, he would announce to the council that Glaucus was dead. And Tessa would belong to Spiro.

*Unless I remain here a few moments more, until Hermes is silenced forever. Then I could run back, find a way to keep Glaucus's death a secret a few hours more, and Persephone would be free of Hermes.*

*But Simeon. Marta and Jacob.*

A crack of thunder threatened in the distance, and the storm grew closer.

In the orchestra the epistates stepped to the side.

Hermes stood.

Tessa's breaths grew shallow. Her heart pounded to match the thunder.

"Let it happen, Tessa," Spiro whispered in her ear.

*Let it happen, Tessa.*

*Trade Hermes' life for my own.*

A simple choice.

# THIRTY-ONE

From inside the parados, Tessa could see that the wind had picked up. Hermes's himation whipped around his legs, and he pulled at it as he walked to the center of the orchestra.

The moisture in the air condensed on Tessa's neck, matching the cold sweat that had broken over her body. Spiro still held her, looking into her eyes as though awaiting her decision.

But the freedom to choose was an illusion, just as all freedom was. She had never been free. Never would be. She knew that now, as certainly as she knew she could not stand in the parados while three of the city's finest leaders were murdered in front of the Assembly. She moved to the side slightly and hoped her voice would carry over the howl of the coming storm.

She filled her lungs, opened her mouth to scream, but Spiro's hand clapped over her lips, cutting her warning short. His eyes sliced into hers. She struggled and he twisted his body, now behind her. One arm wrapped around her waist, one hand still covering her mouth, he yanked her backward, deeper into the parados.

The darkness deepened. She dragged in desperate breaths through her nose, and the mustiness of the stone walls assailed her. A wooden door was set crookedly in the stone wall, and Spiro let go of her waist long enough to yank it open and shove her through. They were outside the amphitheater now, though Tessa believed she might still scream loud enough to be heard.

And then the clouds opened.

Rain fell in ragged sheets—a cutting rain that left the crowd pulling their himations over their heads in protection. But they would not leave; such storms passed quickly in Rhodes. Yet there would be a delay, as Hermes and the others would certainly disappear into the proskenion to wait out the storm.

Spiro pulled her up the hillside, heedless of the muddy rivulets that stained her feet and clothing, until they stood under a tree that offered slight protection. He released her and spun her toward him. His face contorted in anger.

"I have offered you everything! And still you resist!"

The rain pelted her face, but she raised unblinking eyes to his. Her voice hardened within her, as did her heart. The words choked from her. "I—do not—wish—to be—owned!"

He pulled her close, his eyes black. "But that is what you are for!"

Through the rain Tessa saw that they were not alone. A giant of a man, the rain washing over his bald head, could be seen running toward them. Spiro was aware of his presence but did not let her go.

"He is dead!" the slave called as he slowed to catch his breath.

"Good." Spiro said to Tessa, "You no longer belong to Glaucus—"

"No." The slave drew close. "He was already dead."

"His illness—"

The slave shook his head. "Glaucus has been dead this long week. His body is gone, disposed of by her," he pointed to Tessa, "and the young Greek of last night."

Spiro turned on Tessa, his face lighting with a sick amusement. "Ah, Tessa. We are more alike than I even knew. You are truly a woman fit for the gods. What a secret to have kept! And you were almost successful."

It was over then.

Spiro knew her secret. She would not sail for Crete.

The rain lessened. Soon Hermes and the others would resume their places on that stage and face their deaths.

Deep inside, a coldness stole over Tessa.

Five days ago a tiny flame of hope had been lit. Then Nikos had fanned it until it burned more hotly than she would have believed still possible. But Nikos could not save her. And she could not save herself. It had been for nothing, all of it.

Two more figures now moved through the rain toward them. From the amphitheater, Andreas strode toward them, scowling his displeasure at something. And to the right came another man, running.

Nikos.

Tessa closed her eyes, fighting an insane urge to laugh, to throw back her head and laugh into the rain.

Nikos and Andreas arrived together.

Andreas strode up to Spiro. "What is the meaning of this?"

Nikos stepped in. "Spiro plans to kill the strategoi at the Assembly meeting." He pointed to the bald giant. "I witnessed this slave hiring thugs at the docks for this purpose."

The slave took one long step toward Nikos and effortlessly wrapped a meaty arm around his neck.

Andreas turned on Spiro. "Is this true?"

"Father, this does not concern you. I have told you that I have the situation in hand."

"In hand? You call murder having the situation 'in hand'?"

To Tessa, the moment seemed suspended, with the rain unable to wash the evil from them. The bald slave, choking the life from Nikos. Spiro, his rampant insecurity in the presence of his father written across his face as clearly as if it had been inked there. Andreas, full of contempt for his first-born son.

She reached a hand across the space that separated her from Nikos, but the chasm was too great. She let her hand drop, and the fingers felt colder than hailstones.

The rain stopped then as though cut off by the gods, a council of deities who wished to see this thing to its conclusion.

The epistates's voice carried up the hill.

*Let the chaos begin.*

## Ω

Spiro heard the epistates begin and knew it would not be much longer now. Something desperate hardened within him.

*I must keep everyone here. I am so close.*

He pulled Tessa to him and turned to Ajax.

"Kill the servant."

Ajax tightened his grip around Nikos's neck. Spiro would be glad to be rid of the young hero.

"No!" Andreas charged at Ajax.

"He works against the League, Father—"

His father spun to face him. "You are a fool, Spiro! Everything you undertake is foolish."

Spiro boiled but said nothing. His father's eyes bore into his own.

"Let him go, slave," Andreas said to Ajax.

Ajax hesitated, then released Nikos but did not back away.

"You still surprise me, Father," Spiro said. "You have more sympathy toward a peasant than—"

"Nikos is your brother."

The words hung in the air, heavier than the clouds before they had released their moisture.

Spiro watched his father's eyes, unable to take in his words. He was barely aware that his arms fell away from Tessa.

She backed away from him, her eyes on Nikos. Eyes wide with shock.

"My brother?" Spiro croaked.

Andreas's face was impassive. "I sent him to Rhodes to learn your true ambition. He has proven a trustworthy heir."

Spiro took a step back at the disdain in his father's voice. He stood alone, with the others circled against him.

Even Ajax had obeyed his father's command.

"No," he said. "No. None of you understands!" He clenched his fists, waving them in futility. "I am so close. So close to ruling the island! Father, you must understand—"

"You know nothing of how to handle power, Spiro. You never have." His father pulled Nikos to his side. "Your brother has more of the leader in him after one year in my household than you ever will."

*Both of them. The peasant has won both Father and Tessa.*

A rage so hot it could have burned the grass beneath his feet built inside him. It built and grew and focused itself into a shaft of hatred pointed to one person.

Spiro cared not that the scream that tore from his throat was that of a wounded animal. With all the hatred in his heart, he threw himself at the man who had taken everything from him.

His brother, Nikos.

Ω

The confusion on the hillside was more than Tessa could bear. Andreas's revelation. Spiro's anger.

When Spiro lunged at Nikos, she ran.

Only one thought was embedded in her mind. The only thing left for her, to redeem her actions, perhaps to please the gods.

She had to save the three in the orchestra circle.

Heads turned to her as she ran down the amphitheater's steps, her sandals slapping the wet stone.

*Nikos is Andreas's son.*

There was nothing but deception everywhere. No one to trust.

Hermes stood in the center of the circle. He lifted his voice to begin his address. "Citizens of Rhodes. Honored Council members." His voice carried to the highest row of seats, where bedraggled Rhodians had waited out one storm to witness another.

Tessa's body functioned without thought. She flew down the steps, a shout on her lips.

"Hermes! Take care!"

All eyes turned on her. Hermes stopped in mid-address, his arm still raised. He stared at her, open-mouthed.

"A plot!" she yelled, reaching the circle at last. "Murderers!"

Soldiers appeared in the parados.

From among the crowd four men, Jews apparently, rose up. An unholy scream sounded from all sides of the theater as they ran toward the stage. Each held a knife aloft.

One of them tore past Tessa. Her blood chilled at his cry.

"Yahweh takes revenge!"

Women screamed.

Soldiers poured into the orchestra, swords drawn. Hermes, Philo, and Bemus fled to the back of the circle, under the portico and into the proskenion.

The four seemed heedless of the direction their plot had taken. They ran forward, their screams echoing up into the theater, as though an impromptu drama had replaced the Assembly meeting that all had come to hear.

Tessa's legs turned to water. She dropped to her knees in the mud.

In the circle, the four Jews encountered a dozen trained soldiers.

The fight was quick and bloody.

The false Jews still bled into the mud when the epistates jumped into the circle and demanded explanations. He turned on Tessa. "On your feet, hetaera!"

Tessa tried to push herself up. Mud squished through her fingers. No strength remained in her arms. From behind her, other hands lifted her to her feet.

Andreas now stood behind her. "Tell them," he ordered her. "Tell them all of it."

She stumbled forward to the epistates, turned and faced the citizens of Rhodes. The rain-soaked crowd held its breath, awaiting her words.

"This day," she called out, her voice gaining strength, "this day, a plot to rob you of your finest leadership has nearly been carried out."

She paused, tried to catch her breath.

Andreas placed his hand lightly against her lower back in support. She looked up and saw Nikos flying down the steps, with Spiro and the bald slave close behind.

She raised a hand toward Spiro. "There! There is the man who conspired to murder!"

The Assembly turned to the three men, who did not slow.

"He sought to destroy the opposition to the League," she yelled, "but he only pretends to support the League. Once democracy has been abandoned, he aspires to rule as monarch of Rhodes!"

A murmur rose among the crowd, like the rumble of thunder that had not long passed.

Nikos went to Tessa's side, while Spiro ran to stand in front of them.

"Citizens!" Spiro shouted. "Think of who makes these accusations! What has happened to us, that we allow a woman such as this to direct the affairs of the city?"

The epistates stepped forward. "What say you to her accusations, Spiro?"

Spiro waved his hand in disgust, as though Tessa's words were not worth addressing. "What must I say? This hetaera has no proof for any of her lies."

Tessa pointed to the bald slave. "There are witnesses in the Jewish district who will testify that Spiro's slave spread the rumors of the water failing, and that he paid someone to claim a Jew killed the fountain house guard. And that he sent these men dressed as Jews," she pointed to the bodies in the mud, "to murder the strategoi, falsely claiming the name of Yahweh!"

Spiro threw back his head and laughed, as though he had prepared for this performance. Tessa felt the first fingers of fear as she watched his face.

He lowered his head and addressed the crowd. "Do not let this woman manipulate you. It is what she does best!" He pointed to the slave. "This man is not my slave! Anything he has done has been at the request of his true master—Spiro turned on Nikos—a man who is not who he pretends to be!"

The epistates looked back and forth between the two men. "I do not understand. The slave belongs to Glaucus's servant?"

Andreas stepped forward then, adding to the confusion. "He is not a servant. He is my son. I sent him here to gain information about the corrupt politics that seem to form the basis of everything Rhodian."

The Assembly bristled as one at this accusation. Tessa's head swam, and the faces blurred in front of her.

The epistates addressed the bald slave. "What is your name?"

"Ajax."

"And who is your master?"

Ajax slowly turned to Nikos and lifted his arm, pointing. "I serve at the bidding of this man."

The crowd's murmur rose again, and Spiro smiled slightly at the bald slave.

"It is a lie!" Andreas yelled.

Spiro raised his voice above that of his father's. "Ask Tessa why Glaucus does not appear here today," he screamed.

The epistates turned to Tessa, his frustration at the continued unfolding of accusations evident. "Where is Glaucus, Tessa?"

Tessa saw his mouth moving, heard the words, but could not answer. The coldness within her was rising again.

Spiro answered for her. "He is dead! Murdered by his hetaera nearly a week ago, when he supposedly fell ill and vanished from the public eye."

Tessa stared out at the crowd, their horrified faces blending into one stare of accusation.

"It's not true!" Nikos spoke at last. "It was an accident. She did not kill him!"

Tessa looked at Nikos. Son of Andreas.

What did she know of him? Ajax claimed to serve Nikos. Perhaps it was true. Perhaps it had all been a ruse to make her think that Spiro plotted against Glaucus and the others. Her mind searched for a reason to believe. Part of her knew that Spiro lied, but she could no longer tell truth from falsehood.

Spiro spoke now in wry tones. "And why should you not believe this man? After all, he has done nothing but conspire to cover up the murder of a good man and bed his hetaera."

Tessa saw Nikos's face twist in anger. As though each moment lasted a day, she saw Nikos fly at Spiro. His hands wrapped around his brother's neck.

At a flick of the epistates's hand, soldiers rushed in.

"Enough!" the epistates screamed. "Enough!"

The soldiers pulled Nikos and Spiro apart. Andreas now stood between them. The brothers snarled at one another like two mad dogs.

Tessa watched in fascination, certain now that the whole day had been an elaborate play, staged in the theater for the amusement of the citizens of Rhodes.

*Yes, amusing. So well performed.* She thought about applauding but sensed the drama was not concluded. *Better to wait.*

The epistates's face had turned a deep shade of purple. He addressed the soldiers. "Hold them all!" To the Assembly, he cried, "Go home, people of Rhodes! Council, remain. We shall sort this out and pass judgment this day."

The crowd remained motionless.

"Go home!" he screamed again.

Slowly submissive citizens rose to their feet and moved.

As the majority of spectators climbed out of the amphitheater and council members moved forward to fill in the lower seats, the epistates directed the soldiers to separate those who stood in the circle.

Nikos and Andreas were pulled to the left, Spiro and Ajax each stood alone with a guard, and Tessa remained to the right of the circle.

When only the council remained and the amphitheater grew silent and heavy with waiting, the epistates turned to those in the circle.

"Now we will learn the truth."

## Ω

Tessa saw Nikos look at her but knew her face revealed nothing because nothing was happening within her. She returned his look with a blank stare.

Spiro was speculating that perhaps it was Nikos who had murdered Glaucus. "It is well known that my father desires Rhodes to join Kalymnos in declaring allegiance to the Achaean League. And now he has sent his bastard son to murder all those who oppose him!"

The slave Ajax was asked directly if he had orchestrated the chaos in the Jewish district. He bowed his head, as though ashamed. "Andreas and Nikos purchased me in Kalymnos, then brought me here to accomplish their goals," he said. "I do only what I am told."

The council members muttered among themselves.

Nikos protested. "This brute belongs to Spiro and assumes he will be rewarded if you allow Spiro to go unpunished."

"Unpunished for what?" the epistates demanded.

"All of this!" Nikos waved a hand around the amphitheater.

"Glaucus's death?"

Nikos closed his eyes. "No, not Glaucus's death—"

"So you admit to killing Glaucus?"

"I tell you it was an accident."

"An accident that happened when you arrived on Rhodes and assumed a false role in Glaucus's household?"

The clouds had broken, sending streams of sunlight down into the amphitheater. The stone steamed and Tessa felt the sweat build along her neck.

The epistates turned to the council. "Thus far we have only the word of Andreas and his son, Nikos, to speak against Spiro. And the word of Spiro and the slave to speak against our guests from Kalymnos." He turned to Tessa. "What say you, Tessa of Delos?"

Tessa looked from Spiro to Nikos. Brothers. Liars, both.

She smiled at the epistates. "I am simply a hetaera," she said. "What do I know of such matters?"

The epistates turned back to the council in disgust. "We must vote," he said. "The vote will be open. Those who would see Spiro held responsible for the events of today, move to your left. Those who believe Andreas and Nikos are responsible and should be sent home to leave Rhodes in peace, move to your right."

Tessa watched, her face impassive, as the council rose as one, crawled over one another, and moved apart, like a tapestry coming unwoven.

Rows of men before her.

A circle of men around her.

Dead men at her feet.

As it always had been and always would be, men would decide her fate.

The center section emptied and the council sat on opposite sides of the theater. There was no need for a count.

Spiro drew close to her, a slow smile creeping across his handsome face. He leaned in to whisper. "There is the precious democracy you fight for, Tessa. The will of the majority. Decided against you."

# THIRTY-TWO

Two soldiers flanked Tessa as she climbed the steps to Glaucus's house for the last time.

*As if I had anywhere to run.*

She had been permitted to return to retrieve her belongings. They would not stay long. The sun descended behind her, still warming the city after the afternoon's storm.

She passed through the doorway, into the familiar hall. The andrôn was silent, and she idly wondered when another symposium would ever be held there.

As they passed the hearth room, Tessa heard soft voices. She paused at the doorway and saw Simeon bent over Persephone, who sat on the floor beside the fire. A cut above her eye bled, and Simeon dabbed at it with a rag.

"You are hurt," Tessa said, wondering why she felt so little emotion at this scene.

Simeon looked up at her, and she saw that he had been beaten. One purple eye had nearly swelled shut, and a cut split his lower lip.

"What has happened?" she asked.

"A man came," Simeon said. "To kill Glaucus."

She reached a hand toward them both. "He hurt you."

Simeon shook his head and stood. "We will be fine."

Tessa looked at the elderly servant's injured face. "I would not forgive myself if he had—"

Simeon touched her arm and leaned toward her. "It will take more than a mere slave to end my life," he said. "Yahweh has made me a promise, and until it is fulfilled, I will serve Him here among the living."

Persephone started to cry. "I am sorry, Tessa. He forced me to tell him—"

*She is no longer angry with me.*

The thought should have brought comfort. She touched Persephone's hair, and the child reached for her hand and squeezed it, her eyes bestowing forgiveness. A soldier behind Tessa prodded her in the back.

"Keep moving," he growled.

She pulled her hand from Persephone's grip, and with a last look at the girl, left the room. They crossed the courtyard and pushed into the back of the house, where Tessa had stored everything she owned in Glaucus's room.

The blankets on the bed had been thrust aside, mute testimony to the uncovering of her secret. Tessa spread a cloth on the bed, pulled a handful of her few belongings from a chest beside the wall and dumped them into the center of the blanket. At the bottom of the chest lay a necklace given to her by her mother. She left it there.

When all her possessions were in the center of the blanket, she tied the corners and lifted the bundle from the bed.

The two soldiers followed her out of the room, back into the courtyard.

She stopped at Mynah's cage, and the black bird chirped at her. Tessa reached to lift the cage but then dropped her hand. She would not take Mynah to Spiro's home. She pried open the barred door, pushed her hand in, and waited for the bird to hop onto her finger. A moment later she pulled Mynah from her cage and lifted her to the sky above the courtyard in a silent farewell. With a flick of her wrist, she set the bird free.

She turned back to her soldiers and found Nikos and Andreas in the courtyard, accompanied by more guards.

"What are you doing here?"

"We are to be on the next ship leaving for Kalymnos," Andreas said.

Nikos said, "I came to say good-bye to Simeon and Persephone."

Tessa watched his face, waited for something more. The guards escorting Andreas and Nikos grew impatient. Andreas turned away.

Nikos still faced her, the sorrow in his eyes burrowing into her heart.

"Go, Nikos," she said. "You belong to Kalymnos, and I to Spiro. I have no further need for you."

The soldiers pulled at him, and Nikos yanked his arm away, his eyes still on her, angry. "Then I leave you to fight the lovely Berenice for your place as patron hetaera of Rhodes."

She looked away, studied the fountain in the center of the courtyard that bubbled as though nothing could affect its joy. "Go," she said.

Two more appeared in the courtyard, as if all of Rhodes had come to witness her degradation.

Spiro. With Servia behind.

"What are they doing here?" Spiro growled.

Andreas pushed past his son. "We leave you now, Spiro. Leave you to destroy this island as you most certainly will."

Andreas pulled Nikos with him, and they were gone.

Servia sidled up to Tessa. "You are proving to be even more valuable than I imagined the day your mother sold you to me," she laughed. "It is my good fortune that you have disposed of one patron, for now I will receive the price of another." She whispered loudly to Tessa, so that Spiro could hear. "Feel free to go through this one quickly. There will always be more."

Spiro frowned. "Do not think you will soon profit from her again, Servia." He turned to Tessa. "She will be mine for many years to come." He pulled a bulging pouch from under his tunic and handed it to her. Servia hefted the pouch with a smile, judging the weight and the jangle of coins with appreciation.

"Leave us, Servia," Spiro said. "Our business is concluded. I do not wish to see you again."

Servia shrugged, lifted the pouch with another smile, and left the courtyard.

Spiro pulled Tessa through the hall and out onto the portico. He lifted her hand to his lips and kissed it gently. "At last," he said. "Are you ready for your new life?"

Tessa said nothing. Thought nothing. Felt nothing.

The setting sun gleamed across the island, lighting Helios afire in the harbor. She paused to gaze out over the sea and the statue and marveled at what her life had become.

Was it less than a week ago that she had stood here and promised Helios that she would sacrifice herself at his feet? Would that she could return to that moment and keep her vow.

Somewhere across the harbor, a ship prepared to sail for Crete and freedom. It would sail without her.

Ω

Nikos watched the island of Rhodes retreat into the setting sun from his place at the rail of the ship. His father stood beside him.

Soldiers had escorted them to the harbor, seen them onto the ship, and ordered the captain to cast off. They would reach Kalymnos in four hours.

Helios raised his torch in farewell to Nikos. He thought of that first morning when he had found Tessa at the statue's feet, cold and nearly lifeless. He had seen that same look in her eyes in Glaucus's courtyard, when she told him to go.

It had been an illusion, the belief that he could save her. They served the gods, and they served politics, and there was no avoiding either.

"She was an amazing woman, I will give you that," Andreas said.

A flock of sea crows lifted from the harbor. Nikos watched their wings catch the sunlight and trace a path across the sky. They called to one another as they broke free of Rhodes and raced ahead of Nikos and Andreas, over the sparkling blue water.

Nikos smiled. "Yes, she is."

"I would have liked to have seen her become your hetaera—"

"Don't, Father."

"Son, you cannot think that she—"

Nikos held up a hand. "I do not wish to speak of her."

Andreas laughed. "Love is for peasants and slaves, Nikos. You will do well to focus on power."

*Yes, live for power. As Spiro has always done.*

Nikos reflected on his half-brother's obsession to please their father. His willingness to do anything to gain his approval, or at least his respect.

*Like me.*

The truth bubbled up from deep within him, and Nikos moved away from the rail, toward the prow of the ship. Was he not just like Spiro? He had come to Rhodes to please his father, had deceived Tessa for the sake of his father, and now he sailed back to

Kalymnos, again to do his father's bidding. When would he live as his own man?

The statue of Helios faded into the twilight. He would soon return to Dalios Apollo, the patron god of Kalymnos. He thought of the Jews' One God, who offered something no Greek god had ever offered: redemption.

Nikos understood redemption. He had been born in the gutter and adopted as a son. A deep longing to return to the Jews overwhelmed him.

As Rhodes faded in the distance and Kalymnos grew closer, Nikos had the strange feeling that he had left his true home and was heading somewhere false.

Ω

Tessa heard nothing on the brief journey to Spiro's home. If he spoke to her, she had no recollection of it. If the sun shone or the wind blew, she did not know it.

She knew only that she belonged to Spiro now.

She stood in his inner hall, tracing a crack in the wall from floor to roof.

A rotund man bustled toward her, all smiles.

"Here she is, here she is."

Behind her, Spiro spoke. "Did you bring them?"

"Of course, of course." The little man clapped his hands. "All the finest! You shall see, you shall see."

"Where?"

The man crooked a finger at them both. "I have laid them out in her room. Follow me, follow me."

Spiro nudged her in the man's direction and she moved forward, placing one foot in front of the other without thinking. In a small room off the courtyard, a pile of clothing lay strewn on a bed.

"Tessa," Spiro smiled. "This room is for your use whenever you are in attendance. And you see," he pointed at the bed, "I have purchased an entirely new wardrobe for you." He crossed to the bed and held up a handsome chitôn. "Such lovely colors and delightful fabrics, are they not?"

Tessa sensed he expected an answer, so she nodded.

Spiro ushered the little man from the room, talking of money owed, but returned a moment later. Tessa had not moved.

He touched the white chitôn at her shoulder, long ago turned gray from the rain and mud. "I will dress you in finer clothes than Glaucus ever did." He ran his fingertips down her arm, resting them on the underside of her forearm. "He did not recognize the treasure he had in you. Are you not glad that at last you belong to someone worthy of your admiration?"

"I have admired very few men in my life."

Spiro wrapped his fingers around her wrist and tugged her to himself. "Then I am even more pleased to be one of them." He wound his free arm around her waist. "Your life with me will be more than he could ever give you, Tessa. You will be mine in every way, and I will make your name known to islands that are only specks on the horizon."

A coldness was returning, and she welcomed it. Across from her a painted fresco of Athena holding out her arms looked down on Tessa.

Spiro still held her. "I will allow nothing to stand in the way of your renown. There are ways to deal with any interference, and I have no desire for an heir."

Tessa pulled back, a flicker of something still alive. "What?"

He smiled patiently. "Surely the midwife has solved such problems for you before this, Tessa? Or perhaps the gods have smiled on you and it has not been necessary." He shrugged. "Of course, there are many ways to deal with unnecessary complications should they arise, but I have spoken to the midwife, and she assures me there is a method by which we can avoid the inconvenience before it occurs."

"What are you saying, Spiro?"

Spiro held her at arms length and studied her face. "I am saying that the midwife and I will make certain that no squalling brat ever ruins your beautiful body or your favored life."

Tessa tried to breathe, but it seemed the air had gone from the room. She swayed, but Spiro's hands still held her fast. He pulled her into an embrace and whispered to her, "Wash, Tessa. Wash and dress yourself in something beautiful. I will return soon, and together we will find our future."

He released her, and Tessa stumbled backward and fell to the bed. Spiro backed out of the room, his eyes never leaving her body.

She lay there for several moments, against the pile of colorful fabrics. Her fingers played with the edges of something in dark blue. She pulled it to herself, up and over her body, then over her face like a shroud.

And it was dark as death under the fabric, though her breath continued to flutter the blueness above her, proving that she lived still.

But she lived for nothing now.

She closed her eyes, let her mind wash back to the memory she had once believed could be erased.

The docks, the sea, the statue. All there in her memory, though big with the eyes of a child. Few words could be recalled; only flashes of images. Her mother, dirty and street-worn. Servia, gold-toothed and grinning. The smell of sea and fish and sweat. The call of the gulls. Tessa watched a gull peck at a discarded fish bone on the dock, then flap its wings once, twice, and lift without effort above them all. She followed it with her eyes, over the ships at dock, past the waves, into the blue, blue sky until it had escaped and would never return.

And her mother was holding her hand. But pulling, pulling on her hand. Pulling her toward the fat, gold-toothed woman. Pushing Tessa's fingers into the woman's hand, taking something from the woman's other hand.

She had seen the fishermen trade their fish for coins. She knew what it was to be traded. She had been traded. From the fat woman's side she watched her mother escape like the gull. Mother did not soar, however. Her arms hung at her sides like broken wings. Weighted down by the coins, perhaps.

Tessa had never seen her mother again.

The blue fabric grew stifling upon Tessa's face and she brushed it away.

*I would never trade my own child. I would prove that a mother could love her child more than she loved her own self.*

No, she never would. Spiro had made this very clear.

She had heard that the midwives could prevent a woman from ever being able to conceive a child, but what woman would ever choose to give up the only thing that made her valuable?

*But I do not choose. I am traded.*

She rolled to her stomach, uncaring that she crushed the fine fabrics beneath her, and faced the truth in the darkness of that room: No love for her own child would ever remove the pain of that day. She had fought like a threatened animal to save herself from being possessed by another man, and she had fallen into the hands of a man more loathsome than the last. To fight, to run, would only put her on the streets, selling herself to fishermen and sailors in port to spend their money.

And she was too cowardly to embrace the freedom of death.

The coldness crept through her, numbing the furthest reaches, hardening into a solid thing that left no room for pain.

The evening advanced. Spiro would soon return.

Tessa rose from the bed, found the water pitcher and basin. She stripped off her muddy chitôn, poured water over a cloth, and began to wash. Face, arms, chest, stomach, legs. She scrubbed but felt nothing. Washed, in preparation for degradation.

She chose the dark blue chitôn. Dressed, though she could not hide.

And when she was dressed, she turned to the bronzed mirror propped on a small table, and lifted a gold circlet that had been left on the table. The woman in her slow-moving reflection lifted the necklace to her chin, burrowed the clasps under her hair, and fastened them behind her neck. Tessa released the necklace and it fell against her throat, heavy, as a collar for a prized pet.

The doorway curtain was swept aside, and the room's oil lamp danced in response. Tessa did not turn.

"Let me see you," he whispered.

*The marble Athena. She is always safe.*

Tessa spun a slow circle until she faced him. Though she did not lift her eyes, she felt him draw close.

And then he was there before her. And then his hands were on her shoulders. And his lips on her neck.

Across the room the painted fresco of the goddess looked down on her with sympathetic eyes. Tessa focused on those eyes, did not let the goddess look away, even as Spiro pushed her toward the bed.

A gentle throat-clearing announced the presence of another.

Spiro ignored the servant in the doorway, until the man whispered, "Master—"

He rolled to his side and squinted at the servant. "By the gods, this had better be important!"

"I am sorry, Master. I thought you would want to know—"

"Yes, speak!"

"The strategoi are being summoned for Glaucus's funeral, to begin immediately."

Spiro glared at Tessa, then swung his legs to the floor.

"Funeral!"

"Apparently, they have recovered his body from the pit where—where it was hidden, and his wife is insistent that he be given a proper burial to appease the gods."

Spiro slammed a fist into the bedding. "Crazy woman." He sighed and fell back against the cushions beside Tessa. "I suppose I must go. After today's events it would be unseemly to be absent."

The servant disappeared. Spiro rolled to face Tessa. He ran his fingers down her leg and smiled. "You must come with me, of course. And then we will return here." He laughed. "Always you make me wait, Tessa. But it will be worth it."

Again they traversed the city back to Glaucus's home. Tessa felt some surprise at crossing the threshold. What was she doing back here again?

As custom dictated, the house had been cleaned, though hastily to be sure, and hung with wreaths and other foliage. Even from the doorway, Tessa could hear the lament of the mourners. Daphne and Persephone would be there, and probably other female mourners who had been hired for the vigil. Their laments seemed a long string of the same note, a monotone wail that engendered no emotion in her.

The mourners were gathered in the courtyard. Tessa gazed over the crowd, recognizing faces but not acknowledging them. At her side, Spiro held her arm possessively, moving her from one cluster of people to another, dropping comments that made it clear that Glaucus's most precious property had already been disposed of.

Between conversations, he whispered into her ear, "Try to look satisfied, if not happy, Tessa." And later, "You will make them think that you do not wish to be with me. Take more care to look cheerful."

Tessa thought perhaps she would laugh when she saw that Glaucus's body was, indeed, laid out on his bed and covered by a cloth, as she had pretended for so many days. But she did not laugh. She merely stood in the room with the others who had filed in and studied the bulk of the man who had caused her such misery for so many years.

Had they washed and anointed his body with olive oil after pulling him from the pit? Wouldn't his body stink after so many days in the heat? She looked around at the other mourners and was surprised to see looks of disgust, and noses discreetly pinched. She looked back to the body, its feet facing the door as was the custom. Perhaps it did stink. She smelled nothing.

Spiro pulled her back to the courtyard, to a grouping of strategoi. The conversation ceased when they approached.

Spiro frowned. "Men," he said. "It is a sad evening."

Hermes raised an eyebrow. "There was no affection between the two of you, Spiro, as everyone was aware."

"True, true. But I did not wish him dead."

Philo crossed his arms. "We are not all pleased with the decision of the council today. Some of us are not so convinced that you had nothing to do with the recent violence."

Hermes looked at Tessa. "If not for your intervention, a few of us would likely be covered in bier cloths tonight as well."

Spiro wrapped an arm around her waist. "She is an asset, I agree. The gods favored us all by allowing her to discover my half-brother's plot before it came to fruition." He smiled at Tessa. "You were wonderful today, my dear."

Tessa said nothing. She stared at Spiro, wondering why he smiled at her. The silence around the group lengthened, and Spiro's smile faded.

"Tessa is tired from the events of the day, I fear," he said. "I think it is time she withdrew."

"You are not joining the funeral procession?" Philo asked.

Spiro bit his lip. "Let me see Tessa home. I will return."

He pulled her from the courtyard, through the hall and out into the street. She struggled to keep pace with him, and he dragged her by the arm to increase her speed.

"I will take you back to the docks tonight, Tessa. I need to join the procession." He glanced back at her. "But tomorrow," he scowled, "tomorrow our new life begins. I expect you to arrive at my home early in the day, fresh and rested."

Before long he had deposited her at the door to Servia's training house where a bed always awaited her.

"Tomorrow," he said, "I want to see again the spirited hetaera I have long desired. And then," he leaned in to kiss her cheek, "then the pleasure will be mine."

$$\Omega$$

The moon had risen above the city when Spiro returned to his home and strolled through his courtyard, admiring the flowers he had cultivated there.

Glaucus's funeral procession had been customary, with a quick speech and the inhumation at a rock-cut tomb outside the city. Spiro had outpaced the other mourners on his walk back to Rhodes, wishing to be alone to relish the victory of this day. He had not yet gained Rhodes, but he had gained Tessa, and the thought was like a sweet drop of nectar on his tongue.

But the day was not over yet.

Someone had slipped up beside him as he walked the rutted road. Someone whose tall frame and bald head were much too recognizable for Spiro to welcome the conversation.

"We cannot speak here," Spiro said, glancing back at the mourners who followed at some distance.

"What am I to do now?" Ajax asked.

"I have been pleased with your service, Ajax, and greatly regret that you cannot continue to serve me. It is critical that no one know your deeds were accomplished in my name."

"Would you have me take to the streets, then?" Ajax seemed to grow taller, leaning over Spiro by a full head.

"You are free to do as you wish." Spiro tried to leave Ajax behind. "Is that not what every slave desires?"

Ajax grabbed Spiro's arm and turned his body. "But I will need money," he said, his teeth showing white in the darkness. "To start somewhere else."

Spiro twisted his arm out of Ajax's grasp. He could not afford to delay in the road with the other strategoi quickly approaching.

"Very well. Come to me later," he said. "I will have something for you." He looked backward. "But now, get out of here!"

Ajax seemed satisfied with the promise and ran into the night.

And now, hours later, Spiro waited in his courtyard, confident that Ajax would come for his payoff.

Spiro loved his courtyard in the evenings. He had chosen the plantings carefully, nurturing white orchids that opened in the darkness and released their fragrance into the night. He strolled down a walkway overhung with bougainvillea and slowed to run his fingers over a branch laden with magenta blooms.

From the darkness, his name carried to him on a whisper. Ajax had arrived. Spiro straightened his shoulders and inhaled, preparing himself for what he knew he must do.

"Here, Ajax."

The slave peered around a pear tree and spotted his master. "What are you doing back there?" he asked, his voice uncertain. "Come out into the moonlight."

Spiro strolled casually into the center of the courtyard, where Ajax waited beside the central fountain.

The slave bent his head to the water, his back to Spiro, and took a long drink. Turning, he wiped the back of his hand across his mouth and eyed Spiro.

"Do you have my money?"

Spiro smiled. "There was not enough time to speak of my gratitude in the road earlier, Ajax," he said. "Circumstances worked in our favor today, and you played a large role in that. I am in your debt."

"You made it clear you no longer want my service."

Spiro sighed dramatically. If he were to accomplish this, he must first gain the man's trust. "I wish things could be different," he said, approaching Ajax.

"Different?"

"Yes. It would please me to keep you." He touched Ajax's arm. "You know that I have a certain—fondness—for you."

Ajax's shoulders lowered, and he exhaled. "I have been glad to be of service to you," he said. "I plan to leave Rhodes, to sail for Nissiros where I will find other work. Perhaps you could somehow send for me there if the need arises."

"Send for you on Nissiros?" Spiro turned away from Ajax, ambled around to the other side of the fountain.

"Yes. It is a small island. And I am a—noticeable—man. You could find me. If you needed me."

Spiro bent to retrieve something he had placed at the fountain's base earlier. He kept it hidden in the folds of his tunic as he rounded the fountain again to step close to the slave.

"Ajax, Ajax," he said, not taking his eyes from the taller man's face. "You have served well. But I don't believe you understand what it means to have outlived one's usefulness." He was close enough to touch Ajax now, close enough to wrap his arms around the man. A sense of power flowed through Spiro, strengthening his hand to the task and filling his heart with a cool resolve.

The carved dagger had been in Spiro's family for generations. It felt like a familiar friend in his hand, even as it plunged into Ajax's side.

Spiro lifted himself on his toes to reach Ajax's ear. "I will risk nothing now," he whispered. "Nothing that could take *her* from me."

He drove the knife deeper, upward. Then twisted.

Ajax's eyes were on him still, wide with knowing.

Spiro felt the welcome warmth of blood run over his hand, his wrist, down his arm. When Ajax fell at his feet, Spiro still gripped the knife.

He studied the form of the bald giant.

No pity. It had to be done.

*I have her now. And no one will be allowed to interfere.*

# THIRTY-THREE

## ✦ *The Day of the Great Quake* ✦

How long had she lain there? Tessa rolled to her side, aware through still-closed eyes of the early morning light that washed her room on the upper floor of Servia's house. She covered her eyes with the back of her hand and returned to sleep.

The sunlight had yellowed when next she opened her eyes, revealing the peeling of plaster on the ceiling above her. Perhaps the roof would collapse and crush her. No, Servia took better care than that. She pulled the blanket over her head and slept again.

The heat awakened her, having built in the room and under her covering until it sickened her with a soul-weary fatigue she could not rise above.

A low hum in the room caused her to open her eyes. Two girls stood at the foot of her bed, as though she had been laid out like Glaucus, to be mourned over.

"Will you rise now, Tessa? It is nearly midday."

The other girl giggled. "She must have been entertaining at a lovely party late into the night."

Tessa watched the girl's lips, her smile, the way she covered her mouth when she laughed. Tessa's own mouth seemed sticky and tasted bitter. She did not know when she had eaten last.

"Tessa, tell us of the party."

"Yes, tell!"

The two girls sat on the foot of her bed and stared at her, as though waiting for something.

*I am supposed to return to Spiro.*

She pushed off the bed, then slumped again. Something about her arms was not functioning well.

*Will he come for me?*

Perhaps he was sleeping still, too. Glaucus's funeral. It would have gone into the morning hours. Perhaps they all slept today, trying to forget yesterday.

*No, it is only I who wants to forget.*

She closed her eyes against the memories. When she opened them again, the girls were gone and the day was further spent.

Berenice came once, Servia's new sensation, full of good humor. "Rest, Tessa," she said. "There are others who will carry on."

*He will come soon. He will not let me rest.*

When the shadows grew long, a heavy foot fell on the stairs.

*He is here.*

Tessa felt as though she had been cut open, all the lifeblood draining out of her, down into the bed, through the floor, down deep into the earth.

*Is this what it feels like to die?*

A figure appeared in the doorway, and she turned her head to face the future. But it was not Spiro.

Simeon stood there, his lined face creased even more deeply with worry.

"Tessa, I came to be assured that you are well." He approached the bed and laid a weathered hand on her forehead. "You have no fever. Do you feel ill?"

"Simeon." It was all she could think to say.

"Is it your stomach, Tessa? Your head?"

She closed her eyes.

Those two girls had returned, she knew. She recognized their girlish whispers in the doorway.

"What is wrong with her?" one of them asked.

"I fear for her sanity," he answered. "Watch her carefully. I will return."

Tessa wished he would not go. His presence comforted her somehow.

At least until Spiro came to claim her.

It seemed that no time had passed when she heard Simeon's voice at her bedside again. "Tessa, we are leaving here. Can you stand?"

A tugging on her arm. She tried to rise but could not.

She felt an arm under her shoulders and another under her knees. She would not have thought Simeon still strong enough to lift her. She laid her head against his shoulder as they descended the steps. He turned her sideways to carry her through the narrow hall. One of the girls held open the door. Tessa blinked her eyes against the sunlight.

Simeon laid her carefully in a large ox cart, one she had never seen before. He then took a blanket from one of the girls and arranged it over her, in spite of the sun. Tessa pulled it to her chin, so that only if one were to stop and look into the cart would they know that Spiro's hetaera lay there.

A moment later the wheels grated over the ruts in the street.

Did Simeon take her to Spiro? It did not seem like he would. But Tessa had decided it was better not to trust what anyone might do.

Ω

The ship bound for Kalymnos had sailed through the night, with the captain and crew manning the sails and the honored passengers sleeping under a tent shelter on the aft deck. Nikos knew nothing of funerals or courtyard betrayals or Tessa as he sailed through the night.

It was very late when father and son disembarked and made their way to Andreas's estate on an upper hillside. Nikos breathed in the night air and tried to reconcile himself to being home again.

In the morning politics would not wait. Nikos was shaken awake early by a servant. "Your father sends for you," he said.

Nikos groaned and buried his head in the bedding.

"The council meets this morning. You are to be there with your father to report on Rhodes."

*I have had enough of council meetings for a lifetime.*

"Tell my father I will join him for the morning meal shortly."

The servant bowed himself out of the room, and Nikos dressed begrudgingly.

Once they had climbed into his father's ornate chariot, however, and the driver had turned them toward the agora, Nikos felt his spirits lift. To see Kalymnos in the morning, bathed in sunshine and bustling with activity, was to feel alive.

His father seemed to note his change in attitude. "So, it is not so bad to return to Kalymnos after all?"

Nikos shrugged and smiled.

Through the streets Nikos and his father were hailed by peasants and politicians alike.

"Your name is called more often than mine," his father remarked. "The people love you."

"They know me. I was once one of them."

Andreas nodded. "Only one reason why you will make an excellent leader one day. You are trusted, well-liked. The people will follow you gladly, as though one of their own leads them."

"I *am* one of their own." Nikos felt the slight edge in his tone and wondered if his father heard it as well.

"You are my son, Nikos."

Nikos waved to a young man pushing a cart in the street, a friend he had known since childhood.

"Father, sometimes you seem to believe that I was only acting a part in a play when I lived among these people—that I was only masquerading as a peasant, waiting to reveal my true parentage."

"Yes?"

Nikos turned to Andreas. "I did not even know you were my father. You were careful that no one knew about my mother or me until your wife died. For all my life I have been a peasant. It is not as simple as shedding a costume."

Andreas pursed his lips. "You can love these people as your own, Nikos. But I will not have my son live as a peasant as well."

They soon reached the market, the chariot weaving between shoppers anxious for bargains. A meat merchant hailed Nikos.

"Greetings, Nestor," Nikos called. "How is business today?"

Nestor shrugged. "The people of this city, they are determined to rob me." He laughed, and Nikos laughed with him. Nestor hastened over to the chariot and handed up a parcel.

"The best duck you'll ever taste."

Nikos reached for his money pouch, but Nestor waved him away. "Tell your friends that Nestor has the best," he said with a grin.

Nikos smiled his thanks, and they continued on.

The city used a building similar to Rhodes's bouleuterion for official business, but as a monarchy, the council that met there served a different purpose. The debate today would center on Kalymnos's impending allegiance to the Achaean League.

The gallery stood on the perimeter of the agora, just as in Rhodes. This time Nikos would not wait outside. He would sit at the right hand of the island's most powerful man.

*Where I belong,* he reminded himself.

The gallery filled quickly with city leaders, until every stone seat in the half-circle was occupied. The president of the council stood, quieted the crowd, made preliminary announcements, then turned the meeting over to Andreas, who rose to his feet.

Nikos tried to focus on his father's words, but images of Tessa bursting from the Rhodian bouleuterion after humiliating herself kept intruding.

His father reported on the situation in Rhodes, commenting briefly on his displeasure with Spiro's actions, even though Spiro appeared to support the League.

An argument sprang up about how best to convince the leadership of Rhodes to join the League.

"Perhaps Spiro has the right idea," one man called out. "Do away with the opposition."

Andreas scowled. "We are moving toward a more civilized form of government, not away from it!"

Nikos was called upon to tell of his dealings in Rhodes. He stood at his seat and summarized quickly, leaving out all mention of Tessa.

The meeting moved to other topics, and Nikos allowed his mind to travel back to Rhodes. His thoughts at the rail of the ship last night assailed him again as he looked around the gallery.

*What am I doing here?*

Trying to please his father.

So much like his brother, Spiro. Would he do anything to please him? Nikos was willing to be a leader, but would he sacrifice anything for it? The woman he loved? The God he wanted to learn more of?

When the meeting broke, Nikos retained his seat. His father conversed with various leaders, working his way through the gallery, until only he and Nikos remained. His father stood opposite him in the empty gallery, near the door.

"You could have mingled with them more today, Nikos," he called across the open floor.

"My mind is elsewhere."

"Yes, that is obvious." His father crossed his arms and planted his feet wider than his shoulders, a pose Nikos was coming to learn meant that he was ready for the conflict he saw coming.

Perceptive man.

"I am going back," Nikos said.

"No." His father's face remained impassive. "We were run off that accursed island. Besides," he said, "you belong here."

Nikos nodded. "Yes. I do. I am going to bring her back with me."

Andreas exhaled loudly, as though Nikos were a bothersome child needing discipline yet again. "She is so far beneath you, Nikos, that I have trouble even understanding—"

"Is she? I am a peasant, Father!"

"You are not!" Andreas strode across the gallery now, his face reddening. "And even if you were—not even a peasant would stoop to claim a hetaera as a wife."

"No one needs to know."

Andreas slowed. "But they would find out, Nikos. Information like that has a way of being brought to light. Eventually they would know. And then, what of your leadership? How will you maintain their respect then?"

Nikos stepped down the two tiers that separated him from the gallery floor. He drew close to his father and lowered his voice.

"I want you to be proud of me, Father. Very much. I am grateful to you for all you have done. But pleasing you, even pleasing the people of Kalymnos, cannot be more important to me than doing the right thing."

"The right thing! How is—"

"Because I love her." Nikos studied his father's eyes. "As you once loved my mother."

The hard line of Andreas's mouth softened, and he sighed.

"You once told me that love is for peasants, Father. But I do not think you truly believe it."

Andreas dropped his chin to his chest. "Go, then, Nikos. Do what you must."

Nikos hesitated. "I will need money, Father. Quite a bit. And understand that I will not be purchasing a hetaera. I will be paying the slave price to set her free."

Andreas raised his head and looked at his son, and his smile was warm enough to carry Nikos back across the waters to redeem the one he loved.

# THIRTY-FOUR

Something seemed familiar here, even from the rocking floor of the ox-drawn cart. Tessa sniffed. Was it the smell? The buildings on either side of the street they traveled? She gave up and closed her eyes.

"Tessa," a hand shook her shoulder. "Tessa, we are here. Come."

She felt herself pulled from the cart to stand in the street.

The Jewish district.

Simeon led her by the hand through a narrow door and into his daughter's home.

"Father! Tessa!" Marta's warm welcome penetrated the fog in Tessa's mind. Marta's warmth turned to concern. "What is wrong? What has happened?"

Simeon pulled Tessa forward. "She needs a place to rest for a short time."

"In here." Marta led them to the hearth room and, in only moments, had cushions and blankets spread near the fire. Simeon lowered her to the floor. She sat cross-legged before the hearth.

They spoke in low tones, standing behind her, as if she could not hear.

"I heard about the Assembly meeting," Marta said. "Glaucus is truly dead?"

"Yes. He was buried early this morning."

"What will you do now, Father?"

"Do not worry about me. I will continue to serve Daphne for as long as she needs me. Yahweh has my life in His hands."

"And her?"

Tessa heard Simeon's sigh. "She is Spiro's hetaera now."

They remained silent for several moments. Tessa could feel their pity, though she watched the flames.

"Why did you bring her here?" Marta finally asked.

"Since the meeting yesterday her mind has not been well. I believe only Yahweh can heal her now."

Marta dropped to the floor beside Tessa and touched her arm. Tessa tried to smile at the woman.

"What do you fear, Tessa?"

Tessa looked into the kindness of Marta's eyes and wished she could speak of all that was locked up in her heart.

*I fear bondage. I fear pain.*

Children called from other parts of the house. Marta frowned, then patted Tessa's arm. "I will be back."

She was replaced by Simeon. He reclined beside her, leaning on one elbow, his other arm propped on his bent knee.

"Tessa, do you remember the Passover?"

*Lamb. Unleavened bread. Daniel's questions.* She nodded.

"Passover is more than a history lesson, Tessa. It is a map to the future as well. And not only the future of Israel but of all people."

She found her voice. "I do not wish to think of the future."

"But you must think of it!" Simeon leaned forward, his voice rising. "You must be at peace with both your past and your future."

"It is better not to think of such things."

"And then what, Tessa? Will you turn to stone again?"

She looked at him. "Again?"

He turned to the fire. "For years I have watched you try to not feel anything. Pain. Joy."

"It was the only way—"

"No! It is not the only way. The One True God, your Creator, has given you the gift of life. To refuse the life He gives . . . It is not what He wants for you."

"I have never understood the gods."

"That is because your people's gods offer nothing but bondage. Your priests teach you that you must please the gods or suffer their wrath."

"And is your God so different?"

"So different, yes. As the Passover shows us. He offers freedom, Tessa. The freedom to enjoy being His people, because He offers atonement for sin and the past."

Tessa studied the fire, now reduced to glowing embers. Outside the warmth of their room, the family carried on its routine. A family, a routine she would never experience.

The cloudiness in her mind began to clear and she turned to Simeon. "I do not wish to feel pain anymore. I cannot escape my situation, so I will close my heart to anything that can hurt me, and then I will be safe. Do you understand, Simeon?" She heard the anger spark in her voice. "I don't want to feel pain anymore!"

He reached for her, touched her cheek with his fingertips.

"Oh, Tessa," he said. "To feel pain is part of life. To refuse pain is to stop being human. And more importantly, if you will not feel the pain, you do not allow God to refine you through the pain He has ordained in your life."

"You speak like Nikos."

"The man is closer to truth than even he realizes."

Tessa sighed. "I do not want to be refined."

Simeon laughed softly. "No, none of us does, at least at first. But God is patient. He continues to allow the pain, and one day we look back and see that He has used it to purify us."

She shook her head and studied her hands folded in her lap. A lump of charcoal shifted in the fire and sent tiny sparks upward.

"Tessa, when you close yourself off to emotion, so that you will not feel the pain of disappointment, of rejection, you also close yourself off to love and joy and life. It does not work, Tessa. The only thing that comes of denying your emotions is a desire to die."

She looked up at him, wondering if he had guessed her intent when he found her at the foot of the Colossus.

"Of course you wish to see your life come to an end," Simeon said. "A life without joy is not worth living. But a life of joy comes to us hand in hand with a life of pain. You cannot have one without the other."

"So what would you have me do?"

"I have told you already that Yahweh accepts all who will come to Him, even those from outside the house of Israel. He will accept you, if you recognize that atonement for your past can only be found in the forgiveness He provides."

"How can He so easily forgive?"

Simeon reached for her hand. "No, it is not done so easily. There are the sacrifices now. Much blood is shed to cover our sin. And someday," Simeon looked away, as though he could see the future in the empty air, "someday a Messiah will come who will redeem us. I do not know how this will be accomplished, nor when. But I know that my Redeemer comes."

He looked back to her, covered her hand with his own. "Tessa, submit yourself to Him, accept the forgiveness and life that He offers."

"But I will still belong to Spiro."

"Yes. Yes, it appears that this is part of the pain He has allowed in your life to refine you. But with the pain, Tessa, with the pain will come freedom. The freedom to love God with all your heart, and to feel that love for others, and from others."

He stared into her eyes, and the lines in his aged face seemed to fade. "Welcome the pain, Tessa. Feel it with every part of yourself. And then welcome the joy as well."

Tessa breathed in the warmth of the room and closed her eyes to turn Simeon's words over in her mind, like a jewel that needed further examination.

*I am so tired of trying not to feel.*

*But I am so afraid of letting myself feel.*

As though he read her thoughts, Simeon said, "You are afraid of being hurt, Tessa. Let go of the fear. Let the pain find its place in your heart. It is the only way to find a place for joy as well."

She had felt this strangeness before, several times since Glaucus had died. She had called it hope. She had wondered if the bronze framework inside her were melting. But it had not been like this. Sitting here beside the fire with Simeon, drinking in his words, something more frightening than anything she had yet felt now washed over her.

Deep inside, layers of rock that had taken years to accumulate shifted in opposite directions, with a mighty crack that she thought must have been audible. Beneath the rock, trapped for so long, something rushed up, threatening to drown her.

Pain. Deep, long-held, soul-wrenching pain.

She felt the first tear slide down her cheek and swallowed, trying to stop the flow before it started.

"Tessa," Simeon whispered, "let it go. Let it go. You will not die, you will not lose yourself. Yahweh has you in His hand. He holds you with His mighty right hand, and He loves you with an everlasting love."

She was shaking. She clutched her hands together, tried to stop the shaking. But it traveled from her hands to her chest. And then she was sobbing.

And as the pain rushed upward, gushing through the cracks in her heart, she saw every moment in her life that had worked to turn her to stone.

Father, his large hand on her tiny one as he died.

Mother, smiling brightly as she pushed Tessa into Servia's clutches.

*Oh, Mother, did you never wonder what became of me?*

*Did you never care to see?*

The images rushed forward, each one ripping open places in her heart she had long ago forgotten.

Glaucus, his thick-lipped, degrading sneer.

Daphne, with her blank, accusing eyes.

Persephone, desperate for a mother and resenting Tessa.

Spiro. Beautiful and obsessive and evil.

Her sobs turned to wails. She threw herself into Simeon's arms and let the pain of ten years wash over her like a rancid bath eating away at her.

"Feel all of it, Tessa," he said. "All the betrayal and the disappointment. This is what your Redeemer comes to free you from."

*Yes. Yes, I will feel all of it.*

To Tessa, it seemed she wept for the length of a lifetime. Simeon did not leave her, not even when she had no strength to hold herself upright.

But a slow change was now washing over her, as though the gush of pain from within her heart was beginning to exhaust itself, to slow in its intensity. Her sobs grew more sporadic as the supply of pain ran dry, until she felt so empty, she thought perhaps she had finally crossed to the underworld.

Tessa opened her eyes and found Simeon still there, a patient smile on his lips.

She felt frozen in this time, with the layers of rock cracked open, the buried reservoir of pain drained dry, and nothing at all inside.

"He is waiting, Tessa," Simeon whispered. "Waiting to give you life again. There will be pain, yes. But there will be joy. Great joy. A garment of praise for your spirit of despair."

*Can that be true?*

The silence held the promise of something more.

From the hall outside the hearth room, a happy shout erupted. A child ran in, laughing. Then another. And another. They ran a circle around the fire and threw themselves at her feet.

"Tessa!" Daniel rolled onto his back and laid his head in her lap. "You came again!"

"I told you she would," Sarah said from the doorway.

Daniel stuck his tongue out at his sister. "You did not! *I* said she would come again!"

Marta bustled into the room, wiping her hands on her tunic. She opened her mouth to scold but stopped when she saw Simeon's gentle, upraised hand.

And Tessa knew why Simeon kept her from her scolding.

For when the children rushed into the room, their laughter trailing, the empty places in her heart filled with something so pure, so holy, she believed it was a gift from Yahweh Himself.

*What is this? What is this?*

She lifted the question in her heart to Yahweh.

*Love, Tessa. Freedom and love.*

She looked to Simeon, her eyes glistening with fresh tears, this time of a different sort. She put a hand to her lips to stifle a laugh. Simeon pulled her hand away.

Tessa smiled down at Daniel's grinning face.

"Yes," she said. "Yes, I came again."

"Are you going to be our friend?" he asked.

She would not have thought the tears could flow again, but this time they seemed a balm to her heart, sealing off the wounds.

Marta was there beside Tessa, on her knees, nudging her father aside. She took Tessa's face between her hands and brought her own face close. Her voice was a whisper, her words an invitation. "Tell us, Tessa. Are you going to be our friend?"

Tessa laughed again, hardly recognizing the sound of it. "Yes," she whispered. "Yes."

"A friend of God, too, yes?" Simeon asked.

She nodded at the dear man. "Yes, Simeon. Friend of the God of Israel, as well."

More of the family joined the celebration in the hearth room. Somehow a meal appeared. Daniel insisted on sitting on Tessa's right while he ate. When he broke off a chunk of bread and shoved the whole piece into his mouth, she buried her face in his dark curls and laughed once more.

She still belonged to Spiro, it was true. And she did not know how she would live with both the pain of that truth and this new joy. But live, she would. For now she also belonged to Yahweh.

And Yahweh had set her free.

# THIRTY-FIVE

Spiro marked the sun's position, descending into the western sky, from his place on the portico of his house.

He had waited long enough.

When Tessa did not arrive in the morning, he assumed the events of the previous day had kept her in bed late into the morning. When the afternoon waned, he grew irritated at her lack of respect. Now he was simply angry.

*I have waited too long for this day to be denied its pleasure.*

Did she think she could behave as a freewoman?

He had argued with himself for the past hour, wanting to go after her, but knowing the errand was beneath him, that if anyone knew he must beg his hetaera to come to him, he would be disgraced.

And yet the desire to have her in his house was proving too much to ignore. He slapped the column of the portico in decision and called for a slave.

Within minutes, the animal and cart were readied. The slave climbed aboard and lifted the reins.

"No," Spiro said. "I go alone."

He would be less noticeable that way.

The slave nodded and abandoned his position.

The harbor district lay below Spiro's hillside home and across the city. The cart bumped over rocks in his downward journey, throwing him against the front frame and occasionally necessitating a hand to balance on the back of the ox, which Spiro found distasteful.

*She will pay for making me do this.*

There had been moments, over the past few days, when Spiro thought that Tessa might actually desire to be free of Glaucus and serve him instead. But he had no illusions left. She would be a hired companion, not a willing one.

*And I am better served. A slave must do as she is told.*

He smiled at the thought, even as the cart bumped against him once again.

He directed the cart toward the statue of Helios that commanded the harbor, a beacon for those on the sea and on land alike. Though the statue had been completed before he was born, and he had lived in its shadow for his entire life, he never ceased being amazed at such a feat of engineering.

*Truly we are a magnificent people.*

But thoughts of Greek pride soon fled, replaced by a growing fury. Tessa was here in the harbor district, in the house of Servia. She belonged up the hill, in his home. And now it was time to make her place clear.

He stormed into Servia's home, and a young girl, still fresh, peeked around a corner from the hall.

Spiro pointed a finger at her. "Bring Tessa to me, immediately!"

The girl's eyes widened at his harsh manner and she disappeared. He waited, hoping to preserve some dignity by having the woman brought to him. But she did not come.

He refused to go looking for her, like a parent searching for a lost child. "Tessa!" His scream carried through the house. "Come,

Tessa!" He crossed his arms, tapped a sandal against the floor, and waited again. Finally there came a slow step on the stairs, and he pursed his lips in satisfaction.

*At last.*

He had an image in his mind of himself, parading Tessa through the streets of Rhodes, with all the citizens as witnesses.

But it was not Tessa who emerged from the staircase.

"Servia!"

"I am equally surprised to see you, Spiro. We do not often have men of your status down here at the harbor." She smiled and her gold tooth flashed at him. "I must usually bring the girls up into the city." She tipped her head back and studied him. "You are not seeking another girl so soon?"

"I seek Tessa!"

Servia's eyebrows shot up. "She is not with you?"

"Have you seen her?"

Servia motioned to the young girl he had seen earlier, still spying on them from behind a green silk curtain at the end of the hall. "You said that Tessa was here most of the day?"

The girl tiptoed forward and nodded, biting her lip. "She lay abed until after midday. Then the old man came for her."

Spiro growled, "Old man?"

The girl looked at Servia. "An old Jew."

*Simeon.* "Did they say where they were going?"

The girl played with her hair and swayed slightly on her feet. "He tried to get her to speak, but she was silent. He told her that he would take her somewhere safe, where people would care for her."

Servia faced the girl, her hands spread on her ample hips. "Tessa was ill?"

The girl shrugged one shoulder. "Not ill. It was—it was her mind that was not right, I believe."

Servia's mouth curled into a smile. "One day with you, Spiro, and—"

"Enough!" He curtailed the urge to strike the woman. "If she returns, you will tell her to come to my home immediately."

Servia still smiled. "Of course."

He gave them both another angry look, disgusted to have even been here, and slammed out of the house. He jumped to the back of his cart and grabbed the reins. There weren't many places a Jew could hide a hetaera in this city. He would soon find her.

He snapped the reins over the ox and turned the cart toward the end of the harbor street. His thoughts were on Tessa and the Jew, his eyes on the ox's back. When he raised his eyes to a figure running toward him, it took a moment for the shock to penetrate.

*Nikos!*

His half-brother saw him at the same time and skidded to a stop in front of the cart.

"You were removed from this island!"

"I've come for her, Spiro."

"Come for whom?"

"Don't be a fool. She belongs with me."

Spiro laughed. "Your years in the gutter did not teach you the way of the slave market." He tilted his head and spoke the patient tone of a tutor. "She belongs to Servia, Nikos. She is a slave. People pay for her services. I have paid for her; she serves *me*."

"Where is she?"

Spiro wrapped the reins around his palm and scowled. "Leave Rhodes, Nikos. The gods favored you with the council's vote. Myself, I would have liked to see you hanged."

"I have come to buy her from Servia. And then I am going to set her free."

"Ha! Do you have any idea the money Servia receives for Tessa? And a long lifetime of payments is ahead of her." He smiled, leaned forward, and lowered his voice. "Though she is amazing, something tells me Tessa will only get better with age."

Nikos's face contorted with rage and he rushed the cart. He grabbed a handful of Spiro's himation and yanked him from the back. His face was only a breath away from Spiro's.

"Hear this, Spiro. I have the wealth of Kalymnos behind me. I *will* set her free. Because she loves me!" He spat the last words into Spiro's face.

Spiro shoved his brother away. "*Loves* you? She is not capable—"

"It is you who are not capable! You know only obsession and lust. But she loves me, Spiro! And she will come with me willingly!"

The last word struck Spiro like a physical blow. He had resigned himself to Tessa's unwilling service to him. He would not allow her to give herself to another. A rage even he had seldom felt began to climb from his belly and hardened as it grew.

*She is mine. She is mine. She is mine.*

"You will never have her," he said, his voice frozen.

Nikos snorted in derision and turned toward Servia's house, his intent clear.

*You will never have her.*

"I will kill her first."

Nikos whirled at the words, spoken softly.

The horror on his brother's face struck Spiro as humorous. He laughed to himself. Then aloud. A long, wonderful howl of laughter that released something inside of him. All the tension of wanting her, of scheming to get her. He let it go.

*She is mine. But she is not.*

He threw back his head and laughed at all of it. And as the obsession for her seeped out of him, in its place rushed a focused and piercing hatred.

Yes. If he could not have her, then he would kill her.

Heedless of Nikos, he turned to his reins and urged the ox forward. He must find her.

The suddenness of the arm wrapped round his neck threw off his balance. Spiro staggered back. His arms grasped at air. The two men fell together from the back of the cart into the street.

*Not now. I have something to attend to.*

He swatted at Nikos and tried to push away.

Nikos flipped him to his back and straddled him. "Stay away from her, Spiro. Do not touch her! Do not even look at her!"

Nikos's face above him again seemed funny. He spat out a laugh, but the laughter turned to anger. Nikos was keeping him from his task. He grabbed at the man's clothing and tossed him aside.

*You are in my way. I must find her.*

He abandoned the ox cart, knowing he'd be faster on foot, and ran through the harbor street. The pounding sandals behind him told him that Nikos had not given up.

*I must not lead him to her. We must be alone, Tessa and I, when it is accomplished.*

His mind had narrowed and focused on his goal, like an arrow flying true to its mark. But he was able to set the goal aside. First he must deal with his fool of a brother.

To turn and fight him would require effort he did not wish to expend. He veered his path toward the Acropolis Hill, away from the house where Tessa must be. He would lose Nikos there, among the temples and groves.

And then he would finish with Tessa.

## Ω

Nikos struggled to keep up with his brother, who ran through the streets of Rhodes as though Pandora's jar had been opened at his feet.

*Where are you going, Spiro?*

When he had landed on Rhodes, his father's money weighting him heavily, Nikos had known he must remain out of sight of city officials. And he had expected to face a challenge in convincing Servia to let him buy Tessa's freedom. He had not expected to be chasing his murderous brother through the city.

The Acropolis? Why would Tessa be there? Why was she not with Spiro? Had she run? He fought a moment of despair and tried to focus on outrunning his quarry.

He would find her. And redeem her. And love her.

His lungs ached. Blood throbbed in his ears, to the rhythm of his feet on the street. Houses blurred past, then thinned. They approached the path to the Acropolis.

Ahead, a bend in the path obscured Spiro.

There. A flicker of white between the pines.

Nikos lurched from the path, into the grove.

Sunlight fell in pools between the pines, creating patches of light and dark. Spiro's white tunic was only another blur of light, hard to distinguish. He dodged and twisted through trees ahead, still moving upward.

And then Spiro burst from the grove, on the top of the Acropolis hill. Nikos could see him there at the crest, panting, waiting. He cleared the grove and ran toward Spiro.

"Where is she?" he called.

Spiro spread his arms. "You are not easily outrun," he said.

Nikos ran at him, did not stop. He leaped across the last few feet. His shoulders connected with Spiro's midsection. They both went down.

"Did you lead me here to evade me?" he grunted.

Spiro answered with a fist to Nikos's jaw. "It looks as though I will have to kill you first, brother. Before I kill her."

Nikos let the rage build, believing it was his ally. He cracked his own fist against Spiro's jaw.

*Do not kill him.*

They were his father's words, not his own. Nikos pummeled Spiro again, wishing he had not made the promise to Andreas before he left.

*But Spiro fights to the death. I must escape. Find Tessa.*

The edge of the hill grew dangerously close. Below the cliff, waves slapped the rocky coast and spewed seawater upward.

Spiro rushed him. They struggled, tumbling closer to the cliff's edge.

*It will be one or the other of us.*

*I am sorry, Father.*

But at the edge, with a quick look below, an idea dropped from the heavens to him. There was a way to escape Spiro without killing him—to find Tessa before Spiro did.

He gave a final, grunting shove that threw Spiro backward off his feet.

Spiro pushed back up to charge him again.

The moment had come.

Nikos turned to the cliff. Measured the distance with his eye. Backed up as far as he dared. And ran.

With a yell, he cleared the cliff's edge and soared into empty air.

Spiro's angry scream faded behind him.

The wind rushed upward against him.

He thought of Tessa's smile.

His feet hit the scrubby hillside first, then his knees and upper body. He rolled down to the next outcropping, then leaped again.

And then water. Cold, dark, deep.

His lungs screamed.

*Upward, push upward.*

His head broke the surface. He shook the water from his face. Paddling in place, he looked at the cliff above.

Spiro stood at the edge, watching him.

Nikos could not read his brother's expression from this distance. But he had only a moment to study it.

His tunic flying behind him, Spiro whirled and ran from the cliff's edge.

Nikos swam hard for the sand.

The race had begun.

# THIRTY-SIX

In the Jewish district, Tessa and Marta sat at a table in the kitchen, cups of warmed wine before them. Marta had insisted that Tessa begin with her childhood and tell the story that was her life. Tessa laughed each time Marta stopped her and begged for more details.

"You will grow tired of my tale long before it is finished!" she said.

Marta touched the back of her hand. "If it is too much to tell of it, I will understand."

Tessa smiled. "No one has cared to hear my story for a very long time."

Marta rubbed her fingers over her hand. "I care to hear it. I want to be part of it."

Tessa swallowed against the emotion that seemed ever present today. She began again to tell of the wasted years in a voice softened by the release of forgiveness and love.

A cry at the door of the house silenced her. The door burst inward, and Marta jumped to her feet.

Jacob appeared in the kitchen. "Stay here," he said. He disappeared, and the women waited. Tessa held her breath.

*This is about me somehow.*

And then Spiro's oily voice echoed through the house.

"Where is she, Jew?"

"There is no one here that would interest you," Jacob responded.

Tessa heard a crash. Heavy footsteps approached.

Spiro appeared in the doorway. His mouth was strangely slack. His eyes roamed her body. "There you are!"

"How did you find me here, Spiro?"

He laughed. "Did you think you were not noticeable, Tessa? A few well-placed questions, along with a few drachma. It was not hard to discover where the old Jew had taken you."

Tessa placed a hand on Marta's back. "I must go," she whispered. The idea that she could bring harm to the family she loved was more than Tessa could bear.

"Come, Spiro," she said. "Let us return to your home. I am sorry I have been so long."

Marta gave her a squeeze, and Tessa pushed past Spiro, into the hall.

He hesitated. He seemed to suspect her motives.

She tried to smile. "Did you wish to stay with the Jews, Spiro?"

Her sarcasm found its mark, and he followed her to the door.

She felt the family's eyes in the hall behind her.

*I will be back, dear ones. This is how it must be for now. But I will see you again.*

Outside Spiro grabbed her arm and pulled her into the street.

"Where is your cart, Spiro?"

"I came on foot."

"On foot?"

Spiro pulled her down the street, past the Jewish homes and toward the central part of the city.

"Yes. I had a bit of—trouble—getting here."

Tessa walked beside him silently.

*Help me, Yahweh. Help me to remain alive, even now. Teach me to be refined through the pain.*

The residents of the Jewish district slowed in the streets to watch them pass. Tessa smiled at them all, knowing what a strange sight they must be, the scowling strategos dragging his smiling hetaera behind him.

At the end of the street, Spiro turned her to him. "I am not the only one who has been searching for you today, Tessa."

She scanned the street behind him. Simeon knew where she was, had gone back to Glaucus's home hours ago.

"Who?"

"It seems my bastard peasant brother has returned."

Tessa felt something stir within her.

"Nikos has returned to Rhodes?"

Spiro leaned in to whisper, as though he held a sought-after secret. "He has brought my father's money and believes he will buy you for himself."

Tessa pulled her face away.

*He would not do that.*

"I do not wish to be owned by Nikos." She straightened. "Or any man."

Spiro's eyes sparked. "This I know, Tessa." He held both her arms and pulled her close. "But Nikos plans to set you free."

The stirring began again. A flicker of hope. Tessa recognized it, felt her usual tendency to quench it.

Instead she embraced it. Fanned it to flame.

"Nikos comes to free me?" she said and felt the smile break across her face.

Spiro slipped an arm around her waist and brought his lips to her ear. "He says he loves you, Tessa."

She smiled over Spiro's shoulder.

"And do you love him?" It was a low, dangerous whisper in her ear.

She looked into her heart, still fresh-plowed. "Yes," she responded, knowing it was unwise and yet true. Feeling and embracing everything she had long denied. The final bits of stone broke apart within her.

Spiro rubbed his cheek against hers. "He cannot have you, Tessa, you know that."

This was truth, also. "Yes," she said.

"You are mine. Mine to possess. Mine to destroy."

She heard the coldness. It frightened her. She pulled away.

Spiro's eyes had taken on a faraway look. "Yes," he said, focusing on her again. "I will possess you. And then I will kill you."

*Run, Tessa.*

She knew not where the words came from.

But she obeyed.

Through the streets, now turning gray in the twilight. She did not know where to go. Did not know where Nikos might be or where she would find safety.

But her feet carried her toward the place that still called to her even now.

To the harbor.

To the statue.

Ω

And somewhere deep in the sea, below the floor of Rhodes, in layers of rock no human had ever witnessed, tectonic plates shifted.

Unseen, unheard, unmarked for the time.

But not for long.

## Ω

Spiro laughed again when Tessa ran. He could outrun the woman nearly without effort, he knew. And the pursuit would only make the conclusion more fulfilling.

He watched her for a moment, letting her believe she had escaped him. He gathered his himation about him and tied it high enough to free his legs. Tessa's figure grew indistinct in the distance. It was time to run.

He took to the streets once more, this time reveling in the run. His prey was in sight. His enemy did not know their whereabouts.

As he ran, he thought of all that came before, to lead him to this moment. The posturing, the manipulating, and groveling to gain favor. Becoming a strategos. His father's approval for a short time, so quickly withdrawn.

His sandals slapped the road. The distance between them closed.

The aqueduct. The inspector Erasmus and the fountain house guard. Ajax. It had all been for this. All for Tessa.

He realized as he ran that he did not care so much for the monarchy of Rhodes. And did the pleasure of his father really mean so much?

What was any of that compared with Tessa?

Ahead, she stumbled and fell, then picked herself up and ran again.

He was close enough now to hear her panting breath as she ran. The sound of it pleased him.

When his body struck hers, the force nearly carried them both forward to the ground. He caught her, and they spun together, an impromptu dance in the city street.

She pounded fists against his chest.

He grinned and let her flail.

The sun was setting, casting the alleys in shadow. He pulled her into one, deep where they would not be seen, and perhaps her screams would not be heard.

And scream she did.

"Stop!" He wished to hear his own thoughts, not her shrieking. *Not here. Not here.*

No, he must take her home. Not in an alley, which would degrade him.

He shook her. "Stop! We are going home."

Her scream lessened and she eyed him warily.

*She does not believe I truly intend to kill her.*

Though her mistake might make her go somewhat willingly, somehow it troubled him for Tessa not to know what he planned. He thrust his hands into her hair and pulled the pin from it, letting her curls tumble to her shoulders.

"There," he said. "You like it like that, don't you?"

Tears sprang to her eyes.

"Tears, Tessa?" He let his hands linger in her hair, then pulled her head toward his own, until their lips nearly touched. "Do you weep for Nikos? Or do you weep because you know that after I make you wholly mine, I would rather kill you than have you love him?"

The tears coursed down her pale cheeks now, falling to the alley floor. Then her body relaxed. Her eyes closed.

*Yes, Tessa. You know you belong to me now.*

He pulled away, released her hair.

"Let us go home, Tessa." A smile came to him. "I will show you my courtyard in the moonlight."

There was a beat of silence between them.

And then Tessa brought her knee up hard with a well-placed blow.

Spiro screamed. He doubled over in pain.

Tessa ran.

## Ω

Nikos emerged from the sea at the base of the Acropolis cliff. The white beach was smooth under his feet. He ran in the firm sand at the water's edge and circled the coast in the direction of the harbor. Could he outrun Spiro to reach Servia? Or had Spiro already learned that Tessa was not there, before Nikos had even arrived?

He had to try.

The rocky cliffs drew close to the sea and slowed his progress. He climbed over gray boulders, slick with remnants of the sea, and finally took to the water. It was easier to run in the shallows, with the waves breaking over his ankles, than to manage the rocks.

Ahead, the coastline turned sharply to the right.

The harbor lay just beyond the bend.

His chest pounded with the exertion.

*I am coming, Tessa.*

Around the last cliff. There. The harbor.

Small boats drifted at their moorings at the docks, and larger ships waited out at sea for their cargo to come to them. Nikos made his way to a series of steps carved from natural rock and clambered over them onto the docks.

Only a little farther to Servia's house.

He was breathing hard when he pushed into the building he'd been directed to. He could hear Servia's voice from deep within the luxurious home.

"You are too fat," she was saying. "I cannot make enough money from you to pay for the food you eat!"

Nikos heard no response.

"Servia!" he yelled.

She appeared at once.

"Again?" she said. "Three times you have found me, and not once have you paid me for any of my girls."

Nikos pulled the pouch from under his tunic. "Today is different."

She eyed the pouch like a hungry cat.

"Do you like fat girls?" she said. "I can give you a bargain—"

"I want Tessa."

Servia's eyes clouded. "We have been over this already. She is not for sale."

"Do you know who I am?"

Servia waved an impatient hand. "I care nothing for politics. You could be the son of the great Alexander and it would mean nothing to me."

"But my money means something."

She laughed. "Yes, money always means something."

Nikos untied the bag and slowly spilled the contents into a large vase that stood beside the door. He watched Servia's eyes as she tried to count each talent that poured from the pouch.

"How much?" he asked. "How much to take Tessa away from Rhodes forever?"

"Forever?"

"I do not wish to pay for her services. I wish to buy her from you."

"You would pay so much?"

"Give me a number."

She smiled, then laughed, revealing her crooked teeth. "Two brothers, each willing to do anything for one woman." She shook her head, apparently greatly entertained. "It is the stuff of legend. A story of brother gods, fighting over a goddess."

"How much, Servia?"

She grew serious. Studied the treasure she had been offered. Looked at Nikos with a gleam of hatred mixed with greed.

For the first time, he wondered what this woman was capable of. Would she try to kill him and simply keep the money? People had killed for far less.

"My father is the ruler of Kalymnos," he said. "And I am here under his authority. To purchase Tessa and take her from here."

He watched Servia carefully, but suddenly her face went slack, her jowls vibrating in a manner he had never witnessed.

At the same time, a deep and terrible rumble filled the air, as though a storm greater than any the world had seen rushed toward them from the underworld.

Nikos gripped the doorway beside him, his balance stolen. The rumbling went on, so loud and frightful he feared he would lose his hearing. Inside the house, the screams of a handful of girls echoed and mixed with the thunder.

With an insane upswell, the entire house lifted from its foundation and crested a wave, then dropped back to the earth. The ceiling cracked open with a hideous screech, and the house filled with dust and smoke.

Nikos fought to open the door behind him. The twisted frame held the door fast. He shoved a shoulder against it.

The ground shook.

*The house is coming down.*

He fought against the door.

Behind him, Servia screamed.

Nikos broke through and stumbled to the street. He turned to see if Servia followed him, could see her bulk near the doorway. But she was bent to something. Not fleeing.

The money.

She was trying to retrieve the money.

The noisome shaking grew, then ended with a violent twist.

A wave of destruction washed down the harbor street, and the buildings began to fall.

Servia still groped for coins, inside the house that had trained so many girls to sell themselves, when the ground heaved upward yet again and the entire house collapsed upon itself.

# THIRTY-SEVEN

As Nikos bargained with Servia, Tessa had fled to the harbor. A rock had cut her leg when she fell in the alley, and she tried to ignore the pain as her feet carried her swiftly through the city streets, down toward the sea and the statue.

And then where?

Where would she find Nikos? Where would he look for her?

The wind caught her loosened hair as she ran, streaming it behind her. Though the city rushed past, she had the odd sense that everything had stilled, as though Rhodes held its breath for what would come next.

She cleared the residential districts and rushed into the harbor area. The docks hummed with trade and fishing. Ships bobbed in the water. Slaves worked. Merchants haggled.

Somewhere a dog howled. Then another.

Unearthly howls from the underworld.

Tessa ran toward Helios, knowing Spiro followed close behind.

A cart rumbled past, filled with logs that would be cut into building framework. Tessa snatched a log narrow enough to be held with her two hands and not too long to lift. The driver never looked back.

At the statue's base, she turned and placed her back against it, the log held out in front of her.

Spiro slowed to scan the area, until his eyes found hers and he ran for her.

She forced her breathing to slow.

*Focus on your weapon.*

Her hands tightened around the log, and the bark bit into her skin.

Spiro approached her with caution, his eyes on the log she held.

"This is what we have come to, Tessa? You would attack me?"

"I will not let you kill me!"

Spiro spread his hands as though innocent. "I want only to make you mine, Tessa. That is all I have ever wanted."

"I will never belong to you, not in the way you want."

His eyes darkened. "I could have accepted that once, Tessa. When you were the marble goddess who cared for no one. I knew that you would never trust anyone with your heart. You had been mistreated by too many."

Tessa blinked and shifted the log in her hands. Her arms were wearying.

Spiro took two steps closer. "But after all these years of coldness, you have suddenly decided to trust him? My peasant brother? To love him, even?"

*Can I? Can I trust Nikos?*

Spiro smiled. "You have never been anything but a possession of men, Tessa. And you never will be. There is no love for you. You cannot trust anyone. You were better off as the marble Athena."

*I hold you with My mighty right hand.*

The words of Simeon's Yahweh flooded her heart.

She felt new strength in her arms and held the log higher.

"I have found someone to trust, Spiro. Someone who will not fail me."

His eyes seemed to spit fire.

*He thinks I speak of Nikos. He could not understand.*

Spiro's eyes went to the log she held like a gladiator's spear. He lunged for it, and Tessa felt as though she might laugh at the game they played. An ox ran past, escaped from its owner, and Spiro tore the log from her hands. She felt a sharp rip in her skin and saw blood drip from her palm. He tossed her only weapon aside, and somewhere behind him a child screamed.

"I will have you, Tessa," he said. "By the gods, I will have you. Your life is in my hands."

He was still yelling when the noise began.

A hideous and frightful noise. Like thunder broken free from the sky and poured out on the city.

Tessa looked above Spiro's head toward the city.

*What is happening?*

And then the ground lurched. The surface of the earth and everything on it lifted up, then rolled forward from the direction of the sea.

Tessa's stomach heaved and she fought to keep her balance.

Spiro's eyes went wide, and he backed away from her.

Behind him, the harbor street buildings rose and fell, rose and fell, on waves of dirt and stone.

She threw her arms wide to steady her feet but fell to her knees anyway.

*An earthquake.*

She fought to keep from screaming.

The rolling earth threw Spiro to the ground as well. Far from frightened, Spiro had begun to laugh. He rose to his knees, threw his head back to laugh into the sky. "The sea god bangs the floor with his trident," he howled. "Poseidon himself approves! It is a sign!"

Tessa could not take it all in at once.

Buildings leaned, then returned upright. Foundations ripped and fractured and screeched. All across the docks, cracks opened, water spewing from the fissures. People were writhing on the ground and shrieking in terror. Animals tore through the streets. Tessa watched as the abandoned ox charged and gored a man.

And then the shaking ended with a horrible scream and the buildings fell.

Some collapsed on their wailing inhabitants. Some fell forward, into the street, to crush panicked citizens running in circles.

Tessa cried out, reached for those she could not save.

Fires erupted everywhere, and dust filled the air.

She was still on her knees when Spiro crawled to her, reached for her.

She pushed to her feet and ran past him, away from Helios, who watched the destruction from his lofty place in the sky above them all.

Her head jerked backward. Spiro held her by the hair.

Unable to move forward, she thrashed at the hand behind her. He forced her to turn to him.

All around them, people screamed and died.

*Still, he wants only to possess.*

"Yes, Tessa," he said. "I will have you." His hands went to her throat. "I had thought it would be different," he said, "my possession of you." His eyes gleamed.

A goat ran past. Buildings continued to crash to the ground behind her. Over Spiro's shoulder, Tessa saw a large wave surge over the docks. Seawater rushed toward them, past them, soaking them to the knees and scraping her legs with debris.

Spiro's hands tightened on her throat. "I don't know," he said, "why I didn't realize this would be better. To hold your very life in my hands, to crush it slowly, to feel it run down through my fingers and drain into the ground. *This* is complete possession." His expression was focused, questioning, as though the world were not coming to an end around him. "Do you not agree, Tessa?"

She could not speak. Could not breathe.

*And yet I am more alive at this moment than I have been in many years.*

A peace stole over her. The peace that, even in this, Spiro did not truly possess her. A Mighty Outstretched Hand held her fast, and would continue to hold her, even as the blackness grew.

Her eyelids fluttered. The harbor and the sky appeared and disappeared.

And then just before she would have closed her eyes, another wave roared in from the sea. Larger, swifter, it hammered Spiro's back and pitched him forward. He lost his grip on her neck. She pulled in a dust-filled breath and let the water carry her backward, several paces away from Spiro.

The wave exhausted itself and rushed back to the sea. Yet the roar remained.

No, the sound Tessa heard now was different—a deep and prolonged groaning, as though the gods themselves mourned the devastation of Rhodes.

She lifted her eyes to find the source. Above her head, at Spiro's back, she had the strange sensation that Helios had grown dizzy and swayed on his feet. Like a tree succumbing to harsh winds.

*Helios is falling.*

In a moment of clarity, Tessa held her breath and locked eyes with Spiro. She let her expression challenge him. Watched his own eyes respond.

Felt the shadow of the colossus spread over them both.

*Hold. Hold.*

And then Spiro sensed the danger somehow. Jerked his head around, then back to her.

With every bit of strength she still possessed, Tessa rushed toward Spiro. She wrapped her arms around his chest, planted her feet. He grunted in surprise, then terror. Fought her embrace. She held. The sky darkened to bronze above them.

*Now.*

A final shove against Spiro. A leap out of the statue's path.

A rush of wind stole her balance, and Helios crashed onto his back in the harbor district, taking down everything in his path.

Dirt and rocks sprayed upward and struck Tessa. The force of the statue's fall threw her onto her back. Debris rained down on her, as though she had been buried.

*But buried alive.*

She lay there only a moment, then shook the dirt and stones from her face and shoulders and regained her feet.

The chaos continued around her.

The collapse of Helios had struck a fear of divine retribution into the people. Combined with the physical destruction, the city exploded with terror.

Helios had broken at the knees. His lower legs and feet remained on the platform above her. The rest of him lay in the dirt, buried in part from the force of the impact, unseeing eyes facing the sky.

And somewhere, under the massive weight of bronze, lay Spiro.

## Ω

Later Tessa could not say what it was that prompted her to climb the statue's base once more. To stand beside the broken legs. To think about the past, to wonder about the future.

But she did climb there.

And that was where she stood when Nikos found her.

# THIRTY-EIGHT

The sun descended over the ravaged island of Rhodes.

In the western sky, a sunset hazy with dust and smoke settled shades of pastel upon the hills.

The citizens of Rhodes cried and searched for their loved ones and salvaged what they could of their homes and their lives. In time, they would rebuild. They would restore Rhodes to her former wealth, if not her former glory.

The statue would remain fallen at the edge of the sea, mute testimony to another age.

But Tessa would not be part of the rebirth of Rhodes.

She stood now on the deck of one of dozens of outbound ships. Ship captains up and down the harbor had spent the two hours since the quake making haste to set sail immediately. Night was falling on a city in chaos; it was safer to be at sea.

Tessa was not alone.

She grasped the aging hands of one of the men with her.

"You are certain, Simeon?" she asked again.

Simeon smiled in his patient way. "They were in the market, all of them. Marta and Jacob had brought the whole family to choose the bird for the evening meal. Praise Yahweh, they were in the open market when the quake struck. Nothing to fall on them. Just shaken and frightened, that is all."

Tessa closed her eyes. Felt another hand on her back, warm and reassuring.

She looked to Simeon again. "And Daphne and Persephone?"

"Also well. Daphne had pushed the wedding forward as she is now a widow forced to rely on her daughter's husband. But Hermes . . ." Simeon hung his head. "Hermes was killed during the ceremony." He looked at both of them. "Persephone asked after you both. What shall I tell her?"

Tessa felt Nikos close behind her and leaned her head back against his shoulder. "Tell Persephone that the Tessa and Nikos she knew died in the quake. But two others sail to begin again." She smiled. "And help Daphne find a good man, Simeon. One who will treat Persephone with respect."

Simeon nodded, then removed his hands from Tessa's and pulled her to himself. He whispered to her. "I will miss you, dear girl."

Tessa clung to Simeon, a sudden ache swelling in her chest. "And I you." She pulled her head away to look at his precious face. "Come with us."

Simeon smiled. "My family is here." He gazed over her head, to the sea. "But perhaps we will all make a voyage. I think perhaps it is time to return to Jerusalem."

"Your home."

"Yes, but I am longing for more than my home. I am looking for the consolation of Israel." His eyes returned to hers, and a youthful light sparkled there. He whispered again. "Do not fear for me, for the Spirit of God has revealed to me that I will not taste death until I see the promised Messiah."

Tessa hugged him again, unsure of what these strange words meant, but certain that she loved this man and owed him more than she could repay.

"Do take care, Simeon," she said.

Simeon turned to Nikos. "I am trusting you with a part of my heart," he said to the younger man.

Tessa smiled back at Nikos, who clapped Simeon's shoulder. "I will not disappoint you," he said.

And then Simeon was gone.

Ω

It was fully night when the ship lifted anchor and turned its sails for the sea. A favorable wind blew, as though to speed the escape of those who could.

The destruction of the city held the attention of all, and departing ships and their passengers were unimportant.

Tessa stood at the rail of the ship, watched Rhodes grow distant, and felt the city's hold on her release. She would leave the position of most respected and admired hetaera in the hands of Berenice and pray it would not destroy the girl.

Nikos wrapped an arm around her waist and pulled her close. "You are free, Tessa."

She leaned her head against him. "Am I truly? I cannot believe it."

"Servia is dead. And well paid for her trouble," he added. "Glaucus is dead. Spiro is dead. And in the confusion, the rumors of your death will be believed."

The coastline of Rhodes seemed barren without Helios. Instead of the torches that had flared each night at the statue's base, scattered fires burned throughout the city.

Tessa thought of Helios, the colossus that had been a central figure in her life for so long. How she had almost become like the statue herself. Cold, unfeeling. Stone and bronze.

But that person had broken at the knees as well. Humbled by her need for redemption. Made alive by her acceptance of it.

She smiled at Nikos. He was a man, not a god, and would disappoint her. But she would take that risk. The risk to trust another,
to be alive to both joy and pain, because she knew in whose hands
she truly rested.

In the darkness, with Rhodes fading behind her and the future
before, Tessa let Nikos turn her to himself, raise her face to his, and
remind her again of why it was so good to be alive.

# Author's Note

The list of the Seven Wonders of the Ancient World evolved slowly, from their first mention by the Greek historian Herodotus in 450 BC, to the poet Antipater in the second century BC. Though only the oldest of the seven, the Great Pyramid of Giza, still stands, their mystique has endured, each a wonder of engineering and a testimony to the creativity of ancient peoples.

The Colossus of Rhodes was built by Chares of Lindos, beginning in 290 BC. The statue reportedly took twelve years to build and was erected by creating an iron framework, filling it with stone, and then overlaying it with plates of bronze "skin." During construction, builders moved piles of dirt to surround the statue, building up the dirt ramps as the statue grew. When the Colossus was complete, the dirt was removed and the statue towered over the harbor. It stood approximately 110 feet high. (The Statue of Liberty, at about 120 feet, was patterned after the Colossus; the New York statue's base is much higher, however.)

The Colossus remained upright for only fifty-six years, until broken at the knees by an earthquake. Though Ptolemy III of Egypt offered funds for its rebuilding, the people of Rhodes declined, believing they had offended Helios by building it. They chose to allow the god's likeness to remain beside the sea. And there it lay for nine hundred years. Empires rose and fell around the fallen Colossus until, history tells us, a traveling Arab salesman purchased the bronze remains as scrap and had them transported to his home on the backs of nine hundred camels.

I was privileged to visit the island of Rhodes during the writing of *Shadow of Colossus*, and I invite you to visit my Web site, www.TLHigley.com and click on the Readers link. You'll experience the sights, sounds, and people of this beautiful island and be better able to picture the harbor, streets, and the Acropolis where Tessa fought for her freedom and found redemption. You'll also learn what is fact and what is fiction within the book, find giveaways that will sweep you off to other times and places, and the chance to join an Ancient Treasure Hunt.

And I ask, where are you in your own struggle to find life and joy amidst the pain? I love to hear from readers about the adventure of their own lives. Please visit my site and share your heart with me!